W9-CFK-755

"This substantial book will kindle the desire and provide the guidance to help its readers study the Scriptures wisely on their own. I encourage every serious Christian who wants to know the Bible better and more accurately to read this impressive book."

— TREMPER LONGMAN III, Robert H. Gundry professor of biblical studies, Westmont College

"Dr. Klein has pulled together in succinct and readable form the kind of information many people wish they had as they begin to study the Bible. This book isn't just a methodology for Bible study; rather, it draws the reader into Bible study by answering nagging questions about how the Bible came to us and why we can trust it as the Word of the living God. I highly recommend this book to small groups as well as to individuals who care about hearing and understanding God's Word to them."

— ALICE MATHEWS, PhD, academic dean, Gordon-Conwell Theological Seminary

"One size can fit all. Klein's work is so complete and varied that a layperson can keep coming back to it for more, with twenty-two methods of Bible study, helpful biblical backgrounds, additional resources, and more. Written by a scholar, accessible to the nonspecialist, with a proper emphasis on God's transforming power at work in His Word. It will help lift you out of the doldrums of ineffective Bible study."

— BILL MOUNCE, Ph.D., president of BiblicalTraining.org

"Followers of Jesus are people of The Bible. It is our compass for life and eternity. The better we know it and follow it, the better we will navigate our life journey. This handbook has it all: the story of the Bible, how to study it, how to interpret it, how to be transformed by it. Get it? Got it? Good."

— JIM TOMBERLIN, church consultant, ThirdQuarterConsulting.com

"Dr. Klein asks the key question, Is my relationship with God worth cultivating? This handbook is an incredible help if you want to grow and deepen your faith or help others do the same. It is like finding a detailed treasure map, pointing you on the right path with clear and thoughtful directions."

— NICK LILLO, lead pastor, Waterstone Community Church, Littleton, Colorado

THE NAVIGATORS REFERENCE LIBRARY

HANDBOOK FOR PERSONAL
BIBLE STUDY

Enriching Your Experience with God's Word

DR. WILLIAM W. KLEIN

NAVPRESS

Discipleship Inside Out™

NAVPRESS

Discipleship Inside Out™

NavPress is the publishing ministry of The Navigators, an international Christian organization and leader in personal spiritual development. NavPress is committed to helping people grow spiritually and enjoy lives of meaning and hope through personal and group resources that are biblically rooted, culturally relevant, and highly practical.

**For a free catalog go to www.NavPress.com
or call 1.800.366.7788 in the United States or 1.800.839.4769 in Canada.**

© 2008 by Dr. William W. Klein

All rights reserved. No part of this publication may be reproduced in any form without written permission from NavPress, P.O. Box 35001, Colorado Springs, CO 80935.

NAVPRESS and the NAVPRESS logo are registered trademarks of NavPress. Absence of ® in connection with marks of NavPress or other parties does not indicate an absence of registration of those marks.

ISBN-13: 978-1-60006-117-2

Cover image by Shutterstock

Some of the anecdotal illustrations in this book are true to life and are included with the permission of the persons involved. All other illustrations are composites of real situations, and any resemblance to people living or dead is coincidental.

Unless otherwise identified, all Scripture quotations in this publication are taken from the HOLY BIBLE: NEW INTERNATIONAL VERSION® (niv®). Copyright © 1973, 1978, 1984 by International Bible Society. Used by permission of Zondervan Publishing House. All rights reserved. Other versions used include: the *New American Standard Bible* (nasb), © The Lockman Foundation 1960, 1962, 1963, 1968, 1971, 1972, 1973, 1975, 1977, 1995; *THE MESSAGE* (msg). Copyright © 1993, 1994, 1995, 1996, 2000, 2001, 2002, 2005. Used by permission of NavPress Publishing Group; the *English Standard Version* (esv), copyright © 2001 by Crossway Bibles, a division of Good News Publishers. Used by permission. All rights reserved; the *New Revised Standard Version* (nrsv), copyright © 1989, by the Division of Christian Education of the National Council of the Churches of Christ in the USA, used by permission, all rights reserved; *Today's New International®* Version (tniv)®. Copyright 2001, 2005 by International Bible Society®. All rights reserved worldwide; the *Holy Bible, New Living Translation* (nlt), copyright © 1996, 2004. Used by permission of Tyndale House Publishers, Inc., Carol Stream, Illinois 60188. All rights reserved; the *New King James Version* (nkjv). Copyright © 1982 by Thomas Nelson, Inc. Used by permission. All rights reserved; and the *King James Version* (kjv).

Library of Congress Cataloging-in-Publication Data
Klein, William W. (William Wade)
Handbook for personal Bible study / William W. Klein.
p. cm. -- (The navigators reference library)
Includes bibliographical references and index.
ISBN 978-1-60006-117-2
1. Bible--Study and teaching. 2. Bible--Criticism, interpretation, etc. I. Title.
BS600.3.K54 2008
220.071--dc22
2008003632

Printed in the United States of America

2 3 4 5 6 7 8 9 10 / 14 13 12 11 10

I dedicate this book to a mentor of many years, a servant of God whose life has blessed many hundreds—if not thousands—of men and women over the course of his long life, Dr. Vernon C. Grounds. I first heard Dr. Grounds give a lecture at Wheaton College in the mid-1960s when I was an undergraduate, and he was one of the reasons I chose to attend Denver Seminary as a student. Over the course of several years, when I needed to make key decisions in discerning my vocation, Vernon supplied a willing ear and wise counsel. What a delight to have him welcome me in 1978 to the Denver Seminary faculty, where we have served together ever since. I know of no more convincing evidence of the power of God's Word in a human life than Dr. Grounds. The Scriptures are part of the very makeup of his life. Through his preaching, teaching, counseling, and leading, Vernon Grounds has exemplified a life committed to God and God's Word. Thank you, Dr. Grounds.

CONTENTS

CHAPTER 2:
PREPARING TO STUDY THE BIBLE: ITS STORY AND WORLD

CHAPTER 3:
THE BASICS OF BIBLE STUDY

CHAPTER 4:
THE SPIRITUAL DISCIPLINE OF BIBLE INTAKE

CHAPTER 5:
INTERPRETING THE BIBLE

CHAPTER 6:
BIBLE STUDY METHODS

CHAPTER 7:
RESOURCES AND HELPS FOR STUDYING THE BIBLE

CHAPTER 8:
USES OF THE BIBLE

Chapter 9:
A Lifetime of Bible Study

PREFACE

The Bible has always occupied a central place in my life. When I was growing up, my parents were members of churches that preached and taught the Bible. At the early age of seven, I decided to follow Jesus myself—with the encouragement of a children's Bible teacher. My mother was an outstanding lay Bible scholar, effectively teaching children and adults throughout her life in the days when conservative churches didn't encourage women to be teachers.

I took Bible courses in college and attended seminary after that. Upon graduation with a master of divinity degree, I served on the staff of a large church in California. Teaching the Bible and training others to lead Bible studies became central goals of my ministry. At first, among other pastoral duties, I taught classes and led small-group Bible studies for college students and young couples. Then, as minister of evangelism and discipleship, I focused more exclusively on teaching and overseeing small groups for the entire church. I recruited and trained many small-group Bible study leaders over several years. I developed training materials and Bible studies. The teaching bug really bit me!

I then acquired a PhD in New Testament exegesis and have been teaching courses about the New Testament ever since. In addition to teaching undergraduate and graduate courses, I remain strongly committed to the local church, and I've had many opportunities to teach classes and lead Bible studies of various kinds throughout the years.

I'm telling you this bit of personal history not to call attention to myself in some narcissistic way, but to emphasize this point: God has blessed my life with profound and life-giving connections to Scripture. I've come to deeply value the study of God's Word. It has the power to transform lives. I've seen it happen repeatedly—in my own life and in the lives of others.

With great insight, the writer of Hebrews penned these words: "The word of God is alive and active. Sharper than any double-edged sword, it penetrates even to dividing soul and spirit, joints and marrow; it judges the thoughts and attitudes of the heart" (4:12, TNIV). Not only can God's Word discern who we are, but God can use it to transform us to become what God intends us to be. Or as the apostle Paul put it, "Every part of Scripture is God-breathed and useful one way or another—showing us truth, exposing our rebellion, correcting our mistakes, training us to live God's way" (2 Tim. 3:16, MSG).

I'm certainly not saying that God limits his working in the world to the Bible and to those who have access to it. However, the Bible definitely serves as the centerpiece of God's special revelation. We're blessed to have God's Word, and when we engage it, God accomplishes extraordinary things!

I want to thank and acknowledge several people for their roles in bringing me to a love for Scripture and its Author. These individuals set me on a course that enables me to write this book. My parents, William and Eleanor Klein, were committed to the Bible, and my mother modeled serious study from my earliest days. Reverend Herbert J. Freeman was my first pastor as a child; we have reconnected in recent years, and I've come to see—as I never could as a child—his deep love for Scripture. Sadly, I don't know the name of the woman who led me to "take Jesus as my savior" in 1953, but I thank her for helping me to make that decision and for giving me my first copy of the New Testament. Dr. Charles W. Anderson, my pastor during my teen years, helped me see how vital and life-changing Scripture can be. These people, along with dozens of faithful Sunday school teachers and youth leaders, laid a sure foundation for my life.

Thanks also to many people who've given me the privilege to teach them or lead them in Bible studies. I especially want to mention the members of churches where I've been integrally involved in teaching the Bible since graduating from seminary: Calvary Baptist Church in Los Gatos, California; Gilcomston Park Baptist Church in Aberdeen, Scotland; WaterStone Community Church in Littleton, Colorado; and Pathways Church in Denver, Colorado.

I also acknowledge the support of Kent Wilson of NavPress, who pursued me to undertake this project. Affirming The Navigators' long history of commitment to Bible study, Kent wanted to place in one volume numerous resources that would help and encourage people to continue that crucial pursuit. More than that, Kent encouraged and allowed me to incorporate and adapt some materials previously published by NavPress. That material forms parts of chapters 3, 4, and 6. I offer my thanks to those authors, some who wrote anonymously, for their insights that augmented my own thinking. Astute readers will recognize some terminology and concepts from some of those works.

In addition, my editor, Brad Lewis, helped convert my sometimes elevated or obtuse prose into more readable sentences. I, and you as readers, owe him a debt of gratitude.

As always (and this is not a mere formality), my dear wife, Phyllis, went out of her way to provide the support and space I needed to write this book in the midst of a full teaching load, my role as a church elder, and life's other responsibilities. Her spiritual strength and vitality are sustaining graces in my spiritual journey. Her commitment to Scripture and the life with God inspire my own (often-too-feeble) efforts.

My fondest hope is that this *Handbook for Personal Bible Study* will encourage many people to embrace the Bible, perhaps in new ways, as God's living and active message to them. That's my hope and prayer for *you*—that your reading and studying of God's Word will enable you to encounter the living God in both fresh and profound ways.

WILLIAM W. KLEIN
Denver, Colorado

INTRODUCTION

You've probably seen many books on "how to study the Bible" in bookstores, and perhaps you even have some on your own shelves. Some provide theoretical help in the task of understanding God's Word, while others strive to be practical and hands-on. Some pastors write from their perspectives in the church, while others instruct readers in Bible study from their vantage points in various parachurch ministries or academic institutions. Many of them are excellent, helpful, and encouraging.

So why do I presume to write yet another book, and a hefty one at that, to add to the stack? Perhaps the "heft" supplies at least part of the answer. While other authors address specific elements to help Christians study the Bible, no one provides the scope of coverage that I'm offering here. Of course, even with the bulk of this book, it easily could have been much larger. Still, you'll find that it covers more territory than most books that provide specific and more-limited instruction on how to study the Bible.

Let me highlight several features that motivated my writing. Most Christians need encouragement to persevere in their engagement with the Bible. While we want to understand the larger perspective on why the Bible is important for our lives, we also want and need practical and concrete help on how to conduct our study. Because we all come in different shapes and sizes (meaning culture, gender, race, denomination, and other factors), because we all have been on the journey for longer or shorter times, and because we're more or less familiar with the Bible and the Christian faith, we need different approaches and tactics that will serve us well. And those approaches and tactics might need to change as our faith grows.

While no one book can supply everything you might need for studying the Bible, my goal is to supply as much help as possible within a reasonably sized volume. I wanted to create a book that individuals can use profitably on their own and that small groups could also find useful to answer specific questions before they went too far into their study. I wanted it to be practical and readable while not "talking down" to anyone. I wanted it to portray the best tactics for understanding the Bible and give readers suggestions to study specific issues in more depth on their own.

All of this means that you might read some sections or chapters only once but return to other parts repeatedly as you seek more help or further insight or to refresh your memory about certain ideas. You'll discover a bit of overlap in several chapters, as I need to say similar things in different ways or from different perspectives. If you find that some concepts seem familiar, you can skim through those rapidly until you encounter new territory. I might cover some points in detail in one place and then more briefly in another. You can return to the fuller explanation if you need a refresher.

So what does the book include? Let's briefly look at what each chapter contains.

Chapter 1 sets the stage for reading and study of the Bible. It helps us understand the nature of the Bible and how it came to us by way of the ancient Hebrew and early Christian communities. It also answers questions such as: Why do we have so many versions and translations available today? Can we trust some or all of them? And why do some Christian groups but not others include the Apocrypha in their Bibles?

Chapter 2 surveys the cultural and historical settings where the Bible came into being. What was it like to live in Old Testament times? We survey the history of ancient Israel. What else was going on in the world? What do we need to know about the four hundred or so years between the close of the Old Testament and the arrival of the Messiah? What light does that period shed on our understanding of the New Testament? And what was the Roman world like that Jesus and then his church were born into?

Chapter 3 introduces the basic and essential elements of Bible study to prepare for further developments of some of these in later chapters. We need to understand ourselves and what we bring to the task of Bible study. In addition, we tackle the central steps in Bible study: observation, interpretation, and application.

Chapter 4 points us to our need to take in the message of the Bible and includes some basic tactics we can use to accomplish that goal. We supply practical steps for each of the following: hearing, reading, memorizing, and meditating on the Word.

Chapter 5 covers how to interpret the Bible. An authoritative text is of little value if we don't understand how to interpret it. So, after tracing briefly how the Bible has been interpreted in history, this chapter provides some general principles of interpretation as well as specific tactics for interpreting the Bible's various genres.

Chapter 6 presents twenty-two different methods of Bible study. You can accomplish some of them in just a day, while you might extend other approaches over weeks or months as circumstances and interest allow. Most of us need variety to keep our study of Scripture fresh and invigorating, so using different methods at various times is crucial.

Chapter 7 consists of my list of the best tools and sources for researching important issues in the course of your Bible study. I organize them in the following categories: Bible introductions and surveys, historical-cultural background sources, concordances and lexicons, theological dictionaries and encyclopedias, grammar helps, commentaries, original Hebrew and Greek language sources, and electronic tools and resources.

Chapter 8 offers a compilation of some of the essential ways to employ the Bible in our lives and Christian communities. Throughout the book I stress the need for personal application of the Bible's message, but this chapter in particular includes helpful discussions about using the Bible for: personal growth, worship, liturgy, theology, the ministry of the Word (teaching, preaching, and leading Bible studies), pastoral care and counseling, and spiritual formation.

Chapter 9, finally, provides my "parting shot" as author and encourager. I hope to instill in you a fond love for God's Word since it comes from the heart of the God who loves us. I want to encourage you to do whatever it takes to make your encounters with the Bible a source of joy and profit. Our goal—one I try to stress not just in this chapter but throughout the book—isn't just studying the Bible; our goal is to love God and our neighbors. The Bible provides a vital means to reach that goal, so I hope you'll keep at it.

Most chapters end with a "For Further Study" section, directing you to books you might wish to consult for further insight or help on the topics of that chapter. And the *Handbook* ends with a glossary. Inevitably, either in this book or in some of the other resources, you'll encounter terms you're not sure about. I try to anticipate many of them and include definitions right in the text for you, but you can also turn to the glossary to refresh your memory.

Now you simply need to read the rest of this book. Perhaps,

more importantly, you need to pick up and read The Book! I love the eloquent and truthful words recorded in Martin Luther's *Table Talk*:[1]

> The Holy Scripture is the highest and best of books, abounding in comfort under all afflictions and trials. It teaches us to see, to feel, to grasp, and to comprehend faith, hope, and charity, far otherwise than mere human reason can; and when evil oppresses us, it teaches how these virtues throw light upon the darkness, and how, after this poor miserable existence of ours on earth, there is another and an eternal life.

May God enrich your life immeasurably as you read and study his Word. To him be glory forever and ever. Amen.

CHAPTER 1

HOW THE BIBLE CAME TO US

Have you ever wondered how a book written by many authors, mostly unknown, over the course of so many centuries, in three different languages, and to a diverse group of people and cultures who lived a long time ago could become the world's best-selling book of all time? Why does this book occupy such a crucial place in history?

Of course, I'm speaking of the Bible.

All branches of the Christian church—whether Roman Catholic, Orthodox, Protestant, or any subgroup or group in between—agree that the Bible is foundational to what they believe and how they practice the Christian faith. Indeed, because of Scripture's pivotal role and so that God's people can easily access its contents, the Bible has been carefully preserved throughout the centuries and translated into hundreds of languages in the modern era.

Yet it's important to ask if such a diverse collection of writings speaks with one voice, several harmonious voices, or many discordant voices. Also, can such a collection speak authoritatively today?

Before we get too far along, we need to ask precisely *what* Scripture is. How many books make up the Bible, and what are they? After all, the branches of the church previously mentioned don't always agree. And while we're thinking about the origin and makeup of the Bible, we need to ask how we can be sure that what we have before us in our modern versions is what the original authors wrote. In addition, can we be certain that our modern versions adequately represent what the ancient authors intended to say?

THE NATURE OF THE BIBLE

If a police officer or a representative of your local court system came to your door to deliver a subpoena, you'd be legally obligated to appear in court as directed. If you ignored the summons, you'd find yourself in contempt of court. While a subpoena is just a piece of paper, the weight of the whole legal system and the entire rule of law stands behind that simple document.

What kind of weight does the Bible carry? Why do Christians hold it in such regard? What is the nature of the authority behind the Bible? Or perhaps, more simply, what do Christians believe about the nature of the book (or collection of books) we call the Bible?

Once we come to terms with these kinds of questions, we can decide what role the Bible will play in our own lives. Will we study it? How seriously? Will we obey its teachings or merely treat them as ideas that we'll weigh against our own opinions or the advice of others? Will the Bible's words guide how we live, how we think, and what we believe?

Let's look at these issues in four sections: revelation and inspiration, the role of the Bible's human authors, the authority of the Bible, and unity and diversity in the Bible.

Revelation and Inspiration

Christians have always defended a central belief about the nature of the Bible: It owes its origin to God. The Bible is God's disclosure and revelation of himself. While composed by human writers, the contents of the Bible are divinely inspired.

The Old Testament (OT) frequently includes language such as, "The Lord says . . . " to reflect the author's view that the words following that phrase come directly from God (out of numerous examples, see Gen. 22:16; Ex. 5:1; 10:3; Num. 14:28; 1 Sam. 10:18; 1 K. 11:31; 2 K. 1:6; 1 Chron. 17:4; Ps. 12:5; Is. 10:24).

In the New Testament (NT), the apostle Paul reflected on the phenomenon of God speaking words through human authors, noting that the OT writings were "inspired" or "God-breathed" (2 Tim. 3:16). While emphasizing the same point, the apostle Peter used a different image: God "carried along" the writers of the OT (see 2 Pet. 1:20-21) so that what resulted wasn't merely what human authors wanted to say but what God desired to communicate. In addition, NT authors regularly referred to texts from the OT as support for claims or proof of their arguments (see Mt. 1:23; Acts 2:17; 4:25; Ro. 9:17; Ex. 9:16; Ro. 12:19; 1 Cor. 14:21; 2 Cor. 6:16-18; Heb. 10:16). Both OT and NT writers were conscious of God's role in speaking his words through human speakers and writers.

What early Christians saw as true for the OT led to the eventual formation of the NT. By the time Peter wrote his second letter, he claimed that at least some of Paul's letters were equal to the OT—the "other Scriptures" (2 Pet. 3:16). Paul wrote specifically that the origin of his teaching was the same as the origin of the OT, namely, the Holy Spirit (see 1 Cor. 2:13). In some of Paul's judgments, he was conscious of God's Spirit at work (see 1 Cor. 7:40). And the apostle John thought his writing embodied "the true words of God" (Rev. 19:9).

Eventually, the early Christians settled on a Bible that gave equal status to the Hebrew Scriptures and twenty-seven Christian writings from the first century. We'll address the issue of the Canon in more detail.

Human Authors

While some people might question the Bible's divine origin, almost no one questions that humans wrote the words of Scripture over a span of many centuries. If we accept that the Bible is a divinely inspired document, how did so many people write it over hundreds of years? We might not understand the process that took place, but it seems clear that God directed the writers' efforts so that they wrote precisely what God wanted to convey to his people. Again, although some writers of Scripture acknowledged God's activity in their lives (see 1 Cor. 2:13; 7:40; Rev. 19:9), the biblical writers rarely declared God's role in directly writing Scripture.

Despite the lack of awareness by Scripture's human authors that they were penning God's Word, the Holy Spirit certainly knew that's what they were doing. So Scripture possesses this unique quality: It expresses both the human and divine authors' purposes at the same time. As a result, we believers can hear God's voice in the words of the Bible—words written by people just like us—and we can embrace them confidently.

Authority of the Bible

Remember that subpoena mentioned earlier? If you're required to respond to this court order because the authority of the state lies behind it, how much more weight do God's words carry? The writer of Hebrews argued, "We must pay more careful attention, therefore, to what we have heard, so that we do not drift away. For if the message spoken by angels was binding, and every violation and disobedience received its just punishment, how shall we escape if we ignore such a great salvation?" (Heb. 2:1-3).

Let's break that down. If OT Law, which was mediated by angels, demanded punishment for Law breakers, it would be even more serious to ignore or violate a message from God himself—especially one mediated by his Son, Jesus Christ, and confirmed by signs and wonders! If the message of the Bible is God's message, and if God seeks to speak to his people as they read the words of Scripture, then that message carries God's authority.

With their ample use of the OT, the writers of the NT clearly viewed the OT as the words of God, which were authoritative for them and their readers. Jesus also affirmed the total authority of the OT, stating that "the Scripture cannot be broken" (Jn. 10:35).

If we choose to ignore the Bible's message, our ignorance doesn't negate Scripture's authority or our accountability to it. Even our legal codes assume that ignorance of the law is no excuse. When we ignore the Bible, we risk losing both its benefits and its warnings. How crucial then is our obligation—as well as our privilege—to read and study God's life-giving message to us.

Unity and Diversity in the Bible

When you read through the Bible, you can quickly and easily see the diversity between its two covers. The Bible was penned over the course of many centuries, by and for people of diverse languages (Hebrew, Aramaic, and Greek) and cultures (from ancient Semitic to Greco-Roman). According to tradition, Moses compiled the Pentateuch—the first five books of the Bible—some time around 1300 BC, relying on a rich oral history that predated his time by many centuries. At the other end of the Bible, the apostle John penned Revelation just prior to AD 100.

In addition, the Bible contains many different genres of writing. Narratives, poetry, prophecies, letters, and apocalyptic writings record the exploits, aspirations, preaching, prayers, and exhortations of a wide diversity of people. In fact, it's truly remarkable that such a collection could find its way into one book!

We also see another kind of diversity in the Bible's two "testaments" (meaning "covenants"). The "older testament," the Scriptures of the Jews, functions as the first part of the Christian Bible. Early Christians clearly saw the OT as God's Word because it testifies to the continuity of God's working in history. Of course, what the Christians call the OT, Jews simply call the Bible or Tanach (*Tanakh*). For Christians, the "newer testament" relates the fulfillment of God's promises to provide the Redeemer and proclaim the message of salvation in Christ throughout the world. The name "New Testament" represents the "New Covenant" in Christ, who fulfilled the prophecies of the OT (see Jer. 31:31; Ezk. 37:26; see Lk. 22:20; 1 Cor. 11:25; 2 Cor. 3:6; Heb. 8:8; 9:15; 12:24).

If the Bible is so diverse, what can we claim about the unity of Scripture? Of course, we can speak of the unity of the OT as the collection of ancient Israel's Scriptures, and the NT as the early church's collection. Further, both the OT and NT affirm allegiance to the one true God: *Yahweh*. The Israelite affirmation has always been clear, as expressed in the *Shema* (the Hebrew word translated "hear"): "Hear, O Israel: The LORD our God, the LORD is one" (Dt. 6:4). And while the early Christians (mostly Jews who had embraced Jesus as the Messiah) continued to affirm monotheism (for example, see 1 Cor. 8:4), they quickly came to attribute the devotion due solely to *Yahweh* to Jesus as Lord, too (see 1 Cor. 8:6). Eventually, after several centuries of deliberation, Christians formally expressed what Scripture has always implied—that God is triune, one essence in three persons: Father, Son, and Holy Spirit (reflected in texts such as Mt. 28:19; 2 Cor. 13:14).

Beyond seeing the one true God as a unifying center for the Bible, we can also identify a unifying narrative: the story of redemption. Following the "good" creation, humans—although made in

God's image—disobeyed and fell into sin. Genesis 3–11 details some of the results of this fall. Then, starting in Genesis 12, the rest of the Bible charts God's efforts to redeem what was lost. This story of God's redemption culminates in a new creation: a new heaven and a new earth (detailed in Revelation). Even portions of Scripture not directly engaged in telling this redemption story—whether the Law, wisdom, and prophets of the OT, or the epistles of the NT—provide guidance for how God's people can live as redeemed people.

Of course, we should note that the Bible's unity doesn't imply uniformity. Books have different emphases—even the Gospels, which all tell the story of Jesus' life and death. The OT Law prohibited God's people from eating shrimp and pork, while in the NT "Jesus declared all foods 'clean'" (Mk. 7:19). While the terms and issues might change as we move through the story, the Bible moves confidently forward under God's sovereign direction. Perhaps that represents the ultimate unity: God works all things according to the purpose of his will (see Eph. 1:11) to save a people who love and worship him alone.

THE CANON OF THE BIBLE

If you head to your nearest major bookstore and check out the Bible section, chances are that you'll quickly be asking yourself an important question. If you have friends of various faiths—Protestant, Catholic, and Eastern Orthodox Christians—who talk about the Bible, the same question might surface: Why do the Bibles of some groups have books between the OT and NT?

This section in some Christian Bibles, called the Apocrypha, consists of thirteen books written by the Jews prior to the first century AD. However, the books were never included in the Jewish

Scriptures. Do the groups who include the Apocrypha in their Bibles place the same value on these books as they do on the books of the OT and NT?

In other words, what's the extent of the "Canon" of Scripture? The English word *canon* comes from the Greek word that means "rule" or "standard." Canon refers to the measuring stick that defines what's "in" and what's "out" of Scripture. Catholics and various Eastern Orthodox Christians—although they differ on what to include or exclude—add various Jewish writings written during the time between the OT and NT. Anglicans include readings from the Apocrypha in their lectionary as profitable but not to establish doctrine. Mormons add books written in the nineteenth century that no others recognize.

As we examine the process Jews and Christians used to formulate their canons, we can gain some understanding why disagreement still exists among these various groups today about what actually makes up the Bible. At the same time, we should admit that the whole process used to canonize books is both somewhat shadowy and untidy, leaving us to draw conclusions from reports and data that don't always answer all the questions we want to raise.

However, the overall picture is clear enough. So let's consider the issues surrounding how the various canons were formulated by looking at them in four sections: how the OT Canon was formed, how the NT Canon was formed, how Christians arrived at what to include in their Bible, and how to view the Apocrypha.

How the Old Testament Canon Came into Being

As we noted earlier, the OT contains writings that claim to have divine authority. Naturally, the Jews collected and revered the books making those claims. Eventually, Jews combined the five books of the prophet Moses into a unit, known as the Pentateuch. Deuteronomy ends with Moses' death and the implied acknowledgment that this biblical unit was complete. By the fifth century BC, the Jews recognized these books as Scripture.

The Jews also viewed the words of other prophets—such as Joshua and Samuel—as authoritative and coming from the Lord, so these writings were also retained. And this process continued, even for writings by those not identified as prophets. Some of the authors were kings (David is an obvious example) or other wise individuals. David's words in 2 Samuel 23:2 reflect this recognition: "The Spirit of the LORD spoke through me, his word was on my tongue."

Eventually, in addition to the collection of Moses' books, which are also called "the Law," the compilation of "the Prophets" (Joshua, Judges, Samuel, Kings, Jeremiah, Ezekiel, Isaiah, and the Minor Prophets) became part of the Hebrew Bible. In addition, the Jews collected "the Writings" (Ruth, Psalms, Job, Proverbs, Ecclesiastes, Song of Songs, Lamentations, Daniel, Esther, Ezra, Nehemiah, and Chronicles). While this threefold grouping isn't found in Christian Bibles, it nicely reflects the literary character of the books.

We can't be sure when individual books in the Hebrew Bible were acknowledged as canonical or when these three groupings first appeared. In about 160 BC, the victorious Jewish warrior-priest Judas Maccabeus[1] made a concerted effort to collect the holy books that had been scattered during the war of independence[2] because at that point the Jews believed that the writings of the prophets had ceased.[3] By the end of the second century BC, the Greek translation of the prologue to the apocryphal book Ecclesiasticus mentions these three sections of the Hebrew Canon. Jesus (see Lk. 24:44) and the first century AD Jew named Philo[4] acknowledged these three divisions (although they gave "the Writings" the name "Psalms").

Reading later texts of the Talmud (records of rabbinic interpretations of the OT pertaining to Jewish law, ethics, customs, and history), some scholars argue that around the year AD 90, rabbis debated the status of the Canon. Apparently, some Qumran and

Septuagint (the translation of the Hebrew Scriptures into Greek, abbreviated as LXX) manuscripts included some apocryphal books along with the canonical ones. But if this meeting of the rabbis actually occurred, it merely removed the apocryphal books to arrive at the authoritative Jewish Canon: twenty-two books that correspond to the thirty-nine books that Christians call the OT.

How the New Testament Canon Came into Being

While the OT was the Bible of Jesus and his followers, the gospel message about him quickly led his followers in the first century to acknowledge their own collection of Scriptures, which they added to the existing Jewish Scriptures. The early Christians didn't consciously set out to write Scripture, but some of the books that began to emerge—letters first and then other documents—were eventually recognized as having divine authority.

By the time of Peter's second letter, for example, early Christians viewed some of Paul's letters on par with the OT. Speaking of Paul's letters, Peter observed, "There are some things in them hard to understand, which the ignorant and unstable twist to their own destruction, as they do the other scriptures" (2 Pet. 3:16, NRSV). In other places within the emerging NT, writers urged Christians to conform to conduct based on the Lord's words (for example, see 1 Cor. 7:10; Acts 20:35). The early church based the Communion or Eucharist ceremony on remembered words of the Lord (see 1 Cor. 11:23-25). And Paul noted that the essential message of personal salvation through Christ's death and resurrection was something he "received" and passed on (see 1 Cor. 15:3-5; see Gal. 1:9,11-12). As the apostles spread the good news of salvation, they realized the importance of retaining the traditions about Jesus (see Acts 10:36-40).

Theologically, the emerging church concluded that in Jesus Christ, God was fulfilling the promise of a New Covenant (see Jer. 31:31-34), which Jesus' death confirmed (see Lk. 22:20; 2 Cor. 3:6;

Heb. 8:8-13). Just as the Law of Moses applied to the generations of Israel, the apostles naturally applied Jesus' words to his followers. These applications—coming in the forms of the Epistles, Acts, the Gospels, and Revelation—assumed positions of authority as well. God was now speaking through Christian apostles and prophets. And while these writings don't make explicit claims to be Scripture or even authoritative, their usefulness and divine status became evident almost immediately.

However, this raised the issue of how to define what books to include in the NT Canon. The early Christians produced many books, continuing well after the age of Jesus and the apostles. If books written hundreds of years after Moses could enter the Canon of the OT, could the Christian Bible also include books written decades to hundreds of years following Jesus?

Several lists of canons from the first three centuries AD provide some interesting findings. Initially, some sectors of the church disputed some books in our NT, which gained or lost favor over several centuries before finally being embraced. Books such as Revelation, Jude, 2 Peter, and James fall into this category. In addition, some of the early lists included books not in our NT, such as Barnabas, Hermas, and Clement (these are called NT apocrypha, not the OT Apocrypha included in Catholic and Orthodox Bibles). But most early Christians never acknowledged the authoritative status of these books, so their favor was generally short-lived and they were excluded from the final Canon.

How Did Christians Arrive at Their Bible?

To determine how Christians decided what to include in the universally recognized Canon, the first question to consider is one of Jewish origins: What Jewish writings did the early church adopt as Scripture? In the earliest period following the apostles, the Christian Canon of the OT corresponded to the Jewish Canon of thirty-nine books. The

NT itself refers to the three sections of the Jewish Scriptures and cites most of the individual OT books authoritatively. However, the NT never cites any of the Jewish apocryphal books.

Over the next several centuries, Christians developed their own standards for what to include in Scripture, and several lists of canons emerged. In this process, some Christians found value in some apocryphal books, and these books found their way into some Christian copies of the Septuagint. Some scholars refer to this as the "wide canon." However, several prominent early Christian leaders (for example, bishop Melito in the second century, Origen in the second to third centuries, Epiphanius in the fourth century, and Jerome in the fourth to fifth centuries) defended a "narrow canon" that put the apocryphal books in a separate, noncanonical category.

Regarding the NT writings that ended up in the Christian Bible, evidence from the second century shows that early church leaders referred to and used books that eventually found their way into the NT. Polycarp (a Christian bishop and martyr who lived from about AD 70–155, said to be a disciple of the apostle John) used Matthew and Luke. The Christian book called *2 Clement* and the *Epistle of Barnabas* also cited Matthew, Mark, Luke, and John (in about AD 130).

By about AD 200, with the increased presence of heretics and their false teaching, church leaders realized that a canon was required. The heretic Marcion hastened this process when he published his own canon with one gospel and ten Pauline epistles (omitting Hebrews, 1 and 2 Timothy, and Titus). Irenaeus, the church father, apologist, and disciple of Polycarp, in his *Against the Heresies*, played a key early role in defending the authority of what became the canonical books. By the third century, the important church leaders Tertullian (c. 155–230), Clement of Alexandria (died between 211 and 216), and Origen (c. 185–254) all made ample use of most NT writings in the Canon we now possess, although they also cited some of the early church fathers' works as authoritative.

By the early AD 300s, the situation largely stabilized. As early church historian and bishop Eusebius wrote in his *Ecclesiastical History* (3.25), certain books were "acknowledged," meaning they certainly belonged in the NT Canon; other books were still "disputed," meaning their status was uncertain; some books were judged "spurious," meaning they were thought to be false; and yet other books considered heretical were rejected outright. At this stage (c. AD 325), James, Jude, 2 Peter, and 2 and 3 John fell into the disputed category, with Revelation in the spurious category. Later in the fourth century, the Canon was solidified. Most likely, the Thirty-ninth Paschal Letter of Athanasius (AD 367) settled the Canon for the eastern church, while the Councils of Hippo (AD 393) and Carthage (AD 397) ratified the same list for the western church. As a result, the NT consisted of the twenty-seven books in our Bibles today.

One question remains unanswered: What criteria did the Christians of these early centuries use to include or exclude books from the NT Canon? This much is clear: being a part of the Canon did not confer authority on the books; rather, books that were acknowledged as authoritative were put into the Canon. So how did the early leaders of the church recognize inspiration? Three terms summarize the process they used: apostolicity, catholicity, and orthodoxy.

Apostolicity

This term refers to writings that originated with, or at least were closely connected to, one of Jesus' apostles. Proximity to Jesus, the founder of the New Covenant, was one requirement for adding a book to the Canon. Although some books were not written by apostles, the authors had close connection to an apostle (for example, Luke as a close associate of Paul).

CATHOLICITY

This term, referring to widespread use over the entire realm of Christendom, carried significant weight in determining that a book was authoritative. When churches from east to west and north to south recognized a book's authority and found it universally useful, its case for inclusion in the Canon was strong.

ORTHODOXY

This term means that to be worthy of the Canon, a book needed to affirm the church's emerging understanding of truth and theological soundness. Most likely, the texts of the gnostics and other heretics were rejected on this score.

Again, by about AD 400, the church had finalized its canon. The NT emerged after a long process of sifting that resulted in its twenty-seven books. The Bible of the Jews, taken over intact as the Jews had preserved it, became the OT. While some Christians added the apocryphal books to their canon of the Bible, others considered them secondary, and still others rejected them altogether.

What About the Old Testament Apocrypha?

The OT Apocrypha consists of thirteen books: eleven written in Hebrew or Aramaic, and the other two in Greek. Though some early Jews considered these books inspired, the final consensus of Jewish leaders in antiquity was to exclude them from the Canon. Jews today don't consider them part of the Bible, adopting only books authorized in their authoritative commentaries on the Scriptures and oral laws: the Mishnah (c. 200) and the two Talmuds (c. 300s and 500). However, several major fourth- and fifth-century Christian Greek manuscripts of the Bible (given the names Vaticanus, Sinaiticus, and Alexandrinus) did include these thirteen books. In fact, the OT apocryphal books are preserved only in these Greek versions of the Bible, not in their original Semitic languages or by the Jews. These

Christian "Bibles" contained the thirty-nine books of the OT, the Apocrypha, some so-called Pseudepigrapha (books falsely attributed to more famous writers), and other Christian compositions, resulting in the label "wide canon."

In the late fourth century, when Jerome translated the Hebrew and Aramaic OT into Latin, he included only its thirty-nine books and considered the others apocryphal. Later, however, the Western church expanded the Bible to include these thirteen books, labeling them "deuterocanonical," or secondary to the universally accepted books of the Canon. In the sixteenth century, when reformer Martin Luther rejected the biblical status of the apocryphal books, the Roman Catholic Church responded by endorsing their inspiration and reaffirming their place in the Bible as deuterocanonical.

Why did Protestants ultimately reject the Apocrypha as part of Scripture? We can observe at least four reasons.

The first goes to the heart of the Reformation: *sola Scriptura,* which means "Scripture alone." The Reformers were reacting against perceived abuses by the Roman Catholic Church, including use of tradition and sources such as the Apocrypha rather than the Bible alone to support doctrine. A classic example comes from the apocryphal book 2 Maccabees 12:44-45, which encourages praying for the dead. Using this text as support, the Roman church developed the practice of praying for the dead to speed their way through purgatory. Protestants note that the NT never affirms prayer for the dead and does not acknowledge the existence of purgatory.

Second, Protestants assert that Jesus and the writers of the NT used only the thirty-nine books of the OT. They never directly quoted the books of the OT Apocrypha.

Third, Protestants point out that the Jews themselves limited the Bible to the thirty-nine books of the OT. First-century Jews such as Josephus and Philo, and later rabbis up to the writing of the Talmuds, claimed that prophecy ceased with Malachi.

Fourth, the acceptance of the Apocrypha as Scripture didn't start until at least a full century following the age of the apostles, perhaps after the church lost sight of its debt to the Jews. This underscores an important point: While Protestants reject the Apocrypha as Scripture, they don't view the books as useless or heretical. In fact, the thirteen books of the OT Apocrypha supply many valuable historical and theological insights into the Jewish world in the time between the OT and NT.

In contrast, Roman Catholic and Orthodox Christians defend the biblical status of the Apocrypha because that was the uniform position of the church through the centuries. They follow the historical Christianity established by church founders and refined in the ecumenical councils of the fourth through eighth centuries. The Roman Catholic Council of Trent in 1546 affirmed the Apocrypha as part of the Bible (labeling it as deuterocanonical) and thus part of inspired Scripture.

In summary, the Protestant church generally acknowledges that we can find useful and inspiring information in the OT Apocrypha, which can help us more fully understand the world and thinking of the Jews during the period between the OT and NT. And while Roman Catholic and Orthodox churches agree with that, they also affirm the Apocrypha's rightful place in the Bible, even if labeled deuterocanonical.

WRITING IN THE ANCIENT WORLD

If you want to write something—for instance, a quick shopping list—you might pull out a pen and a piece of scrap paper. Or you might start up your PC to write an e-mail or compose a more formal letter. Of course, writing in the ancient world wasn't quite so easy. So let's switch gears and examine how writers of the books that became the Bible recorded their words, briefly exploring both the history of languages in and around Palestine and the materials that people in the ancient Near East used to record their writings.

History of Languages in and Around Palestine

Possibly as many as four to five thousand years before Christ was born, the Mesopotamians developed cuneiform. Other civilizations also used this wedge-shaped writing. The Egyptians developed hieroglyphic writing, based on symbols and pictures. Eventually, ancient peoples developed systems of writing based on the concept of the alphabet. While scholars dispute the dates and locations of the origin of the alphabet, reducing language to a system of twenty to thirty letters rather than hundreds or thousands of signs greatly facilitated the ability to write.

Evidence of the use of an alphabet for writing in Palestine dates from the fifteenth to sixteenth century BC. As the use of alphabet systems grew, cuneiform and hieroglyphic writing styles disappeared.

When the Israelites first appeared in Palestine (c. thirteenth century BC), the people occupying the land had already used writing for several centuries. As with other language systems in the Semitic world, writing proceeded from right to left. From about 1000 BC, the Greeks began to develop their own alphabetic writing system, proceeding from left to right. Around the same time, a distinctive Hebrew language and script began to develop in Israel, related to but distinct from other Northwest Semitic languages such as Aramaic. Archaeologists have found clay bullae (seals for papyrus documents) in Judah dated c. 600 BC. Other ancient Hebrew writing has been discovered on seals, ostraca (broken pieces of clay pots used as writing surfaces), vases, weights, stone or rocks, as well as amulets.

The Aramaic language began with the Aramaeans, a nomadic people who lived in northern Mesopotamia and Syria. They developed an alphabetic script also used by the Canaanites and Phoenicians, even to the point of embracing the twenty-two letters of the Phoenician script. By the eighth century BC, because Aramaic was so much more useful than their cuneiform script, the Assyrians also adopted it as their official language. Before long, it became the international language for diplomacy and commerce, extending from Asia Minor (modern Turkey) to Afghanistan, Egypt, and Northern Arabia. When the Persians ruled Palestine, they made Aramaic the official language and script of the land; archaeologists have found evidence of Aramaic on seals and ostraca from that period (c. 539–332 BC).

The Hebrew language survived only in a few bullae and seals, most likely out of reverence for the biblical texts. Eventually, even biblical texts were written in Aramaic. By Ezra's time (c. 400 BC) and later, Aramaic became the common script for copying the Torah. Writers used Aramaic to write original portions of the biblical books of Ezra and Daniel (see Ezra 4:6–6:18; 7:16-26; Dan. 2:4–7:28). By the Hellenistic period (c. 300 BC and later), Aramaic virtually replaced Hebrew for writing, except for inscriptions on coins, some biblical texts, and the writing of God's name.

Based on archaeological discoveries of writings on ossuaries (stone boxes, buildings, or other places used for burials), ostraca, letters, and contracts, we know that Aramaic also became the everyday spoken language by the Jews into the first century AD. Then, as Alexander the Great successfully spread Greek language and culture beyond the boundaries of the Greek peninsula, both spoken Greek and the Greek script eventually became common in Palestine. Archaeologists have discovered Greek texts of biblical manuscripts in Qumran and Masada. The presence of Roman officials in Palestine after 63 BC even introduced a limited use of Latin. Members of the army and other officials from Italy likely spoke Latin, but this was a temporary imposition used only by foreigners.

Beyond the borders of Palestine to the west, Jews spoke and wrote Greek more and more. By the second century BC, Jews translated their Bible into Greek (the LXX), the dominant language in Egypt.

Greek became the common language of the ancient world from about the second century BC until the third or fourth century AD, and authors of the books that eventually made up the NT all wrote in Greek. Although Jesus spoke Aramaic for much of his teaching, and while oral stories about his words and activities might have circulated among Aramaic speakers at first, soon those traditions entered the Greek language. This means that if the NT gospels were written as early as three decades following Jesus' resurrection, the accounts of Jesus' life and death were already fixed in Greek.

Writing Materials

How did people in the ancient Near East write? What physical materials did they use? At first, they pressed writing into soft clay that hardened or they chiseled inscriptions into stone. Beginning around 3000 BC, clay tablets were commonly used (although not widely in Palestine) because they could easily be passed around. Inscriptions in stone also occurred (see Job 19:24); the Ten Commandments provide a prime example (see Ex. 24:12; 27:8; 31:18). Ink on stone was another medium, although it didn't survive long in the elements. Although we find references to writing on metal in Israel (see Ex. 28:36; see the apocryphal book 1 Macc. 8:22; 14:18,27,48), it was rare. The Romans wrote on bronze tablets, but usually only for official pronouncements or functions. The Egyptians wrote on wooden boards with ink. Examples of writing on thin wooden leaves also survive in Latin from Roman Britain and in Aramaic in a cave near the Dead Sea.

Many ancient peoples wrote on wax-covered boards by pressing a stylus into the soft medium. Examples occur among the Egyptians,

Babylonians, Hittites, Assyrians, Greeks, and Romans. This might explain several OT references to prophetic oracles written on tablets (see Is. 30:8; Hab. 2:2). Broken pottery fragments called potsherds or ostraca were also put to use as writing surfaces. Writing could be applied to ostraca with ink using a brush made from a rush or reed or scratched into the surface by a sharp implement.

Papyrus, made from strips of pith from the papyrus reed that grew in the marshes of the Nile River, was the most common material to receive writing in the Greco-Roman world. A tradesman would lay together the strips of pith side by side in one direction and then hammer another row of strips into the first layer at right angles to form pages. The sap in the pith kept the strips together. Once the dried pages were polished with a stone, they could receive writing, usually across the horizontal rows. The ends of the sheets could be glued together to form scrolls, resulting in the usual form of ancient books. The account of Judah's king Jehoiakim burning the prophet Jeremiah's scroll in Jeremiah 36 probably refers to a papyrus scroll. The Egyptians exported papyrus throughout the known world, and it was used in Europe until replaced by paper during the Middle Ages.

While Egypt controlled the supply of papyrus, other nations discovered that leather—when tanned, stretched, and scraped—served as an obvious medium for writing. Skins could also be sewn together and rolled into scrolls. More durable than papyrus, leather could more easily be erased and reused. Invented in the ancient Greek city of Pergamum, parchment was an especially finely processed leather produced by scraping the hair from sheep or goat skins and smoothing the tanned hides with lime.

Most OT books were probably written on leather scrolls. Most NT books, especially letters, were probably composed on sheets of papyrus. Writers of short letters such as Philemon, 2 John, and 3 John probably wrote their words on a single sheet. Early collections of epistles were joined in a scroll. Starting in the first century

AD, individual sheets of either papyrus or parchment began to be sewn together at the edges, one on top of the other, to produce what is called a codex, the forerunner of modern books. Scribes wrote on both sides of the sheets, allowing them to be read sequentially. This became the dominant method that early Christians used to reproduce and distribute their Bibles. Whether in scrolls or codices, scribes usually divided each sheet into two or three columns for ease of writing and reading. The Dead Sea Scrolls, famous examples of ancient leather rolls, date from the final two centuries BC and into the first century AD. The one scroll of Isaiah measures 24 centimeters high by 7.34 meters long (approximately 9.5 inches by 24 feet).

Ink was made from a source of carbon, usually soot or lamp-black, mixed with gum. This became a hard cake that scribes moistened with water to yield an acceptable ink for writing on papyri or skins (and even on ostraca). This type of ink tended not to fade. By the second century AD, scribes also used iron compounds to produce ink, though this process yielded ink that faded after time.

BIBLE MANUSCRIPTS — UNDERSTANDING TEXTUAL CRITICISM

Most of us love bookstores and libraries. Books we buy or borrow allow us to share authors' stories, information, poetry, and other literary creations. More amazingly, if you visited one of the Smithsonian Institute's museums, you might see a letter actually written by Abraham Lincoln nearly 150 years ago. Or in the British Museum in London, you can view one of the four surviving copies of the Magna Carta, which dates from AD 1215.

Astonishingly, the Bible includes literary works that have survived for two to three thousand years, yet we don't possess original copies of any portions of the Bible. That leads us to ask how the words of the Bible were preserved.

Using preexisting traditions and materials, and working on papyrus or skins within Israel, writers composed the books of the OT over a span of six hundred or more years. Most likely, their work began during the reigns of King David or King Solomon. The authors of the NT books wrote during a much shorter span — probably about fifty years — but over a much larger geographical territory in the Roman world: Israel, Syria, Greece, Italy, and the present area of Turkey. Again, they wrote on papyrus or skins.

Eventually, Israel and the church revered these books. But how were they preserved? Moreover, since we don't possess any original documents, how do we know that our copies of these books correspond to the original works? Can we be confident that our Bibles accurately reflect what Moses, David, Isaiah, Paul, and Peter wrote?

To answer these questions, scholars turn to the discipline known as textual criticism, which we can most simply describe as the process of identifying and removing alterations or errors from texts and manuscripts. Let's look briefly at two aspects of textual criticism: the "autographs" of the writers, and the ancient process of making copies of manuscripts.

The Autographs

Imagine King David writing out Psalm 34, or the apostle Paul composing his letter to the Romans. We don't know if David wrote out his psalms himself or dictated them to a scribe. With Paul, we know that a scribe named Tertius actually penned the epistle of Romans (see Ro. 16:22). In either case, as part of textual criticism, we call the original copy that came from an author (no matter who actually put pen to manuscript) the "autograph."

When Scripture's writers composed their books, the pages looked different from the one you're reading. Of course, these pieces were handwritten in Hebrew, Aramaic, or Greek. In addition, the writers didn't usually leave spaces between words, perhaps because writing materials were costly. Also, the languages employed only capital letters. What's more, in Hebrew and Aramaic, scribes wrote only consonants, not vowels. Imagine the first verse of Psalm 34,

I WILL BLESS THE LORD AT ALL TIMES;

HIS PRAISE SHALL CONTINUALLY BE IN MY MOUTH

written in all capital letters, with all vowels and spaces between words removed:

WLLBLSSTHLRDTLLTMS;

HSPRSSHLLCNTNLLBNMMTH

You'd probably wonder how anyone could read this. Words did have vowel sounds, but the written forms of Hebrew and Aramaic didn't record them. Native speakers learned the words with the vowel sounds and supplied them when reading. Still, this practice created a real problem for scribes who copied these books. So the Masoretes (Jewish scribes who worked in Palestine and Babylonia from about AD 600–1000) developed a system of dots and other markers to identify vowels and accents to assist readers in pronouncing the texts correctly.

Greek words do include vowels, so NT readers didn't face that problem. However, Greek writing at the time didn't include spaces between words, meaning that Paul's initial verse in Romans looked something like this:

PAULASERVANTOFJESUSCHRISTCALLEDTOBEAN
APOSTLESETAPARTFORTHEGOSPELOFGOD

With a bit of practice, you can make out the words. But you might run into problems with some sentences. Consider this one:

GODISNOWHERE

Depending on where you divide this into words, you could end up with very different meanings, including:

God is nowhere.

God is now here.

These issues demonstrate the need for textual criticism, including consideration of how copies of the autographs resulted in many variations of manuscripts.

Manuscript Transmission

When you have a keepsake or a memento—perhaps a watch that belonged to a grandfather or a favorite aunt's antique china—you regard that item as significant and valuable. What's more, you treasure and protect it.

What about the autographs of the books of the Bible? First, considering the perceived value of these books, many people would want to read them. Some might even want copies for themselves or their assemblies. In ancient Israel, individual synagogues wanted their own copies of the Torah. And in the NT era, churches scattered around the Mediterranean Sea wanted to apply the instructions Paul recorded in his epistles to their own congregations. So trained and untrained scribes produced copies of these books for wider circulation. Eventually, copies were made from copies and so on through the centuries.

Today, a copy machine or scanner will produce a nearly perfect copy of an original document; however, human scribes copying biblical books didn't. Inevitably, the laborious process of copying a biblical document introduced errors. Some of these mistakes were inadvertent and unintentional. A scribe's eyes might slip to a different line of the text, causing him to omit a line of words. Or a scribe might misunderstand a letter and substitute another. Other alterations were more intentional when scribes copied manuscripts. Sometimes they desired to "correct" the text they were copying to "improve" its style or to harmonize conflicts.

As copies proliferated during the centuries prior to printing presses, scribes continued to commit errors. As copies were made of copies, scribes often perpetuated prior errors and introduced new mistakes. Perhaps as these various copies were able to be compared, scribes corrected some errors. Still, not all corrections necessarily reverted to the way the autographs read. As the number of copies reached hundreds and then thousands, the resulting state of biblical texts became quite complex.

Let's look at an example of the confusion that these various copies of biblical manuscripts create. In Matthew 5:22, Jesus says, "I say to you that if you are angry with a brother or sister, you will be liable to judgment" (NRSV). However, the KJV reads, "But I say unto you, That whosoever is angry with his brother without a cause shall be in danger of the judgment." Note that the KJV inserts the phrase "without a cause." This difference reflects the fact that some copies of manuscripts in the original languages of Scripture include these words and others don't. For a variety of reasons, most scholars agree that a well-meaning scribe added the words "without a cause" to the manuscript he was copying and that the words were not original to Matthew. We can easily understand how a scribe might find Jesus' words difficult and, as a result, try to clarify what he thought Jesus meant. In this case, a scribe might have thought, *Jesus wouldn't prohibit all anger, only anger "without a cause."*

In addition to copying the original Hebrew, Aramaic, and Greek texts, Jews and Christians began to translate the biblical books into other languages. First, in the second century BC, the Jews translated their Hebrew/Aramaic Scriptures into Greek (the LXX). After the early church embraced the OT into its canon, the entire Bible — in parts or as a whole — was translated into other languages as the church spread. In the fourth through tenth centuries AD, Christians could read Scripture in Coptic, Old Latin, then the Latin Vulgate, Syriac, Armenian, Georgian, and Ethiopic. Lectionaries began to include portions of Scripture in local languages for use in church liturgies and other ways.

However, the autographs disappeared. We can't check any manuscript against the original to verify its accuracy. We only have copies, copies of copies, and their various translations. As we compare all these manuscripts and versions, we discover "variants" or differences among them — places where the manuscript copies contain different readings.

In many Bibles, you'll find footnotes in locations where the translators indicated their choices about which of the variant readings to include in the body of the text. Most modern versions alert readers only to places where variant readings make a difference worth mentioning. They ignore hundreds and hundreds of other minor variants that minimally affect the meaning of the text. Modern critical editions of the OT and NT that scholars and Bible translators use include most, if not all, of the variants.

THE PURPOSE OF TEXTUAL CRITICISM

When we have so many manuscript copies with divergent readings, can we really know what the original authors wrote? Can we have confidence that our Bibles contain the words inspired by the Holy

Spirit? Beyond the problem of translating the original languages into modern languages (see page 56-66), can we be certain about the wording of the original languages?

Textual criticism is the process of sifting through the variants with the goal of determining what the original autographs most likely said and to "recover" as much of the original text of a biblical book as possible. The process aims to reverse the years of alteration, copying, and translation. Let's look at how textual criticism works. Because what we can recover and how we go about the task are different for the OT and NT, let's examine each separately.

Textual Criticism of the Old Testament

Because of the length of time that it took to "produce" the OT and the scarceness of manuscript evidence over the course of that period—as well as the length of time from the OT's origin and the present—most OT scholars shy away from the goal of recovering the original wording of an OT book. That goal is simply unattainable.

In about AD 915, the Masoretes produced the main Hebrew text available today (called the Masoretic Text or MT). About a thousand years earlier, Jews had translated the OT from Hebrew into Greek (the Septuagint or LXX), which has been preserved in Christian manuscripts. Beyond that, we possess a few papyri, various texts from the caves at Qumran near the Dead Sea that reflect many books of the OT, Aramaic paraphrases of select biblical texts (called Targums), and references to the Bible in rabbinic sources.

Most biblical scholars believe that from the time of Moses, many OT books went through both oral and written versions, edited along the way, sometimes many centuries after their original appearances. The Jewish community acknowledged the books in the OT as authoritative, and most scholars agree that in about the first century BC, the textual traditions in the OT books became relatively fixed. The amazing correspondence between the scroll of the book of Isaiah found at Qumran (c. 100 BC) and the edition of Isaiah in the Hebrew MT about a thousand years later supports this conclusion.

So if biblical scholars don't have the goal of arriving at the autographs of the OT books, what does textual criticism of the OT achieve? Because Jews did not specify what were the authoritative versions of the biblical books during the many centuries leading up to the first century AD, OT scholars mine the LXX, the Targums, the Qumran texts, and the MT in an effort to discover an authoritative text that emerges from an eclectic assessment of these various texts and their readings. OT textual criticism seeks to discover the earliest renditions of the biblical texts—texts that most likely gave rise to the others—even if the goal of the autographs remains out of reach.

Because the process of sifting through manuscripts and variants is the same for both the OT and NT, we'll look at that in the next section.

Textual Criticism of the New Testament

In some ways, the task of textual criticism for the NT is easier than for the OT. The authors composed the autographs over a considerably shorter period of time (c. 50 years). And relatively quickly, Christians began to copy these texts and distribute them to churches around the Roman Empire. As a result, many copies survived. With a few exceptions, the production of the texts themselves didn't go through a long period of development. For those that did undergo a series of edits (perhaps the gospel of John), they emerged in "final form" in a matter of decades, not hundreds of years. In all likelihood, all the NT books had been composed by AD 100 and were likely already being copied and circulated.

The number of both copies and variants makes the task of

textual criticism complicated. The autographs were copied, perhaps numerous times. Then copies were made of copies, and so on. Eventually, as the church moved into areas beyond its Greek-speaking origins, Christians translated sections or the entire NT into other languages.

Arriving at the Original Texts

So now that we've explored some factors that require the practice of textual criticism, let's look at the processes that can take us as close as possible to a recovery of the original texts. If we want to play the part of textual critics, we need to consider two main factors in our attempt to recover the original (or earliest) forms of a text: external evidence and internal evidence. External evidence concerns the manuscript itself—the number, dates, and types of manuscripts that we can access and read. Internal evidence consists of two forms: (1) what we know about how scribes operated and were likely to do when making copies of texts; and (2) what we can know about the original authors of the texts—their thought, theology, language, writing style, and background.

Of course, the field of textual criticism is very complex and nuanced. In what follows, I'll try to explain the process in a simple way. Arriving at the best possible reading among various copies and versions of manuscripts of biblical books involves deciding on a number of probabilities. On balance, textual critics decide that one reading (variant) is more likely to be the original (or preferable) reading than others. The process involves putting manuscripts with variant readings side by side.

Textual critics seek to determine which option matches what the author most likely wrote. As we look at the manuscripts themselves (the *external evidence*), a variant is more likely to be original if it is earlier than the others, is found in better-quality manuscripts, and has the widest geographical distribution. While there are exceptions to these guidelines, most often the longer the time between the original text and a copy, the more likely an error was introduced. Also, if a scribe located in Caesarea made an error when copying a text, that error wouldn't be present in copies in other locations. As scholars assess the variants of manuscripts, they often come to trust some manuscripts more than others because those seem to contain the more likely readings more often than not.

The *number* of manuscripts supporting a given variant isn't necessarily significant, but it might be. As centuries passed, the number of manuscripts grew exponentially; therefore, an error introduced in the fifth century AD might subsequently have hundreds of copies spring from it. So even though all these copies perpetuated the error, that reading became an accepted one. Manuscripts that contained a better reading (that is, close to the original that the biblical author wrote) might never be copied again. So that reading, though original, would occur in fewer manuscripts.

Textual critics also need to weigh *internal evidence*, and they usually use two sets of criteria. First, they look at how scribes worked; often the shortest reading is more likely to be original because a scribe probably expanded, improved, or enhanced a reading rather than abbreviated it. That also implies that a more difficult reading is probably original.

Second, textual critics look at a text's author and conclude that the most likely reading closely conforms to the author's typical vocabulary, style, and theology. In addition, given the background of the biblical authors, a variant that seems more Semitic has a better claim to originality than one that's more Hellenistic or Greek. In the case of parallel passages, such as in the Synoptic Gospels, a reading that diverges from parallels is more likely original because a scribe would probably try to change a passage to conform to another gospel rather than introduce or leave a conflict. A reading that diverges from its OT background, from church theology, or from liturgical expressions in the church is more likely to be the original. Again, scribes would likely alter texts in the direction of conformity to orthodoxy and church practice rather than against them.

The entire process of textual criticism boils down to this: The correct reading is the one that best explains how the others came into existence. To go back to the earlier example from Matthew 5:22, it's more likely that the *absence* of the phrase "without a cause" explains why a scribe would add it. It's less likely that the phrase existed in the original and that a scribe deleted it.

Certainly, the way critics use these criteria isn't exact. Sometimes the criteria work in tension with each other. Textual criticism is both an art and a science, and critics must often *weigh* more than *count* the evidence as they work. They constantly make judgment calls, and decisions result as they consider different probabilities. This approach, sometimes called "reasoned eclecticism," lies behind the current Hebrew and Greek testaments and serves as the basis for all modern translations of the Bible.

Largely since the nineteenth century, both OT and NT scholars have sifted the evidence and, along the way, developed the principles outlined here. As more evidence surfaces — often in the form of earlier or better manuscripts — scholars evaluate and revise the published original language versions of both testaments. The result is an overwhelming consensus among scholars of all backgrounds around the world that our versions of the Hebrew/Aramaic and Greek testaments are as close to the originals as the current state of the evidence allows. For the OT, that text is *Biblia Hebraica Stuttgartensia*, 5th edition. For the NT, the texts are Nestle-Aland, *Novum Testamentum Graece*, 27th edition (German Bible Society) and *The Greek New Testament*, 4th edition (United Bible Societies). The texts of these two Greek NT versions are identical.

TRANSLATING THE BIBLE

Now that we understand how we've arrived at texts that are as close as possible to what the original authors wrote, and thus what God inspired, we still face the work of translating those texts faithfully into the languages of the people of God. Of course, even if we have the original words that biblical authors penned, most of us can't read them. We need the expertise of biblical scholars who can read the ancient Hebrew/Aramaic and Greek languages to translate the Bible into languages we understand.

One glance at the Bible section in a bookstore shows not only how many versions are available in English but also how many different types of Bibles exist. We find Bibles that contain only the translated words of Scripture, various kinds of study Bibles, and Bibles targeted to specific audiences. And they come in many versions.

Why are so many different Bibles available? How do you know which one is *best* or whether some are *more reliable* or *more faithful* than others? Why do some people insist on retaining the King James (or Authorized) Version of 1611 (or its updated NKJV), while others argue that modern versions provide a better choice? Let's look at the following three issues about translating the Bible that will help answer these questions: the nature of translation, the available English versions of the Bible, and the process of selecting a version for yourself.

The Nature of Translation

Most of us studied a foreign language at some point, at least in high school, or we know someone who speaks a language other than English. Even minimal contact with another language is enough to convince us that different languages use different ways to convey the same idea.

When translating the Bible into English, translators need to know both what the original language means and how English (or any target language) best conveys that meaning. In the transfer from the original language to another, translators use different tactics depending on the goal of their translation. How closely should they keep to the words or structures of the original language? What role does the target language have? Let's look at a few of the issues translators need to address that make their task complex.

Meaning or Exactitude?

In producing a translation, does the translator place priority on reproducing the *effect* of the word, phrase, or sentence of the original, or on finding terms to reproduce exactly in English what the Hebrew or Greek words mean? In other words, what's the goal of the translation: transferring the intended meaning of the original, or trying to duplicate the original's exact wording?

Priority on Text or Audience?

Translators must also decide whether to place a higher priority on the needs of the audience or on reproducing the forms of the original language. To use an extreme example, if you had to translate "Your sins will be white as snow" (Isa. 1:18) to a tribal group in a tropical climate with no concept of snow, would you substitute a different word for *snow* in order to meet the needs of that audience? Or would you use the word *snow* (or invent a word for *snow*) because it most closely matches the original language?

Balancing Potential Ambiguities

Moving from one language to another requires decisions on how to handle ambiguities in one or both of them. A literal translation might introduce more ambiguity into the target language than what existed in the original language.

For example, 1 Corinthians 7:1 might read literally, as in the

KJV, "*It is* good for a man not to touch a woman," the translation also adopted by the NRSV. Is that more or less ambiguous in meaning than, "It is good to live a celibate life" (NLT)? The NIV, "It is good for a man not to marry," takes the modern reader in a different direction. The TNIV altered it to "It is good for a man not to have sexual relations with a woman" (much closer, I'd argue, to the intention of Paul's words). *Touch* in the KJV and NRSV is a literal translation of the Greek word *aptō*. But translating it literally might result in readers missing the sexual connotations of the word in this context. In this instance, the NLT and the TNIV correctly remove the ambiguity. So which is really more literal?

This might be a good time to mention that the word *literal* often isn't useful when speaking of translations. A better phrase to capture what most people mean by literal is *formally equivalent*. For example, in 1 Corinthians 7:1, *touch* is more formally equivalent to the Greek word *aptō*, but it's not necessarily more literal. We can be certain Paul didn't intend to prohibit men from shaking hands with women.

Another troublesome ambiguity concerns gender. In Greek, the words for man (*anēr*) or woman (*gynē*) can also mean husband or wife. Another word, *anthrōpos*, means person or human, but in the Greek NT it can also refer specifically to a man (male person). In the past, the words *man* or *men* often functioned generically in English. So when people of the past read, "All men are sinners," they understood it to mean, "All people are sinners." Translators didn't face any trouble when they translated the Greek *anthrōpos* as "man" or its plural as "men."

However, an ambiguity for modern translations occurs when *anthrōpos* refers to people generically. For example, in Matthew 18:7 Jesus says, "Woe to the world because of the things that cause people to sin! Such things must come, but woe to the *man* through whom they come!" (NIV, emphasis added). The word translated "man" here is *anthrōpos*. See what the NRSV does with this: "Woe to the world because of stumbling blocks! Occasions for stumbling are bound to come, but woe to the *one* by whom the stumbling block comes!" (emphasis added). By translating *anthrōpos* as "one," the NRSV avoids the ambiguity for modern readers who might think that Jesus announces judgment only on males who cause others to stumble.

Another tactic for avoiding gender ambiguity is to take statements that are singular in the original text and make them plural in the translation. For example, the NIV renders Psalm 1:1 as follows: "Blessed is the man who does not walk in the counsel of the wicked or stand in the way of sinners or sit in the seat of mockers." Does the psalmist believe that only an individual male can be blessed in this way? Answering this question with a no, the NRSV reads, "Happy are those who do not follow the advice of the wicked, or take the path that sinners tread, or sit in the seat of scoffers." In this case, the NRSV gains a more inclusive appeal to all readers, male and female, to seek God's blessing, and women don't need to feel that the text doesn't speak to them. Yet the NRSV loses the original formally equivalent use of singular nouns and verbs. Another loss might be a sense of individual responsibility to choose carefully the counsel we follow. (By the way, note in the previous sentence that I used the plural pronoun *we* to appeal to all readers of this book.)

FORMALLY OR DYNAMICALLY EQUIVALENT?

Earlier, I mentioned the phrase *formally equivalent*. All translations fit on a continuum from formal equivalence to dynamic equivalence to free paraphrase. Although these labels are far from precise, let's look at each one.

A *formally equivalent translation* tends to be word for word. The most formally equivalent is an interlinear version that simply substitutes the word in the target language for each word in the source. However, that isn't really a true translation. Formally equivalent translations do adjust the structure and wording to produce an acceptable version in the target language. Of our modern English translations, the NASB and the ESV represent this approach.

A *dynamically equivalent translation* tends to be thought for thought. The translators ask how the original text *functioned* for readers and employ the best expressions in the target language that will achieve that same function. When concepts or images of the original don't function in the same ways today, contemporary versions often substitute modern forms to achieve dynamic equivalence. For example, the Hebrew text of 1 Samuel 25:22 speaks of urinating against the wall (see KJV; the LXX reads "make water against the wall"). But this graphic image isn't required in order to make the point. Examples of versions seeking dynamic equivalence include the NIV, TNIV, and GNT.

Finally, a *paraphrase* tends to take more liberties in departing from the wording and structure of the original language texts, using more distinctive language targeted to a specific culture. Examples of paraphrases include *The Living Bible* and *The Message*.

The following chart reflects where the most popular modern versions fall along this continuum.

FORMAL EQUIVALENCE	DYNAMIC EQUIVALENCE		PARAPHRASE
Interlinear ESV RSV NRSV	NIV	NCV	*The Message*
NASB KJV NKJV	TNIV	REB GNT NLT	

All of these versions have potential merits and pitfalls. While formally equivalent translations appear to begin with a worthy and useful goal, these versions might run the risk of using language that misleads modern readers; in only one sense do they maintain proximity to the inspired version. Dynamically equivalent versions might offer a better chance of causing modern readers to get the message, but these versions and paraphrases might omit or distort the structure and wording—and possibly the intention—of the original text.

Available English Versions

The continuum chart in the last section lists just some of the versions available in English today. How did we end up with so many translations of the Bible into English?

Though versions produced by John Wycliffe, Miles Coverdale, and William Tyndale—as well as the Geneva Bible (1575)—appeared earlier in English, King James VI of England commissioned the translation that became the Authorized Version throughout the British Isles and then eventually the entire English-speaking world. His team of scholars compared the available Hebrew and Greek manuscripts and in 1611 produced the version that dominated English language usage for several centuries. Working under difficult political and religious conditions, they produced an amazing translation. However, since Elizabethan English language became archaic and obscure, the KJV was revised many times over the centuries to keep current with language usage. The most thorough updating became the NKJV. Note the differences in the various renditions of John 3:8:

The wind bloweth where it listeth, and thou hearest the sound thereof, but canst not tell whence it cometh, and whither it goeth: so is every one that is born of the Spirit. (KJV)

The wind blows where it wishes, and you hear the sound of it, but cannot tell where it comes from and where it goes. So is everyone who is born of the Spirit. (NKJV)

With the discovery of better and earlier manuscripts, biblical scholars eventually saw the need to produce a new English translation based on the best available manuscripts and the best principles of textual criticism. In 1885, British biblical scholars produced the Revised Version (RV), and in 1901 the American Standard Version (ASV) appeared in the United States.

As archaeologists discovered additional ancient texts in the twentieth century, including the Dead Sea Scrolls, American scholars produced the Revised Standard Version (RSV) in 1952. While some groups of Christians shunned the RSV and insisted on using only the KJV, the RSV marked a monumental achievement based on thoroughly modern principles of textual criticism, translation theory, and the best manuscripts. In 1971, scholars updated the RSV and in 1990 thoroughly reworked it to produce the New Revised Standard Version (NRSV). As we observed earlier, this translation adopted gender-inclusive language. The RSV and NRSV have become the mainstays of many Christian groups.

While some Christians shunned the RSV, many of them saw the wisdom of incorporating the latest advances in textual criticism and moving beyond the KJV. Therefore, in the U.S., conservative biblical scholars produced a formally equivalent translation, the New American Standard Bible (NASB, 1971), updating the ASV. British biblical scholars produced the more dynamically equivalent New English Bible (NEB, completed in 1970), subsequently updated as the Revised English Bible (REB) in 1990. Meanwhile, an international team of scholars produced a version that fell somewhere between formal and dynamic equivalence, resulting in the New International Version (NIV, completed in 1978). Further updates to the NIV resulted in the New International Readers Version (NIRV) for young readers, the NIV Inclusive Language Edition (in Britain in 1996), and finally Today's New International Version (TNIV).

Appearing more recently, the English Standard Version (ESV,

2001) terms itself "essentially literal," stating its goal of formal equivalence. The Holman Christian Standard Bible (CSB, 2003) fits into this camp as well. These Bibles do not employ gender-inclusive language.

In addition, a desire emerged for more accessible versions that could be more easily understood by people with little biblical background. These translations often used more paraphrasing in their language. In the dynamic part of the continuum, the Bible societies issued Today's English Version (TEV, 1966), expanded later into the Good News Bible, and then the Good News Translation (1976). More to the paraphrased side of the continuum, J. B. Phillips paved the way in Britain with The New Testament in Modern English for Schools (PH, 1959). Starting with Living Letters, American Kenneth Taylor eventually completed the entire Bible, the Living Bible, Paraphrased (TLB, 1971). While their goal was to paraphrase the biblical text to be understandable to modern readers, both came under some criticism for the liberties they took in their translations. The Living Bible was eventually redone as a dynamic equivalent translation under the auspices of a team of scholars, resulting in the New Living Translation (NLT, 1996). Also on the paraphrased side of the spectrum is Eugene Peterson's *The Message* (MSG, 2002), which has proven very popular but has also received criticism for departure from formal words and structures of the original languages.

A similar paraphrasing process took place in translations to other major languages and, to a decreasing extent, in languages fewer people speak or where there are fewer Christians. Luther produced the Luther Bible in German, which has undergone revisions. The same holds true for other European languages, as the production of more dynamic versions paralleled the practice in English. Through the work of the Summer Institute of Linguistics (Wycliffe Bible Translators) and the combined efforts of the United Bible Societies, all or portions of the Bible have been translated into more than two thousand languages. In many cases, some languages that previously had just formally equivalent versions now also have dynamically equivalent translations.

In fairness to translators and versions, we should evaluate Bibles by considering what the various translations seek to accomplish. In other words, it's not fair to criticize a translation for not doing something it was never intended to do. Criticizing a dynamically equivalent translation for not translating a word "literally" means we're misunderstanding the nature of that version.

For example, interlinear is perhaps the purest formally equivalent version, but it's not really a translation at all; it's more of a word-for-word interpretation from one language into another. An interlinear word-for-word rendition of John 3:16 from Greek into English would read like this:

> So much for loved God the world, that his son the unique
> he gave, in order that every one who believes in him not
> may perish but have life eternal.

While this retains the structure and formal translation of the original words, the result isn't acceptable English and it doesn't convey clearly what the original Greek intended. Every version, then, must decide how much it will depart from this extremely formal equivalence to communicate the text's meaning to its readers. Most translators and Bible publishers decide who the intended readers will be and then determine whether the translation will stay closer to the original wording of the source language or to its original function.

Selecting a Version for Yourself

When choosing a Bible version for yourself, you'll need to consider several factors. One is where a translation of the Bible falls on the formally equivalent/dynamically equivalent/paraphrase spectrum.

Again, the target audience often determines where a version lands on this continuum. For example, if a version targets readers with no more than a third-grade level of reading (such as the New Century Version), then it can't achieve formal equivalence. The vocabulary will need to be limited and the lengths of the sentences shorter. What this version gains in accessibility it sacrifices in precision. So if you are a young person or are buying a Bible for a young person, you might consider a version like this.

Another issue that looms in the minds of some readers is the decision about gender language. Some recent versions made conscious choices to employ gender-inclusive language. Others made equally conscious choices to retain the exclusive-language approach. The greatest benefit of gender-inclusive versions is precisely that: They seek to be inclusive. They avoid the appearance of excluding females where the original languages didn't intend to. When James wrote in Greek, "Consider it pure joy, my brothers," it would be unfortunate for readers to conclude that James was writing to only the men in his congregations, so some versions clarify as, "Consider it pure joy, my brothers and sisters." For those who don't know the biblical languages or who don't possess and know how to use an interlinear translation, a gender-inclusive version helps them distinguish between when the original languages referred generically to "man" and when the original referred specifically to males.

So how should you choose a Bible? One important question to ask yourself is, *How will I use this Bible?* Believers use their Bibles in a variety of ways, and one version might be the best choice for a specific task. For example, for a close study of a text in preparation for teaching, you might want to use a version from the formally equivalent end of the spectrum to stay closer to the structure and wording of the original languages. This won't necessarily result in a better understanding of the text's meaning, but you'll have a better sense of how the original language presented the message. You can see structure and gain a closer view of what words were used originally, but you'll still need to decide what *"touch* a woman" means (1 Cor. 7:1). Many teachers use several versions to see where translations differ and how best to interpret.

For devotional or more "daily guidance from Scripture" reading, a dynamic version might offer the best choice. This middle ground serves many Christians well. Readers have the best chance to grasp the intentions of the author and how those intentions apply to their own lives.

If you're a new Christian or investigating the Bible for the first time, you might choose a paraphrased version that uses more modern wording and structures. Reading one of these versions can be less intimidating and more inviting for those unfamiliar with Scripture. It can also be a refreshing change for a more mature Christian who wants to read familiar texts from a different point of view, perhaps devotionally or in some new regimen of reading.

Most of us enjoy the blessing of abundance, and we can use several types of Bibles for various uses. If your pastor tends to preach from one version, you might bring that one to church; for a neighborhood Bible study, you might use another; and for personal reading or study, still a third. In fact, the use of several Bibles will help you see where differences in the translations occur and why the translators did what they did. Even more important than what version you select is the commitment to read and study the Bible consistently and with a commitment to put into practice what you learn (see Mt. 7:24-27; Jas. 2:22).

FOR FURTHER STUDY

The Nature and Authority of the Bible

Dockery, D. S. *Christian Scripture: An Evangelical Perspective on Inspiration, Authority, and Interpretation.* Nashville: Broadman, Holman, 1995.

Erickson, M. J. *Christian Theology*. 2nd ed. Grand Rapids, MI: Baker, 1998, 196–259.

Morris, L. *I Believe in Revelation*. Grand Rapids, MI: Eerdmans, 1976.

Vanhoozer, K. J. *Is There a Meaning in This Text?* Grand Rapids, MI: Zondervan, 1998.

Wenham, J. *Christ and the Bible*. 3rd ed. Grand Rapids, MI: Baker, 1994.

Woodbridge, J. D. *Biblical Authority*. Grand Rapids, MI: Zondervan, 1982.

The Biblical Canon

Beckwith, R. *The Old Testament Canon of the New Testament Church*. Grand Rapids, MI: Eerdmans, 1986.

Bruce, F. F. *The Canon of Scripture*. Downers Grove: InterVarsity, 1988.

deSilva, D. A. *Introducing the Apocrypha*. Grand Rapids, MI: Baker, 2004.

Harris, R. L. *Inspiration and Canonicity of the Bible*. 2nd ed. Grand Rapids, MI: Zondervan, 1971.

Metzger, B. M. *The Canon of the New Testament: Its Origin, Development, and Significance*. Oxford: Clarendon, 1997.

Waltke, B. K. "How We Got the Hebrew Bible: The Text and Canon of the Old Testament." In *The Bible at Qumran: Text, Shape, and Interpretation*, ed. P. W. Flint. Grand Rapids, MI: Eerdmans, 2001, 27–50.

Writing in the Ancient World

Derrenbacker, R. "Writing, Books, and Readers in the Ancient World." *American Theological Library Association Summary of Proceedings* 52 (1998): 205–229.

Elsom, H. "The New Testament and Greco-Roman Writing." In

The Literary Guide to the Bible, ed. R. Alter and F. Kermode.
Cambridge, MA: Belknap of Harvard University Press, 1987,
561–578.

Millard, A. *Reading and Writing in the Time of Jesus*. The Biblical
Seminar 69. Sheffield, UK: Sheffield Academic Press, 2000.
Includes a massive bibliography of the subject.

Bible Manuscripts — Textual Criticism

Black, D. A. *New Testament Textual Criticism: A Concise Guide*.
Grand Rapids, MI: Baker, 1994.

Brotzman, E. R. *Old Testament Textual Criticism: A Practical
Introduction*. Grand Rapids, MI: Baker, 1993.

Holmes, Michael. "Textual Criticism." In *Interpreting the New
Testament: Essays on Methods and Issues*, ed. D. A. Black and D.
S. Dockery. Nashville: Broadman, Holman, 2001, 46–73.

Versions, Translations, and Paraphrases

Beekman, J., and J. Callow. *Translating the Word of God*. Grand
Rapids, MI: Zondervan, 1974.

Brenner, A. et al. *Bible Translations on the Threshold of the Twenty-
First Century*. Sheffield, UK: Sheffield Academic Press, 2002.

Carson, D. A. *The King James Version Debate: A Plea for Realism*.
Grand Rapids, MI: Baker, 1978.

Carson, D. A. *The Inclusive Language Debate: A Plea for Realism*.
Grand Rapids, MI: Baker; Leicester, UK: InterVarsity, 1998.

Kubo, S., and W. F. Specht. *So Many Versions? Twentieth-Century
English Versions of the Bible*. Grand Rapids, MI: Zondervan,
1983.

Poythress, V. S., and W. A. Grudem. *The Gender-Neutral Bible
Controversy: Muting the Masculinity of God's Words*. Nashville:
Broadman, Holman, 2000.

CHAPTER 2

PREPARING TO STUDY THE BIBLE: ITS STORY AND WORLD

Have you ever planted a shrub or tree in your landscape? Or maybe you really worked up your courage and planted a whole vegetable garden. If so, you probably quickly learned that the success of your landscaping or gardening rested on what you did to prepare the soil before planting as much as the watering and other care you gave your plants each day.

In a similar way, before we embark on our own study of the Bible, we need to prepare our minds. While the Bible is "God's word to us," it originated as his Word to other people who lived a long time ago in places vastly different from the ones where we live today. So let's look at the world as it existed while Scripture was written. This will allow us to accomplish two important tasks.

First, we need to understand the message of the Bible — its overall story. Who are its characters? What's the overall plot? Why was it written? Who was it written to?

Second, to grasp the message in the Bible, we need to understand the various worlds where the Word of God came to his people. Who were the authors and the original recipients of the Bible's various books? What were their lives like? As we study the Bible, we can understand its message better if we put the people and places it mentions into some kind of historical and cultural framework. When did these events happen and these people live? What was life like back then where they lived?

While many authors have dedicated entire books to answer these questions, we'll engage in a brief survey of the world of the Bible to set the stage for our own study of its individual sections.

THE WORLD OF THE OLD TESTAMENT

As we briefly look at the historical and cultural backgrounds of the Bible, it's important to examine both the macro and micro levels. This chapter tackles a big-picture survey on the macro level, helping us put the entire Bible into its historical and cultural setting. Later, when we take up the tasks of studying individual sections or passages of the Bible—the micro level—we'll return to this issue. That is, when we study individual texts, we need an understanding of the specific historical and cultural features they include.

For now, let's examine two major time spans in the world of the OT: what was going on in history at the time, and what life was like in OT Israel.

What's Going On in History?

The first eleven chapters of Genesis declare God's creation of the world, its fall, and the disastrous aftermath in human history. Death, murder, Babel, and the flood provide glimpses into a world in chaos. But in Genesis 12, the story of God's plan to restore humankind's relationship with him begins with Abraham. Called by God from Ur in Mesopotamia (modern Iraq), Abraham eventually settled in what became Israel.

Abraham's descendents, the Jews, tell the entire OT story from their location in this land. While historians and scholars can't easily determine precise dates, Abraham probably lived somewhere between 2000–1900 BC. Escaping slavery in Egypt under Moses' leadership in around 1350 BC, the Israelites settled in the Holy Land. The period of the judges ran until about 1050 BC, when Israel crowned its first king, Saul. King David succeeded Saul (c. 1000 BC), and David's son Solomon built the first temple (c. 965 BC).

After Solomon's death, the kingdom divided into Israel (ten tribes) in the north and Judah (two tribes) in the south (c. 933 BC). This divided kingdom continued until the Assyrians toppled the northern kingdom (c. 721 BC) and exiled many of its inhabitants. Although Judah held out a bit longer, this kingdom eventually succumbed to the Babylonians (c. 586 BC), which exiled many of its citizens. After the Persians defeated the Babylonians and took over control of Israel, the Persian king Cyrus issued a decree to allow the Jews to return from exile to their homeland (c. 538 BC).

In the following hundred years or so, a remnant of the Jewish population rebuilt the Jerusalem temple and the walls of the city. Before, during, and following Israel's times of exile, prophets appeared on the scene to warn the people of God's judgment, call them to repent, and promise future blessing if they would turn back to God. The OT closes on this note, with Malachi appealing to his people to return to God.

We read the records of the events of these periods in the books of the OT. Genesis covers the time from creation until the death of Joseph, after Jacob and his sons settle in Egypt (c. 1680 BC). The remaining books of the Pentateuch cover the span from the Exodus from Egypt until the conquest of Canaan (c. 1360–1240 BC). Joshua details the conquest, followed by the period of the judges (c. 1210–1050 BC). The story in Ruth takes place in the period of the judges as well.

The books of Samuel span the final years of the judges and the beginning of the monarchy; Kings and Chronicles encompass the rest of the monarchy until the Exile (c. 586 BC). The Poetic and Wisdom Literature (Psalms, Proverbs, Song of Songs, and Ecclesiastes) begins to emerge at the time of Israel's first kings, although they incorporate writings passed down from earlier periods. The writing of the prophets emerges c. 800 BC and continues to the end of the OT. Meanwhile, in the period at the end of the Exile and the return to the land in the Persian rulers, we find the books of Ezra, Esther, and Nehemiah.

This rapid overview mentions several ancient world powers that intersected with Israel during this period. Of course, history records many other significant nations and events that occurred during this span. In brief, between about 2000–1500 BC, the Druids appeared in Britain, the Hyksos ruled in ancient Egypt, Hammurabi issued the law codes in Babylon, the Hittites ruled in Anatolia, the first seven periods of Chinese literature emerged, and the Minoan culture developed in Crete.

In many parts of the world, religious polytheism (the worship of multiple gods or deities) and various ethnic and local religions dominated. Around the same time the Israelites conquered Canaan, the Egyptians moved to a monotheistic worship of the sun-god Ra, and the great Nile delta building projects appeared. During the time of the judges in Israel, the Hittite Empire collapsed and the Philistines and other Sea Peoples settled in the coastal areas of the eastern Mediterranean Sea. When Kings Saul, David, and Solomon ruled Israel, the Etruscan (pre-Romans in Italy) civilization began, Baal worship flourished in Canaan, and the beginnings of polytheism and various folk religious practices appeared in Greece.

At the time of Israel's divided kingdom and the Exile (c. 800 BC and later), Greece began its golden age (Socrates, Homer, the Acropolis in Athens, and the founding of democracy). At the same time, Zoroaster, an Iranian poet and religious reformer, founded a religion in Persia (Zoroastrianism or Parsiism in India) that had monotheistic elements in contrast to the pervasive religious climate of Persia. As the prophets of Israel proclaimed their messages, some of the world's most powerful empires rose and fell: Assyrian, Babylonian, Persian, and Greek. Also about this time, Confucius and Taoism arose in China, and the Upanishads and Jainism in India.

What Was Life Like in Old Testament Israel?

Though we don't have space to describe daily life in the entire world, we do know some details about the land of Palestine during the time of the OT. This quick overview provides some glimpses into the lands and peoples who played their roles in the unfolding of God's story.

LIFE PRIOR TO THE EXODUS

With the Exodus from Egypt, the Israelites entered the Promised Land, taking possession as God's inheritance for them. Prior to this conquest, the Land had many local inhabitants. When the OT mentions their land, the Israelites recall that they didn't always possess it; it was the land of Canaan (see Gen. 12:5; 23:2; Dt. 32:49).

Who dwelled there? Exodus 3:17 provides a classic list: "I promise that I will bring you up out of the affliction of Egypt, to the land of the Canaanites, the Hittites, the Amorites, the Perizzites, the Hivites, and the Jebusites, a land flowing with milk and honey." Genesis 15:18-20 provides an even more expansive list: "On that day the LORD made a covenant with Abram, saying, 'To your descendants I give this land, from the river of Egypt to the great river, the river Euphrates, the land of the Kenites, the Kenizzites, the Kadmonites, the Hittites, the Perizzites, the Rephaim, the Amorites, the Canaanites, the Girgashites, and the Jebusites.'"

Often, the OT refers to all these Northwest Semitic peoples through the use of two headings: Canaanites and Amorites. While we might recoil at the thought of God's people simply taking control of a land from its original inhabitants, the OT bases the transfer to Israel on God's ultimate ownership of all things and God's right to give his people what he wants them to have.

While some of the peoples and cultures of Canaan were relatively localized, many (for example, the Amorites) lived throughout a large geographical region. The varied cultures of these people during this Late Bronze Age ranged from wandering nomads to scattered villages to highly organized cities with impressive walls and fortifications.

According to the Song of Deborah in Judges 5:24-27, the Kenites likely lived in tents and pastured dairy herds, perhaps like Bedouin in today's Middle East. Before the conquest of Canaan, the spies reported to Joshua that the Hittites, Jebusites, and Amorites lived in the hill country, while other groups lived on the coast or in the Negev (see Num. 13:29). Joshua 11:3 confirms this situation.

At times, local inhabitants organized politically, such as when they joined forces in an attempt to prevent Joshua's advances. Often, larger foreign powers such as Egypt controlled and exacted tribute (payments of submission or allegiance) from the local peoples. Overall, when Joshua led his forces to conquer the land, Canaan was thinly populated and economically depressed.

Of course, the peoples who inhabited Canaan worshipped gods other than *Yahweh*, and God commanded the Israelites to kill them all and destroy their religious shrines (see Ex. 23:23-24; Dt. 20:17). Israel's failure to completely eradicate the people resulted in continuing temptations to follow their gods and detestable cultural ways (see Jdg. 3:5).

Canaanite religion centered in a fertility cult with Baal, a title for the Semitic storm-god Hadad, who dwelled on a mountain in the north. The cult included female deities named Asherah, Astarte, and Anat, although the OT gives them different names. Religious practices included sacred prostitution, homosexuality, and various orgiastic rites—all repulsive to *Yahweh* and a primary cause for destroying the worshippers of Baal.

WANDERING IN THE WILDERNESS

The early chapters of Exodus describe God's deliverance of his people from slavery in Egypt, and the march to Mount Sinai, where *Yahweh* gave Moses the Ten Commandments. The book of Numbers takes the wandering Israelites from Mount Sinai to the threshold of the Promised Land, the conquest of which the book of Joshua details. Although the Israelites complained about the inhospitable environment of the wilderness (see Ex. 15:24; 16:2-3; 17:2-3), this period of wandering solidified their worship of *Yahweh* (see Dt. 33:2; Jdg. 5:4-5). With Moses as leader, Israel's faith takes on its distinctive nature.

Israel's loose collection of wandering tribes didn't have an easy time deciding how to claim the Land God promised them. Moses was the acknowledged leader, but the crowd was unruly. Whether or not to trust Moses—and the God that Moses served—became a major test of whether Israel would succeed or fail. Often the people rebelled during God's tests of their loyalty (see Ps. 95:7-11). They failed to gain access to Canaan from the south, wandered a great deal as a result of God's punishment for their rebellion (see Num. 14:28-35), detoured into the Edom and Moab territories (see Num. 21–25), and conquered the kingdom of Heshbon (see Num. 21). The wanderings finally ended when God chose Joshua to be Moses' successor (see Num. 27:12-22; Dt. 31:1-8; 34:9), the one who would lead Israel in the conquest of the Promised Land and divide the Land among the twelve tribes.

The Conquest of Palestine

Joshua 1–12 presents a graphic picture of Israel's twelve tribes conquering the inhabitants of the Promised Land. The conquest took place in fits and starts, paralleling the pattern of the Israelite's obedience or disobedience of God's instructions. When the conquest ended, Joshua divided the land among the tribes (see Josh. 13–21). However, Judges 1 confirms evidence within the book of Joshua (for example, see Josh. 13:2-6; 15:63; 23:7-13) that the conquest was far from complete; many pockets of resistance remained that the Israelites contended with for years to come.

Archaeological evidence confirms that during the 1200s BC, major upheavals and the destruction of many towns occurred in Palestine, just as the biblical record recounts during this conquest period. In many cases, the Israelites rebuilt and occupied the cities they destroyed. They settled the land in the manner of the former inhabitants, eventually planting orchards, fields, and vineyards, and herding sheep, goats, and other animals.

Just who were these people who wandered in the wilderness and now occupied their own lands? After Abraham's entrance into Canaan (see Gen. 12:5; 13:3), his descendents multiplied in the land. Abraham's son Isaac fathered Jacob and Esau. God gave Jacob the name Israel (see Gen. 32:28); because the Hebrews descend from Jacob, they came to be known as Israel. While Jacob's twelve sons and their families relocated to and multiplied in Egypt because of Joseph's intervention (see Gen. 46:5-27), other Hebrews likely remained in Canaan to weather out the famine as best they could with the land's other inhabitants.

Eventually, Moses directed a mass exodus from Egypt, leading to the eventual conquest of the Land. Some Egyptians probably joined the Exodus, as did Moses' Midianite father-in-law and his clan (see Num. 10:29-32). Others joined the assembly along the way—becoming "converts" to Israel (for example, see Caleb in Josh.

14:14; Othniel in Josh. 15:17)—and during the conquest (Rahab in Josh. 6:25). As the Israelites demonstrated that their powerful God, *Yahweh*, provided their victories, many people converted and joined the religion of their conquerors.

When the Israelites entered Canaan, some of their kin who inhabited Canaan (descendents of Abraham and Isaac who never left with Jacob's family) likely joined with them in the struggle against their foes. Eventually, Israel absorbed the Gibeonites (see Josh. 9, especially 9:27; compare with 2 Sam. 21:1-9). The accounts in Joshua show that this wasn't an isolated example; other conquered peoples became part of Israel as well (for example, see Josh. 17:2-3; 12:17,24).

What we know about Israel parallels what holds true for many countries: By the process of conquest and assimilation, intermarriage and conversion, the people of Israel became a diverse lot bringing different cultural and religious practices and traditions into their nation. Although far from a homogeneous group, after conquering the land, all Israel came together at Shechem to solemnly commit themselves to the worship and service of *Yahweh* alone (see Josh. 24:1-27). Now Israel as a unified people began.

THE TRIBES OF ISRAEL

For some two hundred years until the crowning of King Saul (c. 1050 BC), Israel existed as a loose collection of twelve tribes with no central government (see Jdg. 21:25) or national army. We commonly refer to this as the period of the judges. Most likely, defense against common enemies served to unify the tribes. Probably most important, the people bonded together because of their common loyalty to *Yahweh* (see Josh. 24).

For the most part, the tribes occupied the lands apportioned to them during the conquest (see Josh. 13–19). They organized in a patriarchal fashion, meaning clan elders exercised local control.

Worship of *Yahweh* took place in the tabernacle (or Tent of Meeting) at Shiloh (see Jdg. 18:31) that housed the Ark of the Covenant. Leaders met regularly for worship to renew their commitment to *Yahweh* and settle matters of mutual importance.

When a foe threatened one or more of the tribes, a "judge" would arise to call the tribes together in battle. Although empowered by God, judges led by their personal charisma; the role wasn't hereditary or equivalent to a monarch. The Israelites' judges served as the focal point for their dependence on God. In words repeated throughout the book of Judges, "Then the Israelites did evil in the eyes of the LORD and served the Baals" (2:11). Eventually, words such as these follow: "The LORD raised up judges, who saved them out of the hands of these raiders" (2:16). That is, when Israel "cried out to the LORD, he raised up for them a deliverer" (3:9).

A hereditary high priest (see 1 Sam. 1–3) oversaw the religion at the central shrine at Shiloh. Being a descendant of Moses or Aaron seemed especially important in determining those who qualified to serve as priests (see Jdg. 18:30). Three annual festivals (see Ex. 23:14-17; 34:18-24) focused Israel's worship on *Yahweh*'s mighty acts on behalf of his people.

The covenant that God established with his people was central to Israel's self-understanding. In this covenant, which actually starts in Exodus 19 and goes through the book of Deuteronomy, God makes three promises: (1) To make Israel his special possession among the people of the land; (2) to make Israel a kingdom of priests and a holy nation, which God followed up with requirements and laws; and (3) to dwell among his people, promising that he would be their God and they would be his people.

Thus, the Ten Commandments immediately followed God's establishment of his covenant with Israel (see Ex. 19–20). A legal system emerged that governed how God's people were to live in obedience to him. During the tribal period, Israel's leaders developed codes for living in their new land, no doubt borrowing some forms from other nations. What is sometimes called the Book of the Covenant (see Ex. 20:22–23:19) reflects the legal system during the period of the judges.

ISRAEL LED BY KINGS

Eventually, this loosely affiliated league of tribes faced a foe it couldn't conquer. While Israel held its own against the Philistines for two hundred years, the nation eventually faced utter defeat. Around 1050 BC at Aphek (see 1 Sam. 4), Israel suffered defeat and lost the Ark of the Covenant (which held the stone tablets containing the Ten Commandments and other sacred objects and so was symbolic of God's presence) to the Philistines (see v. 11). Although the priest Samuel tried to keep the tradition of judges alive, the tribes wanted a king to overcome the enemy. In effect, they thought a human king could do a better job of assuring their survival than *Yahweh* (see 8:4-9).

Saul, a Benjamite from Gibeah, was selected and anointed by Samuel as Israel's first king. Saul spent his entire reign as a warrior but made few structural changes on the national level. In the end, his rule proved ineffective and he never won significant victories against the Philistines.

Ironically, Saul's jealousy of David contributed to David's rise to fame and power. Saul died in battle against the Philistines, and although Saul's son claimed the throne, David was eventually crowned king over Israel (see 2 Sam. 5:1-3). Understanding that the new king would seek independence from them, the Philistines immediately sought to kill David. Through David's stunning military victories, the Philistines retreated and Israel secured its sovereignty.

After ruling a few years in Hebron in the south, David captured Jerusalem from a pocket of Jebusites who lived there. He then proclaimed the more centrally located Jerusalem as his new capital, where he installed the Ark of the Covenant (see 2 Sam. 6) that had been recaptured from the Philistines. David built a palace to show that Jerusalem would serve as both the political and religious capital of the newly unified nation. He also gained control of the remaining Canaanite holdouts and extended Israel's borders by defeating the Ammonites, capturing Moab and Edom, and capturing the territory up to Damascus in Syria.

In effect, David became the unifying figure of Israel. He defeated all enemies and brought peace to the nation. David also instituted a complex political infrastructure with various officers, commanders, heralds, secretaries, and chief priests. Perhaps the census (see 2 Sam. 24:2) signified some major restructuring. Certainly, David championed the worship of *Yahweh* and also contributed personally to the musical vitality of worship.

While David reigned successfully for many years, toward the end of his life he faced rebellion, largely over the question of who would succeed him as king. Both Absalom and Sheba attempted to take the throne from David. Just prior to David's death, a complex palace intrigue developed that finally resulted in Solomon's enthronement (see 1 K. 1).

Not concerned with extending Israel's borders, Solomon consolidated the nation's power, fortified its cities, and increased its prosperity through alliances with Egypt and Tyre as well as extensive trade with surrounding nations. Israel changed from a culture depending only on agriculture with tribal allegiances to become a nation of cities and commerce and the start of a class system, which caused the gap between rich and poor to increase.

In many ways, Solomon's reign marked the golden age of Israel's security and wealth. After constructing a lavish palace for himself, he undertook a major building project to construct Israel's temple in Jerusalem (see 1 K. 7; 2 Chron. 4), where the Ark of the Lord's

Covenant was enshrined. However, fiscal problems set in, and Solomon resorted to heavy taxation, forced labor, and eventually selling territory.

When Solomon died (922 BC), the monarchy of David's descendants soon disintegrated. Alienated by Solomon's policies, the ten northern tribes (which came to be known as Israel) didn't accept Solomon's son Rehoboam as king and elected Jeroboam as their king. Neither Israel in the north nor Judah (the tribes of Judah and Benjamin) in the south had the power or will to keep the former union intact.

Divided, the two kingdoms declined in power and prosperity. For several generations, they even fought against each other, further weakening their status and soon making them prey to outside powers. For a time, the northern kingdom of Israel regained some of its former power, although religious apostasy from (rebellion against) *Yahweh* became rampant. Attacks from border states further weakened Israel's position. The southern kingdom of Judah also suffered attacks on its borders. During the time of the divided kingdom, prophets proclaimed God's message to Israel and Judah, criticizing both nations' kings and their departures from following the terms of God's covenant with his people.

Anarchy left the northern tribes virtually defenseless, and they could no longer hold off the powerful Assyrian army. Israel fell in battle to the Assyrians in 721 BC. Judah was spared, but only by becoming a vassal state of the Assyrian Empire (see 2 K.16:7-8). The inhabitants of Judah embraced the religion of the Assyrians, which met with *Yahweh*'s wrath, although Hezekiah's reforms (see 2 K. 18:3-6) postponed God's judgment for a time.

Later, Judah became a free nation again when Assyria suffered defeats by the Egyptians and Medes. King Josiah (640–609 BC) used Judah's freedom to make wide-sweeping religious reforms (see 2 K. 22:3–23:25). However, the reforms might have been just external rituals rather than true revivals. As a result, Jeremiah proclaimed his message of judgment against the people, who increased only their outward religious practices (see Jer. 6:16-21). After Josiah's death, Judah fell under the rule of the Egyptians (609–605 BC). When Egypt was defeated by the Babylonians, Judah faced a new threat that it was unable to resist. After holding out for a time, various fortified cities of Judah and then Jerusalem fell to Babylon in 587 BC. Israel and Judah ceased to exist.

THE EXILE AND RETURN TO THE LAND

We date the Exile from the fall of Jerusalem in 587 BC. Most of Judah's inhabitants were killed or deported, while those who remained in the Land had to contend with the destruction of nearly all their cities. In this dire situation, many died from disease and starvation during the years that followed (see Lam. 2; 5). The conquering Babylonians deported the highest and best citizens of Judah to Babylon (see Dan. 1). Jeremiah puts the total number of those deported as 4,600, probably counting only the adult males (see Jer. 52:28-30). Although this group found themselves in a foreign land, they were allowed to remain together as Jews, faring much better than their fellow Israelites left in Judah.

During the sieges against Judah, many Jews had left voluntarily, traveling to Egypt (for example, see Jer. 42–44) as well as other lands (for example, 40:11). This marked the beginning of the Jewish Diaspora (the term that refers to the scattering of Jews from their homeland). Understandably, the Jews experienced a severe crisis of faith. Yet this crisis became the eventual source of Israel's survival and resurgence. Was *Yahweh* not as powerful as the other nations' gods? Or was *Yahweh* judging Israel for its lack of obedience to the terms of the covenant? If God was judging Israel, which is what the people concluded, then renewal and restoration could come from an intensified commitment to God's Law and the "ancient paths" (see Jer. 6:16).

During this period of exile, the seeds for the synagogue were likely sown. It would become the place for the community to gather to remember *Yahweh*'s deeds and call the people to follow in obedience. The words of the Torah became central, and some Jews took steps to preserve the writings of the prophets and codify the ancient ways. With this revival, the exiles hoped to return to the Land; Isaiah prophesied that the Exile would end and God would lead his people home (see 40:1-11).

On the world scene, the Babylonian king Nebuchadnezzar died in 562 BC. His successors were unable to stave off the rising power of the Medes and Persians, led by Cyrus. Babylon fell in 539 BC, and Cyrus immediately (538 BC) issued the decree that the Jews could return to their homeland, reinstitute their religion, and rebuild their temple at Persian expense (see Ezra 1:2-4; 6:3-5).

The exiles began to return in successive waves, but those who returned found that crop failures and hostile neighbors made life difficult. At first, plans to rebuild the temple languished and morale suffered, but eventually the temple was completed in 516 BC and dedicated with a great celebration (see Ezra 6:13-18).

Attempts to revive the monarchy of David failed, and the marginal economy couldn't attract many Jews from where they had resettled. High priests answerable to officials in Samaria (who cared little about the Jews' prosperity) administered Judah. The book of Malachi gives evidence that the Jews' religious life was in shambles.

Into this mess, Nehemiah and Ezra instituted reforms to transform the situation and set Judah on a more secure foundation and future. Nehemiah, a Jewish official in the court of the Persian Artaxerxes I, became governor of Judah and organized the rebuilding of the walls of Jerusalem, establishing its security from invaders.

Nehemiah also began religious reforms, a course of action that Ezra, the priest and teacher, greatly augmented with his arrival in 428 BC. With a copy of Jewish law and authorization from Artaxerxes to enforce it (see Ezra 7:11-26), Ezra began the process of teaching the people about the ways of *Yahweh* and what obedience to divine laws entailed. His task succeeded, and Israel became a people ordered under the Law of Moses (see Neh. 10).

In the years that followed through the end of the OT period, Judaism developed the forms that would characterize it in the centuries that followed. The OT story of God's people, Israel, concludes with the writings of the prophet Malachi; Jewish writings do not resume until the time of the Maccabees (c. 175 BC).

THE INTERTESTAMENTAL PERIOD

What happened to the Jews in Palestine from the close of the OT until the Maccabean revolts (when Israel regained her independence as a nation in the 140s BC)? The scanty evidence prohibits saying much with certainty. The Persians contended with revolts in various sectors of the areas under their rule even while Philip II, king of the Macedonians (359–336 BC), extended his power over various Greek states. During the waning days of the Persian rule over Palestine, hostilities between Judah (the Jews) and those to the north (the Samaritans) continued to worsen.

The Samaritans, descendants of Jews who had intermarried and who embraced their own version of the Pentateuch, had resisted the exiles returning from Babylon to rebuild the temple and the walls of Jerusalem (see Ezra 4; Neh. 4). During the Exile, the Samaritans built their own rival temple on Mount Gerizim (reported by Jewish historian Josephus in his book *The Antiquities of the Jews* XI, 7–8). Both Jews and Samaritans claimed to be the true inheritors of Israel's traditions. Aramaic gradually replaced Hebrew as the common language of Palestine, although some use of Hebrew was retained for religious observances.

Influence from the west, especially from Greece, also increased during these centuries. Alexander the Great succeeded his father Philip as king of the Macedonians (336 BC). Within a few years, Alexander completely routed the Persian armies and conquered their lands, and by 326 BC he had extended his rule as far as the Indus River (in present-day Pakistan). Palestine came under the control of this Greek (Hellenistic) and western power.

When Alexander died in 323 BC, his territories were divided among three generals. Ptolemy obtained Egypt and initially controlled Palestine until about 198 BC. So many Jews settled in Alexandria in Egypt that the Jews translated their Bible into Greek (called the Septuagint and abbreviated LXX). The Ptolemies protected the Jews in the practice of their religion. The Jewish high priest, subject to the king of Egypt, governed the Jews. They enjoyed relative freedom and a good standard of living, although information about this period is limited.

Then the Syrians (also called Seleucids) to the north defeated the Ptolemies and ruled the Jews until the mid-160s BC. At first they continued the friendly policies the Ptolemies had established toward the Jews. Under Seleucid rule, Greek thought, language, and culture had enormous influence on the Jews. However, Antiochus IV (the eighth Seleucid king, who ruled for eleven years beginning in 175 BC) ended the relatively good relationship between the Syrians and the Jews, increasing taxes on Israel partly because of his need to pay taxes to Rome, the rising western power. He was dedicated to promoting Hellenism throughout the nations he ruled. He assumed the personal title of God "manifest" (Epiphanes). Conflict with the Jews intensified when Antiochus appointed Jason to be the high priest in place of the proper heir, Onias III, because Jason (Onias's brother) paid a huge bribe.

Antiochus subsequently made all of Judaism's distinctives illegal, offending the Jews' most holy laws and practices. He renamed the temple for Zeus Olympus and set up a pagan shrine. He sacrificed swine on the altar, sprinkling the blood around the temple. He prohibited circumcision and Sabbath observance and banned and burned copies of the Torah. Throughout the land, he erected pagan altars, where Jews were forced to sacrifice to pagan gods. Many Jews believed that this was the fulfillment of Daniel's prophecy of the "abomination of desolation" (see Dan. 9:27; 11:31; 12:11; also see the apocryphal source 1 Macc. 1:54,59 and Jewish historian Josephus, *Antiquities* XII 5:4) that Jesus referred to later (see Mt. 24:15).

The Jews faced a dire situation. They could give in and face extinction, or they could resist. The impetus for resistance came from an unlikely source, an aged priest named Mattathias. He refused to sacrifice to pagan Greek gods, and he killed both an apostate Jew who was about to make such a sacrifice and Antiochus's commissioner, who had come to enforce the sacrifices. Mattathias and his five sons fled to the mountains and called upon zealous Jews to follow them in refusing to submit to pagan ways. They began a guerilla movement that repeatedly surprised and defeated larger Syrian armies. Mattathias died in 166 BC, but his third son, Judas (nicknamed Maccabeus, which means the "hammer"), continued the guerilla movement (166–160 BC). This nickname is the root of the term *Maccabean revolt* and this period of the Maccabees.

During this time, Antiochus faced more urgent matters and couldn't direct his full attention to the Jewish revolt. Judas Maccabeus rallied six thousand men and defeated two separate armies sent by the Syrians. Judas succeeded in entering Jerusalem, where he purified and rededicated the temple in 164 BC. Each December, Jews still commemorate this event in the annual festival of Hanukkah, also called the Feast of Lights or Feast of Dedication.

Leadership of the Jewish revolt passed to Judas's brother Jonathan (161–143 BC) and then to their brother Simon (142–134 BC), who was able finally to throw off the rule of Syria. Israel became a free state politically (142 BC). This established a new ruling dynasty in Israel, the Hasmoneans.

From the time of independence under Simon, the high priest's office became increasingly political in nature. Simon's third son, John Hyrcanus, assumed power after the death of his father (134–104 BC). Hyrcanus eventually discarded the religious ideals of the Maccabees and turned his attention to territorial expansion, mostly south into Idumea. In response, a group of Jews known as the Hasidim (holy ones) attempted to return Israel to its religious heritage and priorities. This group probably became an impetus for what eventually became the Pharisees.

In 128 BC, Hyrcanus destroyed the Samaritan temple on Mount Gerizim, increasing Samaritan hatred for the Jews. Pro- and anti-Greek positions increasingly divided Israel, remaining unresolved into the first century AD. Eventually, a power struggle took place between two grandsons of John Hyrcanus, Hyrcanus II and Aristobulus II. Hyrcanus II ruled briefly in 67 BC; Aristobulus II seized power from 67 to 63 BC. Both appealed to Rome, now the dominant force in the area, to be installed as ruler. After a three-month siege of Jerusalem, Pompey (the Roman general and eventual statesman) annexed Judea as a Roman province in 63 BC, ending Israel's independence.

Several points emerge as significant from the oppression of Israel by Antiochus IV and the resulting Maccabean revolt. These events rescued the Jewish nation from political and religious decay. They stirred Jewish nationalism, uniting the nation with an energy that had not been known for centuries. They ignited a messianic hope in the midst of the terrible persecution. These events reenergized the Jews' interest in the Law; only by faithful observance of the Torah could Israel expect God's rescue, blessings, and peace. The events led to the development of the Pharisees, Sadducees, and Qumran covenanters, each taking a different approach in how to live Torah faithfully. Finally, they increased the dispersion of Jews into various parts of the world as people fled from the terrors of Antiochus.

The intertestamental period ends as Rome begins to rule Israel. From about 280 BC, Rome had grown slowly through deliberate expansionism. In Palestine, Rome ruled first through puppet kings. The Jews couldn't agree how to view Roman rule: Was Rome the hope for Israel's safety? Or were the Romans pagan occupiers who needed to be overthrown, as the Maccabees overthrew the Syrians?

The gifted Idumean (or Edomite) politician Antipater served as a political advisor to Hyrcanus II. When Julius Caesar moved against Pompey in 48 BC, Hyrcanus and Antipater supported Caesar and contributed to his victory. In appreciation, Caesar appointed Hyrcanus high priest and ethnarch (a title of a ruler), while appointing Antipater procurator (a kind of financial officer). Antipater named his son Phasael governor of Jerusalem, and he named another son, Herod, governor of Galilee.

Julius Caesar reduced Israel's taxes, gave permission to rebuild Jerusalem's walls, and allowed the Jews unique freedoms of religion. Following the assassination of Julius, Antipater and Hyrcanus made no moves to rebel. After Antipater's assassination in 43 BC, his sons continued his policies. Anthony Caesar (41–40 BC) appointed Phasael and Herod joint tetrarchs (title of a ruler) of the Jews, and Hyrcanus continued as high priest.

With the help of Antigonus (the son of Aristobulus II and the rightful Hasmonean heir to the throne), the Parthians (the Persian power ruling to the east of Palestine) overran Judea in 40 BC. Phasael was captured and committed suicide, while Herod escaped to Rome, where the Roman Senate declared him king of the Jews. With the help of Antony and the Syrian governor, Herod (the Great) returned to Palestine and secured his kingdom, eventually defeating the Parthians in 37 BC. Herod the Great began his thirty-three-year reign, dying in about 4 BC, shortly after Jesus' birth (see Mt. 2:19).

Herod's reign was both successful and turbulent. Although he was an astute politician and statesman, he also had a troubled personal and family life. His building accomplishments set him apart as extraordinary. He built palaces (Jericho) and fortresses (Herodium, Antonia, Machaerus, and Phasaelis). And he greatly enlarged Israel's port on the Mediterranean Sea, Caesarea.

In addition to building structures and temples in other Roman cities, his most impressive edifice was the temple in Jerusalem. Despite these accomplishments, his relationship with his subjects, the Jews, was stormy at best. He wasn't a Jew, and his loyalty to Rome inevitably caused ongoing friction with Jewish ideals. Further, his family life was tragic. He had many wives and children but had many of them killed when he perceived them as threats to his rule. His attempt to assassinate the baby Jesus illustrates his paranoia.

After Herod's death, a Jewish delegation went to Rome to protest his will. Herod had given a double portion to his son Archelaus, who also went to Rome to defend his cause. Augustus Caesar eventually ratified Herod's will, except that he denied Archelaus's petition and named him an ethnarch instead of king. The area of Palestine was divided among Herod's three sons: Archelaus was ethnarch of Judea, Samaria, and Idumea; Antipas was tetrarch of Galilee and Perea; Philip was tetrarch of Batanea, Trachonitis, and Auranitis.

Antipas and Philip governed ably and ruled for forty-two and thirty-seven years respectively. Archelaus's oppressive rule caused Augustus to depose him in AD 6. Judea was then made a Roman province ruled personally by a procurator appointed by the emperor. Pontius Pilate became the fifth such procurator, ruling in Judea from AD 26–36.

THE WORLD OF THE NEW TESTAMENT

The New Testament era begins with Jesus' birth into Roman-occupied Palestine, where Herod the Great ruled. Herod died while Jesus and his parents took refuge in Egypt. They returned to find Archelaus presiding over Judea. Warned against remaining in Judea, the family returned to Nazareth in Galilee, where Antipas was tetrarch.

In Nazareth, "as Jesus grew up, he increased in wisdom and in favor with God and people" (Lk. 2:52, TNIV). He also learned from his father's craft (stonemason or carpenter) and probably engaged in the same education and religious instruction as other males in Jewish society in the small-town setting of Nazareth. Jesus' birth and the eventual rise and spread of the Christian church raise two questions for us: What was it like to live in the first century AD Roman world? And what characterized Judaism at the time of Jesus' birth?

Under Roman Rule

The NT events and the composition of the documents that became our NT took place during the age when Rome ruled the world. Let's look briefly at several elements of the Roman world that merit attention.

ROMAN POLITICS AND SOCIETY

During the time of the events recorded in the NT, Caesar Augustus (31 BC–AD 14) and his successors ruled Israel through the Herodian family. However, in the province of Judea in AD 6, the Romans governed more directly through the system of procurators, including Pontius Pilate (AD 26–37).

Rome ruled through procurators in some parts of its empire but in other areas governed through client kings, as Herod the Great had been. Although client kings enjoyed some autonomy, the Roman emperors could remove them at will. Choosing rulers who owed their positions to Rome assured their loyalty and a constant flow of taxes to Rome. These local rulers knew that serving Rome's interests well was the most important factor in ensuring their success.

The Roman judicial system and its local courts came with Roman rule. While justice was important for the Romans, it was often weighted in favor of the wealthy and designed to preserve their positions. Paul appeared before the Roman proconsul Gallio in Corinth (see Acts 18:12-17).

Rome also employed a large contingent of soldiers to maintain peace throughout the vast empire. Local taxes funded these armed forces and all other workings of government. Local members of an elite class collected the taxes for Rome (see Lk. 19:2), causing these tax collectors to be hated by their fellow citizens. Local people paid personal taxes based on a census (see Lk. 2:2; Mt. 17:25) as well as a land tax and many other indirect taxes (such as on the transportation of merchandise). Of course, Jews also paid religious taxes, such as those required to run the temple, and tithes on the produce of the land to fund the priesthood. Such taxation placed a considerable burden on the people and often caused unrest and even rebellion.

ROMAN RELIGION

One word describes religion in the Roman world: diverse. According to Greek mythology, the god Zeus oversaw a pantheon of gods. The Romans adopted the Greek god, but gave them their own names—for example, Jupiter for Zeus and Venus for Aphrodite. With the rise of Rome's emperors, the empire's religion transformed itself. The emperor acted as the chief priest (pontifex maximus) for the gods. Upon the emperor's death, the Roman Senate accorded divine status to Augustus (and to subsequent emperors who served Rome well). Some emperors even claimed divine status while they were alive: Caligula, Nero, and Domitian. Christians who refused to worship Domitian as divine were severely persecuted.

Beyond the cult of Rome, many local regions practiced their own religions. Of course, Judaism was one of these. In addition, many Greek, Egyptian, and Oriental mystery religions proliferated in the empire. Many other local cults flourished: Eleusis, Mithra, Isis, Dionysus, and Cybele, to name of few. Magic and superstition, also widespread in the empire, required incantations and special formulas, exorcisms, and other rites to placate the gods and achieve success.

Syncretism—combining elements of a variety of religious practices—was virtually required for people to survive. A citizen of the Roman Empire might worship a local deity to assure a good harvest, give homage to Caesar as Lord, and follow a superstitious rite to cure an illness.

Archaeological finds confirm the variety of household gods and amulets (charms that were believed to bring luck) people used to make their way through the world. Toward the end of the first century AD, a religious movement eventually called gnosticism began to take shape, combining many elements from both western and eastern religions. The gnostics emphasized dividing the material from the spiritual, which led people to deal with the physical world in one of two ways: Some gnostics became ascetic (abstaining from worldly pleasures), attempting to master appetites of the body and lead holy lives; others became sensualists, deciding that because matter is evil and won't survive death, they could freely indulge their bodily appetites.

Alongside these religious options, intellectuals of the first-century world might align themselves with one of the philosophical schools. The chief examples in the first century AD were:

- **Stoicism (see Acts 17:18).** This philosophy claimed that no personal god or personal immortality exists; we live in a purposeless universe. Stoics followed a creed of self-sufficiency, freedom, and acquiescence (or apathy).

- **Platonism.** This philosophy believed that archetypes or models existed—not in any material reality but only as universal ideas. All worldly things are imperfect replicas of their perfect forms—those imperishable ideas found outside of space and time.

- **Epicureanism (see Acts 17:18).** In contrast to Platonism, Epicureans saw reality as completely material. They were hedonists who lived for pleasure with the motto "Nothing to fear in god; nothing to fear in death; good [pleasure] can be attained; evil [pain] can be endured."[1]

- **Cynics.** These ascetics acted against the conventions of society, rejecting pleasure and seeking dishonor to attain hardness. Apathy, simplicity, and freedom were their goals.

- **Skeptics.** This philosophy asserted that nothing is more probable than anything else and that to every argument there is a counterargument.

- **Pythagoreans.** Those following this way of thinking were interested in numbers, asceticism, and philosophy as religions. They believed that the material world was bad (a belief picked up by the gnostics).

While these philosophies existed, most common people lived under the bondage of superstition and syncretism. Certainly, we can see that Christianity entered a complex, pluralistic, and confused religious world, much like our own!

Culture and Society in the First Century

Although cultural practices and patterns were unique to each culture or subculture, the inhabitants of the first century shared certain values. As we read the Bible, we can see how each of these values surface at various times. We can paint four broad strokes to describe these shared values.

1. **Purity.** People in the first century took pains to maintain ritual purity, holiness, and sanctity. They avoided contact with anything that would bring defilement and pollution. When defilement occurred, as it inevitably did, they underwent various rituals to regain purity.

2. **Honor.** In a "shame-based" culture, people exerted great effort to avoid losing face and causing others to lose face. Community was more important than the individual. In the same way, because individual behavior reflected on the group, people controlled their behavior so they wouldn't bring shame on their family or community.

3. **Patronage and reciprocity.** A person was a patron (someone who took care of others), client (someone responsible to a patron), or broker (one who set up the arrangements). These relationships required grace, loyalty, and trust on all sides. A fixed amount of wealth existed in the culture. Some had it, but most did not. To make the system work, people knew their places and operated within the established structure.

4. **The family.** A person's family — traced in a genealogy and dependent on the father's reputation — established his or her position in society. Family rules determined how people treated other family members and outsiders. These arrangements also set the stage for so-called "fictive kinship," the act of giving people a family title and treating them as if they had the actual relationship implied by the title. For example, followers of Jesus called themselves brothers and sisters, understanding both the duties and privileges of family members.

Judaism in the First Century

Beginning with Alexander the Great and continuing with the subsequent powers that ruled Israel in the centuries that followed, Judaism of the first century was definitely Hellenized (influenced by Greek culture and values). Although the Jews resisted, inevitably they took on many of these foreign elements. They translated the Bible into Greek (the LXX) yet retained Aramaic as the common spoken language and Hebrew as the language of religion. People spoke Greek outside Palestine, and Jews in Palestine commonly spoke Greek when they interacted with their Gentile neighbors.

Under Roman occupation of Israel and other lands, Latin was introduced for official functions, but it never became common in any significant way. In the maintenance of their religion, the Jews strongly resisted the inroads of Hellenization and other cultural pressures, as the Maccabean resistance and the Zealot revolt (in AD 68–70) both demonstrated. Let's briefly look at several other features of Judaism.

The Dispersion of the Jews

Luke's comment about the locations that Jews traveled from to make their pilgrimage to Jerusalem for the feast of Pentecost highlights the extent of the Diaspora or Dispersion (see Acts 2:9-11). Jews resided in these far-flung locations for several reasons.

The people faced several exiles or deportations following defeat of their land by foreign powers. Some Jews voluntarily relocated due to hardships or conflicts in Israel. On several occasions, many Jews moved to Egypt. Alexander the Great and the Seleucids also relocated groups of Jews during their occupation of the land. Under the Maccabees, Jews were encouraged to resettle in other places, particularly Rome.

The dispersion of the Jews prior to the first century resulted in two important dynamics as far as Christians are concerned:

1. God's people lived in many of the important world centers of the day. Some estimates suggest that between 4 and 4.5 million Jews lived outside of Palestine at this time.
2. These Jewish communities, and the synagogues that usually resulted, formed the seedbeds where the message of the Christian gospel was sown.

THE SYNAGOGUE

While we don't know the exact origin of the synagogue, we know that the idea of a Jewish house of worship began during the period of the Exile and its aftermath. Even after the rebuilding of the temple in Jerusalem, the synagogue had become an enduring institution with Judaism, certainly in the Diaspora but even within Israel. Each town or hamlet with at least ten adult Jewish males had a synagogue.

Initially, *synagogue* referred to a gathering of people; eventually, it denoted the meeting place for worshippers. An inscription from a first-century synagogue and comments by the Jewish historian Josephus (in his work *Against Apion* 2.175) indicate that the synagogue's central functions were reading the Law and studying the Commandments. The account of Jesus reading from the scroll of Isaiah in Luke 4:16-22 confirms these functions, stressing reading and instruction based on the Law or the Prophets (see Acts 13:13-16).

As the institution developed, a typical service included some or all of the following elements: invitation to worship, including the invocation and reading Psalm 95; Shema (see Dt. 6:4) and reading the Decalogue (the Ten Commandments); reciting the Eighteen Benedictions; the Torah reading; the Prophets or Writings reading; a sermon; and the benediction.

In addition to Jewish males and females (separated during the service), synagogues in the first century AD likely included a category of Gentiles known as "God-fearers." These Gentiles were attracted to the Jewish faith because of its monotheism and high ethical and moral principles, but they hadn't yet become full-fledged converts to Judaism by undergoing circumcision. Several Jewish sources refer to this class as incomplete converts (for example, Josephus, Philo, various inscriptions, and even the pagan philosopher Epictetus). The NT mentions Cornelius, a prominent God-fearing Gentile who became a follower of Jesus as a result of Peter's preaching (see Acts 10–11).

The synagogue contributed to the survival of Judaism; the "calling together" of faithful Jews during the exiles kept traditions and practices alive. The spread of synagogues throughout the Roman world planted and preserved Judaism over a wide area, no matter what political turmoil occurred in the land of Israel itself. Even the final destruction of the temple in AD 70 and the expulsion of the Jews from Israel didn't extinguish Judaism, as the gatherings of local Jews in synagogues continued throughout the known world.

THE SECTS OF THE JEWS

While we can't undertake a complete description, a brief appraisal of the Jewish sects will help us understand the landscape of Judaism when Jesus appeared on the scene. Most of these sects originated during the intertestamental period.

The Pharisees. We first learn of the Pharisees shortly after the Maccabean revolt, a movement aided by the Hasidim (holy ones). This anti-Hellenist group had supported military efforts aimed at overthrowing the Seleucids to cleanse the land of foreigners and reinstate pure worship of *Yahweh*. The Pharisees are probably descendents of these "holy ones." The word *Pharisee* means "separated ones," a name pointing to how seriously they refrained from defilement of all kinds. Theologically, they believed in the resurrection of the body as well as rewards and punishments in life after death.

Numbering about six thousand at the time of Jesus, they rigorously kept not only the Law but also various traditions devised to assure obedience to the Law. They focused on keeping the dietary laws, ritual purity at meals, and the Sabbath holy. For example, because the Law prohibited "work" on the Sabbath, the Pharisees had specified what constituted work as well as what a holy Jew should or should not do to avoid being a Law breaker. With their interpretations of how the Law applied to situations, the Pharisees held a kind of oversight role over the religious life of Israel at the time.

The Pharisees' strict traditions eventually caused some to become legalistic. They externalized God's Law, relying on outward obedience to please God. Of course, this error wasn't new; the OT prophets had challenged people who honored God with their lips while their hearts were far from him (see Is. 29:13).

Not all Pharisees were legalists or hypocrites. Many common Jews admired them for their holiness and commitment to *Yahweh*. Jesus probably had more in common with the views of the Pharisees than with those of other sects. Most likely, some Pharisees became his followers, while others later joined the emerging church (see Acts 15:1,5).

The Sadducees. When the Hasmonean dynasty assumed control of Israel after independence from the Seleucids, a Jewish upper class emerged. The Sadducees of the first century AD likely descended from these powerful people. They held the highest positions within the Jewish society in Israel. High priests, wealthy landowners, and other power brokers joined this sect.

The Sadducees tended to embrace Greek influence more than the Pharisees did. They believed that only the Pentateuch was authoritative, rejecting the Pharisees' oral traditions. Theologically, they denied the resurrection of the body.

Members of this sect wanted to maintain the structures that kept them in power. They controlled the political processes, including the operation of the temple and the Sanhedrin (Jewish legal court). When the Romans took control of Judea and destroyed the temple in AD 70, the Sadducees lost their land, wealth, and power and ceased to exist.

The Essenes. Slightly smaller than the Pharisees, the Essenes (perhaps with four thousand adherents) probably also descended from the Hasidim of the Maccabean era. Instead of the kind of separation from the world that characterized the Pharisees, the Essenes lived more physically separated lives. Some lived in monastic communities, such as those who lived at Qumran near the Dead Sea. From their writings (the Dead Sea Scrolls), we learn that they lived celibate lives and adopted a rigorous devotion to keeping the Law. They believed they were the true elect of Israel, living in the last days and awaiting a royal and priestly messiah.

The Zealots. The name *Zealot* appears in the Gospels as a title for one of Jesus' disciples named Simon (see Lk. 6:15; Acts 1:13). At that point in history (around AD 27), this might simply mean that he was a very zealous Jew—one concerned with *Yahweh's* honor and the purity of the nation of Israel. Paul said he was zealous for the traditions of his fathers (see Gal. 1:14; Acts 21:20; 22:3).

In the AD 60s, the title Zealots described an organized political movement that attempted unsuccessfully to overthrow the Romans in AD 70. They followed in the violent tradition of Phineas (see Num. 25:1-15) and the Maccabees (see the apocryphal source 1 Macc. 2:24). While Jesus' disciple Simon probably didn't belong to the revolutionary Zealot party, he might have subscribed to this kind of revolutionary outlook and willingness to act aggressively to preserve God's honor.

The Herodians. Those who politically supported Herod Antipas constituted a small group in Galilee called Herodians. Because they profited from this association, they wanted to maintain existing structures and keep Rome's interests well served. This stance brought them into conflict with Jesus, to the point that the Herodians made an unlikely pact with the Pharisees to get rid of Jesus (see Mk. 3:6; 12:13).

The Scribes. Not really a political party or religious sect, the scribes held the occupation of writing and copying texts. Some of them copied the Scriptures and naturally evolved into biblical experts. In the Gospels, they also appear with the titles of lawyer, teacher (of the Law), and rabbi. Some of the scribes were Pharisees, and they became experts in interpreting the Law. As such, they developed the oral traditions other Pharisees carefully followed.

THE SANHEDRIN

While the Romans administered justice throughout the empire, they often left political and religious matters to local institutions. In Israel, the Sanhedrin held the highest authority over religious and domestic matters. It was made up of seventy-one members, both Pharisees and Sadducees, and the high priest who presided. To enforce its rulings, the Sanhedrin employed its own police force. Beneath this council, local courts as well as rabbis offered rulings in day-to-day legal matters.

While the Sanhedrin could settle most local issues, Roman law required that their subjects defer to Rome on certain issues, including when they wanted to execute someone for a capital crime. Because of this, the Sanhedrin brought Jesus to Pilate so the Romans could sentence him to be executed (see Jn. 18:31).

FOR FURTHER STUDY

Old Testament History

Dillard, R., and T. Longman III. *An Introduction to the Old Testament*. Grand Rapids, MI: Zondervan, 1994.

Hoerth, A., G. Mattingly, and E. Yamauchi, eds. *Peoples of the Old Testament World*. Grand Rapids, MI: Baker, 1998.

Provan, I., V. P. Long, and T. Longman III. *A Biblical History of Israel.* Louisville, KY: Westminster John Knox, 2003.

Walton, J. H., V. H. Matthews, and M. W. Chavalas. *The IVP Bible Background Commentary: Old Testament.* Downers Grove, IL: InterVarsity, 2000.

Geography

Beitzel, B. J. *The Moody Atlas of Bible Lands.* Chicago: Moody, 1985.

Ancient Near Eastern Religions

Block, D. *The Gods of the Nations: Studies in Ancient Near Eastern National Theology.* Grand Rapids, MI: Baker; Leicester, UK: Apollos, 2000.

Hess, R. S. *Israelite Religions.* Grand Rapids, MI: Baker; Nottingham, UK: Apollos: 2007.

New Testament History

DeSilva, D. A. *An Introduction to the New Testament: Context, Methods, and Ministry Formation.* Downers Grove, IL: InterVarsity, 2004.

Ferguson, E. *Backgrounds of Early Christianity.* 2nd ed. Grand Rapids, MI: Eerdmans, 1993.

Jeffers, J. S. *The Greco-Roman World of the New Testament Era.* Downers Grove, IL: InterVarsity, 1999.

Keener, C. S. *The IVP Biblical Background Commentary: New Testament.* Downers Grove: InterVarsity, 1993.

Witherington III, B. *New Testament History: A Narrative Account.* Grand Rapids, MI: Baker, 2001.

CHAPTER 3

THE BASICS OF BIBLE STUDY

If you're like most people, you've been on a diet at some point in your life. And if you're like most people, you've also probably had a hard time sticking to it. Why do we quit dieting? Most of us would say that it's too hard or too boring. Or we might wonder if it's really worth all the effort of counting calories, carbs, points, and pounds.

The same holds true of many Christians who decide to study the Bible. At some point, you've probably made an effort, but maybe you had a hard time sticking with it.

Why do we quit studying the Bible? Instead of answering that question, let's take a positive tack. Why should we read and study the Bible? Curiosity lures some of us into its pages: We wonder why this book has survived and why some people value it so highly. Others read the Bible because it's central to our religious tradition. Perhaps someone told us how useful the Bible can be, so we decided to read it for ourselves. And some of us read the Bible because someone told us that we *should* read it: "All *good* Christians read the Bible, so you should read it too."

Why do you read and study the Bible—or why don't you? Perhaps this *Handbook* will inspire you to read and study Scripture more. So let's look at the goal of studying the Bible and, even more pointedly, help determine what *your* own goal should be.

KNOW YOUR GOAL

When we look at the goal of Bible study, we immediately need to branch off in two directions, both crucial. First, we must consider the personal question "What's in it for me?" In other words, what do we seek for ourselves when we study this ancient text? What do we want to get out of studying the Bible?

Second, what do we seek in the text of the Bible itself? What do we want from it? These two directions are related, but let's take each one in turn.

The Personal Goal

As Christians, we want to become more and more like Christ — in the apostle Paul's words, to be conformed to the likeness of God's Son, Jesus (see Ro. 8:29). As God's Spirit works in us, this process of becoming like Christ takes time. Paul tells his readers they "are being transformed into [Christ's] likeness with ever-increasing glory, which comes from the Lord, who is the Spirit" (2 Cor. 3:18).

While the Holy Spirit works in many ways to bring about spiritual growth in our lives, the Holy Scriptures fill a primary role in that process. Paul describes the value of Scripture this way: "All scripture is inspired by God and is useful for teaching, for reproof, for correction, and for training in righteousness, so that everyone who belongs to God may be proficient, equipped for every good work" (2 Tim. 3:16-17, NRSV). In other words, if you study God's Word faithfully, pray for understanding, and diligently apply the Scriptures to your daily experiences, you'll grow and change in ways that please God, others, and yourself.

In our better moments, we acknowledge our need to be transformed into Christ's likeness. God inspired the biblical writers to convey his message to us to meet that need. Paul used such terms as *teaching, reproof, correction*, and *training in righteousness*. At various times, we need all of these if we want to become more like Christ.

That's where the Bible comes in. God's Spirit uses it to show us the changes we need to make to be more like Christ. When we take the Bible seriously and study it diligently, using appropriate methods of Bible study that put us in the position where transformation can occur, we can hear God's voice.

As we approach studying the Bible, several basic guidelines can help us be sure we're on the right path to becoming more like Christ. For example, our study should be systematic and consistent. And we need to study the Bible itself, not just books or pamphlets that others have written about it.

However, even the best methods and our most diligent efforts won't achieve God's desired changes in us unless we put into practice what we discover and learn. The apostle James stresses, "Be doers of the word, and not merely hearers who deceive themselves" (1:22). In studying the Bible, then, our primary goal needs to be personal transformation: studying, seeking to understand, and applying God's message to our lives.

The Goal in Reading a Text

Maybe you've been in a group Bible study when someone says something like, "You know what this verse means to me?" The person then shares an explanation that you seriously doubt has any connection to the real meaning of the verse or passage. This kind of experience forces us to look at the question of the goal for our study of the Bible.

Whether written or oral, normal communication between people works best when the meaning one person intends to convey in words is the same meaning the recipient understands. For example, we could easily see that communication failed if someone asked, "Would you please hand me my sweater?" and instead you gave her a hug. A hug might be comforting, but the individual requested a sweater. Obviously, *sweater* and *hug* have different meanings.

Reading and studying the Bible have the same basic premise about communication. When we read the texts of writers who penned their messages many years ago, we know they intended to convey a specific meaning to their readers. When Paul instructed Timothy, "When you come, bring the cloak that I left with Carpus at Troas" (2 Tim. 4:13), we can be pretty sure that he wanted his cloak, not his sandals or a hug. We can't read this text and say, "This verse says to me that Paul wanted companionship in his lonely cell." While this idea might come from a modern reader's psychologizing of what a cloak represented to Paul, we'd be wrong to think the text means this. More likely, Paul anticipated the coming winter and wanted his overcoat to keep him warm physically.

If we want to study the Bible and allow God to speak to us and transform us through its pages, we need to decide what the goal of our reading will be. Will we look for a meaning we want to see in a text? Or will we seek to uncover the meaning that the author meant to convey through the words he or she used in that text? Will we reject the author's intended meaning and replace it with another meaning if we don't like the author's meaning, find it too difficult, or even think it's repulsive?

Later, we'll develop in more detail a crucial distinction for when we study the Bible: meaning versus significance (or application). Briefly, this means that the goal of studying the Bible should be to discover the meaning the author intended and that the original readers most likely understood. This original meaning, however, might have different significance for God's people through the years.

Therefore, they will apply it in various ways, depending on their own circumstances and needs. The meaning doesn't change—a text can't mean today what it did not mean to its author—but its significance will change as time and cultures dictate.

KNOW YOURSELF

The words of the Bible started as a conversation between the author and the original readers, whether the people of ancient Israel or followers of Christ meeting in a house church in the first century AD. Now we modern readers have entered the conversation. In effect, we take the place of the original readers, and we want to hear a word from God for ourselves.

The apostle Paul saw described the purpose of the Scriptures with these words: "Everything that was written in the past was written to teach us, so that through endurance and the encouragement of the Scriptures we might have hope" (Ro. 15:4).

What does it mean, then, that we are now in the conversation? To begin with, of course, we each bring ourselves to the task of studying the Bible. In addition, "who we are" affects what we understand and how we apply what we read. Let's look at three ways this influences our study of the Bible: our qualifications for understanding the meaning of the Bible, our assumptions about the nature of the Bible, and our own beliefs and attitudes.

Our Qualifications

Imagine that a woman traveling in central Asia calls her American mother and the two are talking together on the telephone. They have in common with each other gender, history, culture, language, and a host of shared experiences. However, if a male from the Central Asian nation of Uzbekistan takes the phone from the daughter and starts talking, would he be able to understand the mother? Would communication flow easily?

What about our study of the Bible? As modern-day readers, what qualifications put us in the best possible position to understand the meaning of the Bible? Several stand out as crucial.

BEING A BELIEVER

The writers of the Bible belonged to their own "faith communities": Israel for the OT, and the church for the NT. Readers who share these faith commitments will be in the best position to understand those writers. A "believer" has already embraced the essential point of view of the writers. Because the writers of the Bible wrote to those who believe in *Yahweh* as God and, in the case of the NT, God's Son, Jesus, readers who share those beliefs will study Scripture from the inside. God reveals himself to believers and those who seek him (see Heb. 11:6). The "spiritual person" (a believer in Jesus Christ) occupies the best position to grasp God's truth (see 1 Cor. 2:14).

Beyond basic faith in and relationship with Jesus, a Christian's commitment to Christ's body—the local church—is also crucial. Within the fellowship of believers, we gain needed insights into the corporate or community-oriented dimensions of the Bible's message. In a church setting, we also place ourselves in a position to be accountable for what we learn, hear how others hear and apply God's message, and guard against unlikely or incorrect understandings or meanings found in Scripture. In other words, we enjoy the checks and balances of other faithful believers.

WILLING TO OBEY

When we remain disobedient or unrepentant, we block our relationship with God. This hinders our ability to hear from God. Jesus counseled his followers to deal with personal conflicts with others before seeking to worship God (Mt. 5:23-24). How can we expect to hear and respond to a message from God's Word if we refuse to respond to what we've already heard from God? The psalmist affirms, "If I had cherished sin in my heart, the Lord would not have listened" (66:18). Holding on to or repeating sin effectively blocks our communication with God. A repentant, forgiven, and obedient person occupies the best position to hear God's message clearly. I'm not implying that we have to be perfect and sinless; no person is. What I mean is that we should sincerely seek to follow in the path of obedience.

Praying for God's Guidance

To do our study of the Bible well and to learn what God wants us to understand and apply, we need to recognize that we depend on the Holy Spirit. As we approach reading or studying the Bible, we should pray for the Spirit to keep us from error, help us be diligent in our work, prevent us from arrogance, and spare us from blindness to the truth of what we study. Jesus promised, "The Counselor, the Holy Spirit, whom the Father will send in my name, will teach you all things and will remind you of everything I have said to you" (Jn. 14:26).

As we study, we should pray for the Spirit's teaching ministry, following the example of the psalmist who prayed, "Praise be to you, O Lord; teach me your decrees. . . . Open my eyes that I may see wonderful things in your law. . . . Let me understand the teaching of your precepts; then I will meditate on your wonders. . . . Direct me in the path of your commands, for there I find delight" (Ps. 119:12,18,27,35).

Using the Best Methods and Tools

Even if using the best methods and tools seems obvious, this point is crucial. Because our goal is to understand God's message for our lives, we need to use the best methods and tools available. Why use a shovel to dig a huge hole if a backhoe is available and will do the job more effectively? The same idea holds true for studying the Bible. Two points are relevant here:

1. Without the right tools and methods, we could never discover the meaning of a biblical text. Word meanings are an obvious example; for instance, to understand certain portions of the Bible, it is necessary to know what *propitiation* means. Similarly, we need the right tool to grasp the meaning of an ancient ritual, or the appropriate method to understand how grammar functions.

2. As biblical resources increase and knowledge grows, we need to use the best available tools and methods. This involves a willingness to discard outdated or inferior resources — even those by the most-respected scholars of the past — in favor of the best ones currently available. Sometimes the Internet or computer Bible study programs offer tools and resources free or at low cost. Often, however, these are free because they're old enough not to be under copyright restrictions, meaning they can be reproduced without cost. Usually, better tools have replaced them.

Of course, a new resource isn't necessarily better; likewise, old sources can contain valuable insights. The point is, to accomplish the goal of understanding the meaning of the biblical text, we must be willing to use the best tactics and tools available. We'll look more closely at methods for studying the Bible in chapter 6 and at tools and resources for making the most of Bible study in chapter 7.

Our Assumptions About the Nature of the Bible

Besides the personal qualifications, the assumptions (or presuppositions) that we bring to our study greatly influence our understanding of the Bible. The idea of studying Scripture without presuppositions is an illusion; all of us have them, but sometimes we don't acknowledge them.

We can determine what presuppositions we have. This begins with such questions as: What's your view about the nature of the Bible? Do you think it came from God as his divinely inspired words? Do you think of it as the "last word" on any or all issues?

While we don't have space to explore this issue in depth, let's look at the central issue.

A fundamental presupposition grows out of the Bible's understanding of itself. The Bible embodies God's revelation to his people. Although God reveals some things in the natural world and in the hearts of people made in his image (see Ps. 19:1-6; Ro. 1:19-20; 2:15), the Bible is God's special revelation. The Bible repeatedly affirms that God speaks in and through it, God inspired it (see 2 Tim. 3:16), and God's Spirit moved its writers in what they wrote (see 2 Pet. 1:21). Knowing this (or presupposing it) increases our weight of responsibility to understand the Bible's message accurately because by doing so, we grasp what God has revealed. Do you presuppose this when you study the Bible? You have a choice to make.

If we believe that the Bible is divine revelation, we need to consider several implications as we approach our study of Scripture:

- **Truthfulness.** If God inspired what the Bible's writers composed, then what they wrote is true. And we can trust that message.
- **Authority.** In the Bible, we don't read merely the opinion of another human whose word we might debate or dismiss. If we believe that God inspired the words of the Bible, then we also accept Scripture's authority. When we study and

understand what God says through his words, we're also obligated to obey. Jesus acknowledged the authority of the OT when he said, "The Scripture cannot be broken" (Jn. 10:35). By extension, the NT occupies that same position.

- **Capacity to transform.** When we read words that God speaks in the Bible, we encounter the living God. The psalmist affirms: "Your word is a lamp to my feet and a light for my path" (119:105). Much more than an encounter with another human or some abstract truth, this encounter with the living and active God can transform our lives.

- **Uncommon unity.** In spite (or perhaps because) of its origins, the Bible possesses an overall coherence due to its singular divine authorship. This unity is true, even though the writing took place over many centuries, by many authors, in several languages, and from different locations.

- **Accessible revelation.** Accepting divine authorship means realizing that the Bible readily reveals God's message. In other words, common people—not just clergy, scholars, and those who possess some secret code—can understand Scripture. It would make little sense for God to author a book its recipients couldn't understand.

While we presuppose that ordinary people—just like the Bible's original recipients—can understand its message, we also understand that the best methods, superior expertise, and extensive research using the best tools will uncover more insight and lead to better understanding, especially with complex or difficult passages. Yet even new Christians with minimal education can easily grasp the Bible's basic message: "God so loved the world that he gave his one and only Son, that whoever believes in him shall not perish but have eternal life" (Jn. 3:16). And without trouble, they can comprehend how God wants people to live: "'Love the Lord your God with all your heart and with all your soul and with all your mind.' This is the first and greatest commandment. And the second is like it: 'Love your neighbor as yourself'" (Mt. 22:37-39).

Our Beliefs and Attitudes

In addition to what we presuppose when we read and study the Bible, we also come to the text with our own set of beliefs and attitudes, or preunderstandings. We can easily see that the Bible comes out of its own world, often distant and foreign to us, so we must study to understand words, languages, and cultural practices from that world. As modern readers, we also live in our own worlds, and the features of our worlds color what we see and how we understand. So do other preunderstandings: A woman will "see" a text differently from a man; a Chinese believer will understand things differently from one from Brazil. Several categories of preunderstandings exist that might affect what we see and how we understand when we study the Bible:

- **Readers bring more or less information to their study of the Bible.** Usually, the more information we have, the better—unless it's not correct. For example, if I already know what phylacteries are (small leather cases that contain biblical scrolls and are worn by Jews during prayer), I can understand Matthew 23:5 more readily than someone who has no idea. Of course, if my prior information is incorrect—such as assuming the Bible defines phylacteries the same way modern fantasy fiction and role-playing games do—then that "information" becomes a liability. This goes beyond biblical terms to include history, prophecy, and other information. For example, some readers think they know *when* Jesus will return to rapture his church, which colors how they read all texts dealing with Jesus' return, yet whether their information is correct might be a matter of interpretation.

- **Readers come to their study of the Bible with different ideologies.** Some people have a prior commitment to certain theological systems, perhaps related to their denominations (Baptist, Methodist, Presbyterian, and so on). That might lead to how they understand biblical texts that speak of "baptism," for example. Others might approach their study of the Bible with a strong commitment to social justice issues, and others with a commitment to evangelism. Some readers bring to their Bible study a strong concern for gender equality, while others come with a more traditional or hierarchical viewpoint. Some readers feel more comfortable with a "modern" approach to their lives, while others take a more "postmodern" view of the world. Of course, these are just a few examples of how our viewpoints or ideologies can affect our study of the Bible.
- **Readers approach studying the Bible with different attitudes.** Some people are inherently skeptical, while others are more trusting. Some people need proof of all conclusions, while others more willingly accept things by faith. Some people need closure, while others are content with some ambiguity. Our temperaments and personalities affect our reading of the Bible.

While we might list other categories, the main idea is acknowledging that our attitudes and beliefs likely affect how we read individual texts. Sometimes we choose our preunderstandings, but often we embrace them over time and don't even realize we have them. Not only that, we might be unaware of how influential they are or how strange they are. Our attitudes and beliefs can hurt the way we talk with others who view the world differently, and our preunderstandings can interfere with our own ability to understand a text as the author intended it.

As Christians who desire to study the Bible, we have a responsibility to identify and examine our preunderstandings to the best of our ability. This often occurs when we interact with Christians (or others) who are not "just like us." If we truly desire to hear God's voice, we'll try to discard attitudes or beliefs—even cherished viewpoints—that might prevent the Holy Spirit from revealing God's truth to us.

BASIC STEPS OF BIBLE STUDY

While we'll look at a variety of ways to study the Bible in more detail in chapter 6, we can boil down the process to three essential steps. (In fact, some of the following chapters will elaborate and refine how to perform these steps well and in different ways.) The basic steps amount to answering three questions: What does the Bible say? What does the Bible mean by what it says? How does the Bible's meaning apply to me? In other words, studying the Bible requires observation, interpretation, and application. Let's examine each of these and then look at an example that illustrates these steps.

Observation
Observation involves the act of seeing and taking notice of things as they are. It means developing the art of careful awareness. Observation depends on two basic attitudes: an open mind and a willing spirit. An open mind helps us overcome preunderstandings that stand in the way of grasping what God's Word really says; a willing spirit means being ready to accept what we discover. If we put up barriers, we hinder our ability to hear what a text might really be saying.

Observation requires both attentiveness and perseverance. Accurate observation comes from reading the Scriptures with diligence, purposefulness, thoughtfulness, and a willingness to raise questions and dig for answers. Reading and studying until we really see all that a text says requires both a quality and a quantity of time. As we study, the goal is to grasp the message, not just check off an item on a list of tasks for the day.

Observation also demands studying the Bible in ways that treat its various parts faithfully. We need to learn to understand the Bible as literature. That requires various skills, depending upon what we're studying. For example, parts of the Bible are narratives—books that tell stories—so we need to think about characters and plots when we read such books as Genesis, 1 Samuel, and Acts. Other parts of the Bible are poetry (Psalms), legal material, prophecy, wisdom (Proverbs and Job), gospel, epistle, and apocalyptic (Revelation, as well as parts of some OT books). When we read, "Shall all the trees of the forest sing for joy" (Ps. 96:12), we want to observe that the word *sing* means something different from when we read, "Hear, O kings; give ear, O princes; to the Lord I will sing" (Jdg. 5:3). We need different tactics to make sure that we correctly observe what the authors intended to communicate in these different literary genres.

When you study the Bible, you'll learn more if you record what you observe. As you write down your thoughts, they become clearer. You might want to underline important words in your Bible, write in the margins, and even draw arrows to connect associated terms or ideas. If you don't want to write in your Bible, you can photocopy its pages. In addition, many computer programs allow you to print out passages that you're studying (more on computer tools in chapter 7).

Observation requires defining crucial words and concepts, understanding the background of events or features in the text, and grasping the relationships within each paragraph—the flow of an argument or story. Reference tools become essential here.

Observation also involves determining the tone or atmosphere of a passage. We can watch for clues to mood or emotions (despair, thanksgiving, praise, awe, urgency, joy, humiliation, tenderness, concern, compassion, hostility, and so on).

Six important questions can help us become good observers:

1. **Who?** Who are the people mentioned in or behind the text?
2. **What?** What happened? Do the people do anything? What ideas are expressed? What are the results?
3. **Where?** Where does this account take place? What's the setting?
4. **When?** When did the event take place? What accounts for when it happened?
5. **Why?** Why did this situation occur? What's the purpose, and why now? Why was the text written? Why is this account in the Bible?
6. **How?** How did things happen? How effectively? By what means or methods?

While these questions won't serve all the genres of the Bible equally well, they do provide a good starting point for most passages.

Interpretation

While observation involves seeing things as they are in a passage, interpretation is the process of determining the meaning of a passage. Interpretation helps us more distinctly understand why the Holy Spirit included that portion in the Bible. Interpretation answers the question, "What does this text mean?"

We interpret words all the time—in our everyday conversations. Maybe you've been talking with someone and thought, *I wonder what she means by that?* While you know the meaning of the words in your conversation, you need to interpret the speaker's intentions. Similarly, the Bible is God's Word to his people, and we need to interpret it correctly. The goal of interpretation is to understand what the writer intended to say as reflected in the words on the page.

The central concept in the process of interpretation is context. For example, you probably know more than one meaning for the word *tank*, but only within a context can you decide which meaning an author intended. If the author writes, "The fish is swimming in a tank," then you can conclude that this "tank" is an aquarium, not an armored vehicle.

This concept holds true for studying the Bible: We must relate the passage under consideration to the rest of the chapter, the entire book, and other portions of Scripture. Putting a passage in context prevents us from forcing a meaning on the passage that the writer didn't intend. Someone rightly noted, "The Bible is its own best interpreter." In other words, because we believe in the Holy Spirit's role of inspiring the Bible's writers, we gain insight into how to interpret some passages by seeing them in light of others. However, at times, we find that the Bible itself doesn't answer all our questions about what parts of it mean.

Many NT texts remind us why we should use careful analysis, reasoning, and testing to make sure we understand God's Word correctly. Luke commended the Bereans, who "examined the Scriptures every day to see if what Paul said was true" (Acts 17:11). Paul urged the Thessalonians, "Do not treat prophecies with contempt. Test everything. Hold on to the good" (1 Thess. 5:20-21). Paul reminded Timothy, "Do your best to present yourself to God as one approved by him, a worker who has no need to be ashamed, rightly explaining the word of truth" (2 Tim. 2:15, NRSV, emphasis added). John counseled his readers to "test the spirits" (1 Jn. 4:1).

Interpretation isn't optional. When we merely observe what a text says and then move to the step of application, we risk applying the Bible in the wrong way. Too much is at stake, so we need to be sure we correctly understand what God has revealed.

Application

Application means responding to God's Word by putting it into practice in our lives. Application is the intended outcome of observation and interpretation, but we should apply what Scripture says only after we faithfully complete these two prior steps. In other words, we must first understand what the authors intended to say, and then we can apply that message by putting it into practice.

This makes sense. We can't implement a text if we don't understand what it means, and there's no value in applying an incorrect meaning. For example, the OT prohibits God's people from eating shrimp. Yet why do some Christians feel free to eat shrimp, but insist on keeping some other commands of the OT? What does this prohibition mean in light of the context of the entire Bible?

We don't obtain the benefits of studying the Bible from methods, techniques, or even our diligent efforts to decipher the text. The benefits come from obeying the voice of the Lord—receiving what God says and putting it into practice. Application doesn't just happen by chance; it takes conscious effort. We begin by acknowledging the truth we discover in our study. Then we respond to God's Word with trust, obedience, praise, and thanksgiving.

The Scriptures are God's personal words to us, so we must respond appropriately. We need the attitude of the psalmist who wrote, "When I think of your ways, I turn my feet to your decrees; I hurry and do not delay to keep your commandments" (Ps. 119:59-60, NRSV). Jesus insisted to his disciples, "If you know these things, you are blessed if you do them" (Jn. 13:17, NRSV). Finally, James expressed it this way: "Do not merely listen to the word, and so deceive yourselves. Do what it says" (1:22).

Application involves determining the practical and concrete ways you can glorify God by obeying his Word. The application might include remembering an important truth, changing a wrong attitude, or taking a positive action. It might identify something God wants you to do or stop doing, some habit you need to form or break, or simply a new awareness of a truth to incorporate into your thinking.

Applying Scripture might pertain to God or to others. With God, your application could lead you to appreciate some great truth that deepens your devotion to God, correct an attitude, or strengthen and improve your fellowship with God. It might also mean putting into practice a promise or command that affects your relationship with God. With others, your application might move you toward improving your relationship with other people, fellow believers and the unchurched alike. This type of application usually relates to service or outreach for Christ.

Appropriate application asks, "What's the significance of this text for my life?" Answer in your own words, stating the significance of the passage for you. Use the pronouns *I*, *me*, *my*, and *mine* to make your applications personal. The best applications will also be specific and concrete: "I need to take a meal to the widow who lives across the street" instead of "Christians need to be more loving."

If the meaning of the text doesn't lead you to a plan of action, it remains abstract and theoretical. That isn't the ultimate goal of studying the Bible. Instead, decide on a specific action you need to take to correct a weakness, build a godly quality in your life, or increase your understanding of this truth. Choose a practical action you can take within a specified and reasonable length of time instead of making it like a New Year's resolution that extends "someday" out in the future.

Further, application means responding to God's Word as you'd respond to a loving Father who cares deeply for your welfare and development. A response should be motivated by your love for God, not by a sense of guilt or obligation. The goal is to glorify God by pleasing him in every area of life.

Unwillingness to apply the Scriptures personally will ultimately lead to spiritual insensitivity to the Lord and to other people. The following five questions, which you can remember by the acronym SPECK, can help you think about ways to apply the Scriptures to your life:

S — Is there a *sin* I need to avoid?

P — Is there a *promise* from God that I can claim?

E — Is there some *example* for me to follow or avoid?

C — Is there a *command* I need to obey?

K — How can this passage increase my *knowledge* about God, Jesus, myself, or some other aspect of God's truth?

An Example to Illustrate the Three Basic Steps of Bible Study

Let's look at how these steps work using a simple example from Paul's letter to the church at Thessalonica. He wrote, "Our gospel came to you not simply with words, but also with power, with the Holy Spirit and with deep conviction. You know how we lived among you for your sake" (1 Thess. 1:5).

OBSERVATION

The gospel that Paul preached to the Thessalonians wasn't merely a collection of interesting or useful words. Clearly, God's power transformed Paul and his associates in visible and noticeable ways that affected how they proclaimed the gospel message. In addition, the Christians in Thessalonica were aware of the kind of life that Paul lived in order to proclaim this message.

INTERPRETATION

Paul's exemplary life explains one reason why the gospel had such power. The readers of this letter saw the gospel lived out before them. The Holy Spirit gave power to Paul's words and enabled him to live the kind of life that gave validity to the claims of the gospel message. When we look at the next chapter—using the principle of context—we can see more detail about the kind of life Paul lived when he stated that the readers were aware of his holiness, righteousness, and blamelessness (see 1 Thess. 2:10).

APPLICATION

The application might be stated, "I need to concentrate on living a life of holiness, especially as I seek to tell others about Jesus Christ and his power to change them. In particular, I need to correct my arrogant spirit that communicates to my neighbor Fred that I think I'm better than he is. The next time it snows, I will shovel his sidewalk."

THE ROLE OF THE HOLY SPIRIT

Understanding the meaning of a biblical text requires the methods and tasks of studying the Bible that we discuss in this *Handbook*. The Holy Spirit doesn't tell readers what texts mean. In other words, no amount of prayer by sincere individuals studying the Bible will convey what *phylacteries* means (see Mt. 23:5). That requires study. A humble dependence on the Holy Spirit doesn't rule out research, diligent study, and the use of resources.

At this point, however, it's important to note that the Holy Spirit does make God's Word clear to us. The Spirit doesn't convey new revelation to us on a par with or above Scripture itself. So it's foolish to say, "The Spirit told me . . ." and then proceed to explain an understanding of some text of the Bible. The Spirit doesn't guarantee that our interpretations will always be correct. And the Spirit doesn't give insights that other interpreters have never seen before. Claiming either of these assertions would be extremely arrogant and deny the Spirit's work of illumination throughout history and the world.

In addition, the Holy Spirit doesn't take the place of using common sense and logic. The Spirit doesn't guarantee that we'll clearly understand everything in the Bible equally or promise that we'll gain a comprehensive understanding of God's truth. After all, the Spirit is working with imperfect humans like us, and we bring to our study of the Bible both our sins and our preunderstandings, which can inhibit true understanding.

As we study the Bible, the Holy Spirit doesn't communicate "what a text means." But we do rely on the Spirit to help us grasp and take for our own use the meaning of a text into our lives —what we call application. Without the aid of the Spirit, we're all too likely to misunderstand or avoid the message of a biblical passage for our own lives. We study the Bible best when we humbly depend on the Holy Spirit to allow Scriptures to have the effect God desires for us.

DIRECTION AND GUIDANCE FROM GOD'S WORD

Because we rarely hear from God in an audible voice, we must discern God's guidance through Scripture. When we properly interpret God's Word to us, we can expect it to steer us faithfully through life.

As we'll discuss in chapter 5, sometimes we can determine the response that a biblical author wanted from the original readers. In turn, this gives us godly wisdom about specific actions to take or attitudes to adopt. However, in other places in the Bible, we can't apply the specific instructions in the text (for various reasons that we'll discuss in chapter 5), but we can apply principles for Christian living that incorporate specific elements from the passage. In other words, we can glean definite principles for godly living, even when our circumstances differ radically from the culture of the original readers in the biblical world. And finally, in still other places, we might discover and apply a general truth from the passage that is relevant for current issues.

When it comes to finding guidance for life's decisions, we can certainly be confident that the Bible gives us principles to help us make decisions. As Christians, we should use our sanctified common sense to apply the meaning of the biblical text in appropriate ways. We should imitate what Jesus did when Satan tempted him to disobey or violate God's will: infuse our minds with the teachings of the Scriptures. To do this, we must understand three principles:

1. The guidance we receive from a passage never contradicts what that passage means in its context.
2. Guidance from a biblical text will never contradict what another passage explicitly teaches.
3. Guidance can be as different as God's unique call and gifts to his people; it's not "one size fits all."

We're wise to remember that the Bible records God's Word for God's people. This gives us confidence that the Bible provides all we need to know to be all God wants us to be in every situation in life.

FOR FURTHER STUDY

Duvall, J. S., and J. D. Hays. *Grasping God's Word: A Hands-On Approach to Reading, Interpreting, and Applying the Bible.* 2nd ed. Grand Rapids, MI: Zondervan, 2005.

Fee, G. D., and D. K. Stuart. *How to Read the Bible for All Its Worth: A Guide to Understanding the Bible.* 3rd ed. Grand Rapids, MI: Zondervan, 2003.

Klein, W. W., C. L. Blomberg, and R. L. Hubbard Jr. *Introduction to Biblical Interpretation.* Rev. ed. Nashville: Nelson, 2004.

The Navigator Bible Studies Handbook. Rev. ed. Colorado Springs, CO: NavPress, 1994, 11–26.

CHAPTER 4

THE SPIRITUAL DISCIPLINE OF BIBLE INTAKE

If you want to run a marathon, you face months and months of arduous training. Why? You can't simply strap on the running shoes gathering dust in your closet and suddenly run 26.2 miles. Instead, you might set a goal of running your first marathon in a year. In the meantime, you'll start a program of running an increasing number of miles each day, and you might compete in some shorter races — 5K, 10K, and half-marathon — in the months leading up to the marathon.

Of course, reaching your goal will take practice, preparation, perseverance, and discipline. The same holds true for any difficult but worthwhile task, such as becoming an accomplished musician, learning a new language, or graduating at the top of your class. We have to keep at it — or as my college calculus teacher used to say, we must "keep on keeping on."

The writer of the NT book Hebrews made a statement that has similar implications for our spiritual lives: "No discipline seems pleasant at the time, but painful. Later on, however, it produces a harvest of righteousness and peace for those who have been trained by it" (Heb. 12:11). While this writer referred to benefits that can come through suffering, the point is valid more broadly: "Discipline is a good thing."

How do we become spiritual? No quick prayer, spiritual retreat, or laying on of hands can turn an immature Christian into a mature one. Paul once wrote to his protégé Timothy, "Train yourself in godliness" (1 Tim. 4:7, NRSV). So we need to ask ourselves this question: What disciplines yield the fruit of godliness?

While we don't have the space to develop the full range of spiritual disciplines, we can investigate disciplines that focus attention on the Bible. The disciplines connected with the Bible are not ends unto themselves. We don't study the Bible for the sake of studying the Bible any more than someone practices the guitar each day just to brag to a friend how many days she has practiced.

As we discussed in the previous chapter, the goal (or *end*) of studying the Bible is to know and love God and be transformed into the likeness of God's Son Jesus. One of the primary *means* God uses to accomplish that goal is Scripture. The psalmist asserted, "Your word is a lamp to my feet and a light for my path" (Ps. 119:105). Having God's Word in written form — the *means* to accomplish our goal — is one of God's greatest gifts to his people. Studying the Bible enables God to accomplish his purposes in us, so it's important that we discipline ourselves to understand its message.

The overall spiritual discipline devoted to studying the Bible is often called "Bible intake." Let's look at what practicing this discipline involves.

HEARING THE WORD

The easiest way to take in God's Word is simply hearing it. Why consider this a discipline or practice of Bible intake? If we don't discipline ourselves to hear God's Word regularly, we might hear it only accidentally, when we feel like it, or not at all. For most of us, disciplining ourselves to hear God's Word includes the practice of listening to the Word of God as faithfully preached and taught.

Of course, we should distinguish between merely hearing God-inspired words and actually listening to them. Jesus said, "Blessed rather are those who hear the word of God and obey it" (Lk. 11:28). With all methods of Bible intake, we need to make our goal obedience to what God says. The result of this obedience is godliness. Jesus assumes that this process starts by hearing God's Word.

In Romans 10:17, Paul emphasized the results of hearing as a practice of Bible intake: "Faith comes from hearing the message, and the message is heard through the word of Christ." In other words, much of the faith we need for day-to-day living comes from hearing the Bible's message. For example, a family facing financial struggles might find a measure of faith from a biblical message about God's provision. Or a discouraged believer might receive assurance about his faith from hearing a biblically based sermon on the love of Christ. Such gifts of faith often come to those who discipline themselves to hear the Word of God.

The apostle Paul instructed Timothy, "Until I come, devote yourself to the public reading of Scripture, to preaching and to teaching" (1 Tim. 4:13). Paul knew how crucial it is for God's people to hear God's Word. Hearing and responding to God's Word should become a disciplined priority for us.

Maybe you've heard someone claim, "I don't need to go to church to worship God; I can worship him just as well on the golf course or at the lake as in church." While we might agree that we can worship God almost anyplace, we can't separate the ongoing worship of God from hearing the Word of God.

How do we prepare ourselves to hear the Word of God most effectively? This practice takes some intentional preparation. In 1648,

Jeremiah Burroughs, an English Puritan, wrote the following words of counsel about preparation for the discipline of hearing God's Word: "First, when you come to hear the Word, if you would sanctify God's name, you must possess your souls with what it is you are going to hear. That is, what you are going to hear is the Word of God."[1]

Maybe we need to give more thought to putting ourselves in a place of reverence to listen to and hear God's Word. "Possessing our souls" might involve meditation and prayer to put us in a listening frame of mind and give us better "ears to hear."

Perhaps most importantly, we can stay prepared in a more general way by understanding that hearing the Word of God isn't just passive listening; rather, hearing the Word is a discipline we need to cultivate.

Besides "hearing" God's Word read in a worship service, there are two other practical tactics worth mentioning.

First, you might consider listening to the Scriptures read in an audio format: tapes, CDs, or mp3 players, for example. This works particularly well for people who spend hours commuting or traveling, when their minds are free to concentrate on listening. But we can all benefit from listening to long stretches of Scripture and imprinting God's words onto our hearts. Sometimes this even enables us to concentrate on the words better than when we read them ourselves.

Second, consider the value of reading the Scriptures out loud yourself. This doesn't just help you listen more intently; it aids in the process of fixing the words more firmly into your mind. Reading the Bible aloud also helps you with memorizing. When you read God's Word aloud, you engage your eyes, mouth, ears, and mind—two more faculties than when you read silently. Reading aloud can also be a very useful part of a small-group Bible study, as all hear the same version in preparation for their discussion and meditation.

However you do it, make sure that you regularly hear God's Word.

READING THE WORD

Another method of Bible intake we can practice is reading the Bible. Reading the Word involves going over a verse or passage slowly enough so that you can absorb its message.

When Jesus wanted to gauge people's understanding of the Scriptures, he sometimes asked a question beginning with the words, "Have you not read . . . ?" (Mt. 22:31; Mk. 12:26). He assumed that the people he spoke to had enough access to Scripture to know what it said. Few people in Jesus' day actually possessed any portion of Scripture, but a few people had read at least some sections of the Bible for themselves, perhaps in a synagogue. However, most were illiterate and had access to Scripture's message only by hearing others read it.

Not so for us, because most of us can read. Most of us own more than one Bible. So the question we must answer isn't, "*Can* I read the Bible?" but "*Do* I read the Bible?"

Jesus stated, "One does not live by bread alone, but by every word that comes from the mouth of God" (Mt. 4:4, NRSV). Surely, he meant that people need to pay attention to "every word" so they can live as God intended. Because our goal for studying Scripture is to be transformed into Christlikeness, shouldn't we read every word?

In the book of Revelation, the apostle John delivered a promise from God for those who read and heed his Word: "Blessed is the one who reads the words of this prophecy, and blessed are those who hear it and take to heart what is written in it, because the time is near" (1:3). Certainly this principle extends to all of Scripture, yet we do have to take action and read! Only those who discipline themselves to read God's Word will receive these blessings.

Remember that the main reason to discipline ourselves is to attain godliness. As we walk down the paths of the spiritual disciplines, we should expect to encounter the transforming grace of God. The most critical discipline is the intake of God's Word. If you want to be transformed—if you want to become more like Jesus Christ—discipline yourself to read the Bible.

Briefly, let's look at several practical suggestions for consistent success in Bible reading: making time to read, following a plan, and meditating on what you read.

Make the Time

Perhaps one of the main reasons Christians never read the entire Bible is discouragement. Many of us have never read a thousand-page book before, so we can easily be discouraged by the sheer length of the Bible. However, recorded readings of the Bible prove that you can read the entire book in seventy-one hours. The average person in the United States watches that much TV in a little more than two weeks.[2]

You can read through the Bible in less than a year if you spend just fifteen minutes a day reading. Only five minutes a day takes you through the Bible in less than three years. Yet most Christians never read the Bible all the way through in their whole lives. So that leads us back to the idea that this discipline is primarily a matter of motivation and practice.

Discipline yourself to make the time. It might help to carve out the same time slot every day, perhaps as your first activity of the morning. Of course, you can read the Bible at any time, and you need to find the best time for yourself. But I suggest that you avoid the time just before you go to sleep, for two reasons: First, when you're tired, you'll retain very little of what you read. Second, you can't meditate on what you read during the hours that follow.

So whenever you discipline yourself to read the Word, engage the Scriptures so they will make an impact on your day.

Find and Follow a Bible-Reading Plan

If you simply open the Bible at random to read each day, there's a good chance you'll soon drop the discipline, so I urge you to find a reading plan that works for you and, with discipline, stick to it. *Discipleship Journal* (published by NavPress, also the publisher of this *Handbook*) offers several reading plans that you'll find easy to use (go to www.navpress.com/Magazines/DiscipleshipJournal/BibleReadingPlans/). Or you can search the Internet using the keywords "one-year Bible plans." Remember, the goal isn't to race through a set amount of text in a given amount of time; the goal is to read God's Word, allowing him to use what you take in to transform your life. Work at that objective.

Apart from a specific plan, reading three chapters each day along with five chapters each Sunday will take you through the Bible in a year's time. If you read three chapters in the OT and three in the NT each day, in a twelve-month span you'll read through the OT once and the NT four times! If you read five psalms and one chapter from Proverbs each day, you can read both of these books in the span of a month.

Many denominations suggest lectionary readings for each day. Usually, these include readings from Psalms, the OT, the NT, and the Gospels. In a typical cycle, you'll read the entire Bible in three years and Psalms every year. One advantage of following a lectionary is the variety. Many people who intend to read through the Bible get bogged down in Leviticus, become discouraged in Numbers, and give up completely by Deuteronomy. But when you read in more than one place each day, you'll likely find it easier to keep up the momentum.

Even if you don't read through the Bible in a year's time, keep a record of the books you do read. Place a check beside a chapter when you read it or by the title of a book in your Bible's table of contents when you complete it. That way, no matter how long it takes or what order you read in, you'll know when you've read every book in the Bible.

Find Something to Meditate On

Each time you read, focus on a word, phrase, or verse. We'll look at meditation more closely later in this chapter, but for now, recognize that without meditation or personal reflection on what you read, you might close your Bible and find little to take away. If this occurs, your Bible reading likely won't result in personal transformation. Even with a good plan, reading the Word can become a mundane chore instead of a discipline of joy.

When you read God's Word, take at least one thought or idea and think deeply about it for a few moments. You'll deepen your insight into Scripture, and you'll better understand how God's Word applies to your life. The more you apply the truth of Scripture, the more you'll become like Jesus.

STUDYING THE WORD

What's the difference between reading the Bible and studying it? We might think about reading the Bible as cruising across a clear, sparkling lake in a motorboat, while studying the Bible is more like slowly paddling across the same lake in a glass-bottomed boat. The motorboat crossing provides an overview of Scripture and a swift, passing view of its depths. The glass-bottomed boat, however, takes you beneath the surface of Scripture for an unhurried look of clarity and detail you'd miss if you simply read the text.

Let's examine the idea of studying the Bible by looking at examples from Scripture and some basic study tactics.

Scripture's Examples

Three illustrations from Scripture help us understand what it means to study the Word of God.

The first comes from the OT scribe Ezra: "Ezra had set his heart to study the law of the Lord, and to do it, and to teach the statutes and ordinances in Israel" (7:10, NRSV). The sequence in this verse contains an instructive quality: Ezra (1) "set his heart," or devoted himself, (2) "to study God's Law," (3) "to do [God's Law]," and (4) "to teach its statues and ordinances in Israel." Before Ezra could teach the Word of God, he committed himself to practicing what he learned. Ezra's learning came from a study of God's Law. He engaged in his study from his heart; that is, he devoted himself to his study. Ezra disciplined himself to study God's Word.

The second example comes from the book of Acts. Missionaries Paul and Silas barely escaped with their lives from Thessalonica after their successful evangelistic work provoked some Jews there to jealousy. Paul wrote that when Paul and Silas repeated the same tactics in Berea, the Jews there responded differently: "These Jews were more receptive than those in Thessalonica, for they welcomed the message very eagerly and examined the scriptures every day to see whether these things were so" (Acts 17:11, NRSV). As a result, according to the next verse, "many of the Jews believed." The author commended the Berean Jews for their eagerness to examine the Scriptures because it led many of them to come to faith in Christ. This displayed their receptive (or "noble" in some versions) character.

The third example also involves the apostle Paul. He provides a stirring example of a heart to study the truth of God. From prison, he wrote the last chapter of his last NT letter. Anticipating the coming of his younger friend Timothy, Paul wrote, "When you come, bring the cloak that I left with Carpus at Troas, and my scrolls, especially the parchments" (2 Tim. 4:13). The scrolls and parchments Paul requested almost certainly included copies of the Scriptures.

So in his cold and miserable confinement, the godly apostle asked for two things: a warm coat to cover his cold body, and God's Word to nourish his heart and soul. He continued to study the Scriptures until the end of his life. If this great apostle needed to study God's Word, surely we need to do the same. And we should discipline ourselves to do it.

Study Tactics

If we know we should study the Bible, why don't we? Why do so many Christians neglect the study of God's Word? Could we simply be lazy? Maybe we're uncertain about how to study the Bible or where to begin. Maybe the word *study* frightens us. If you don't regularly study the Bible, be honest with yourself.

Starting really isn't that difficult. The basic difference between Bible reading and Bible study might be as simple as a pencil and a piece of paper. In chapter 6, we'll examine twenty-two methods for studying the Bible. But the easiest way to begin studying is to write down observations about the text as you read and record questions that come to your mind.

If your Bible has footnotes or cross-references in the margins, look up other passages that relate to the verses prompting your questions. Then record your insights, reflections, or additional questions based on those verses. Find a keyword in your reading and use the concordance found in the back of most Bibles to review other passages that use that word. See if the word occurs with a similar meaning in other passages, and again record your insights.

Another simple way to study is to outline a chapter, one paragraph at a time. Isolate the main assertions or themes in each paragraph and any subpoints that support them. If you don't like traditional outline form, simply use main statements for key ideas and bulleted subpoints that support each key idea to create an informal outline. When you finish a chapter, move on to the next until you've outlined an entire book. Start with small biblical books, such as one of the epistles, before you tackle larger ones. Before long, you'll have a far stronger grasp on a section of Scripture than you'd gain by just reading it.

When you practice the discipline of studying the Bible, you'll discover a new richness in the Scripture as your understanding grows about how the grammar, history, culture, and geography surrounding a text affect its interpretation.

Don't let any feelings of inadequacy keep you from the delight of studying the Bible on your own. When you go to a cafeteria and eat food offered and prepared by others, you can choose from only the options offered. But if you learn gourmet cooking, select the ingredients from the best markets, and prepare a meal for yourself, you can savor it with special delight. True, this means more work, but the results are so much more gratifying. Don't just settle for spiritual food that others have "precooked"—experience the joy of discovering biblical insights firsthand through your own study of Scripture!

MEMORIZING THE WORD

Many Christians view the spiritual discipline of memorizing Scripture as a pointless exercise. Why? Perhaps we associate memorization with something required of us in school. Memorizing math tables or verb tenses or scientific calculations took work. A lot of times, the material we had to memorize seemed uninteresting and of limited value.

However, imagine if someone offered you a hundred dollars for each Bible verse you memorized in the next seven days? Do you think your attitude toward Scripture memory and your ability to memorize would improve? Then consider that any financial reward is trivial compared to the value of the treasure of God's Word deposited within your mind. Does that sound a bit crazy? Let's explore the benefits of memorizing Scripture.

Memorization Supplies Spiritual Power

When we store Scripture in our minds, the Holy Spirit can bring it to our attention when we need it most. That's why the psalmist wrote, "I have stored up your word in my heart, that I might not sin against you" (Ps. 119:11, ESV). For example, most of us know when we watch or think about something that's spiritually harmful or sinful. But we experience added power against these temptations when we recall a specific verse such as, "Brothers and sisters, whatever is true, whatever is noble, whatever is right, whatever is pure, whatever is lovely, whatever is admirable—if anything is excellent or praiseworthy—think about such things" (Phil. 4:8, TNIV).

When the Holy Spirit brings to mind a definite verse like this, he provides us with an illustration of Scripture's function: "the sword of the Spirit, which is the word of God" (Eph. 6:17). The author of Hebrews also wrote of this discerning function of God's Word: "The word of God is living and active, sharper than any two-edged sword, piercing until it divides soul from spirit, joints from marrow; it is able to judge the thoughts and intentions of the heart" (Heb. 4:12, NRSV). We need this kind of "arms depot" available to judge our thoughts. A pertinent scriptural truth, brought to your awareness by the Holy Spirit at just the right moment, can be the weapon that makes the difference in a spiritual battle.

Jesus himself provided a perfect illustration when Satan tempted him in the lonely Judean wilderness (see Mt. 4:1-11). Each time the enemy thrust a temptation at Jesus, he responded with truth from God's Word. The Spirit-prompted recollection of specific texts of Scripture helped Jesus experience victory. We can experience spiritual victories if we follow Jesus' example: memorizing Scripture so it's available for the Holy Spirit to take and ignite within us when we need it.

Memorization Strengthens Your Faith

Do you want to strengthen your faith? What Christian doesn't? You can strengthen your faith by disciplining yourself to memorize Scripture. Consider the progression of thoughts in Proverbs 22:17-19: "Pay attention and listen to the sayings of the wise; apply your heart to what I teach, for it is pleasing when you keep them in your heart and have all of them ready on your lips. So that your trust may be in the Lord, I teach you today, even you" (NRSV). To "apply your heart" to the "sayings of the wise" and "keep them in your heart" certainly stresses the need to memorize God's Word. Where can we find a greater source of wisdom than in Scripture?

The reason these verses from Proverbs advise you to keep the wise words of Scripture within you and "ready on your lips" is "so that your trust may be in the Lord." Memorizing God's wisdom as found in the Bible strengthens your faith because it reinforces the truth, often just when you need to hear it again. When you live based on God's wisdom hidden in your heart, you can be ready to face whatever life throws your way. As you reflect on these benefits, your trust in the Author of the words will grow. In future situations—during both trials and celebrations—you'll be more likely to base your actions on God's Word. Your faith will increase, and you'll prove the validity of God's promise: "Those who honor me I will honor" (1 Sam. 2:30). Scripture memory acts like reinforcing steel to a sagging faith.

Memorization and "Spontaneous" Spiritual Insights

Once we lodge the words and principles of Scripture in our hearts, they remain accessible to our minds when we need spiritual insight and wisdom. Many writers of the NT illustrated their command of many portions of the OT, which they frequently quoted or alluded to in their writings. Clearly, they had saturated their minds with Scripture.

For example, on the Day of Pentecost (the Jewish holiday being celebrated when the Holy Spirit first filled Jesus' disciples), the apostle Peter suddenly felt inspired by God to stand and preach to the crowd about Jesus. Much of what he said consisted of quotations from the OT (see Acts 2:14-40). He drew upon Joel 2 and Psalms 16 and 110. His experience illustrates how Scripture memory can prepare us for witnessing, teaching, or spiritual conversations that come our way. Until we hide the verses in our hearts, the words and truths aren't available for our mouths to use.

A Means of God's Guidance

Just as the Holy Spirit retrieves scriptural truth from our memory banks to provide timely guidance for ourselves, he can also prompt us to use the truths we've memorized when we talk to others. The psalmist wrote, "Your statutes are my delight; they are my counselors" (Ps. 119:24). How does this work? Suppose you decided to commit Ephesians 4 to memory. Later, you find yourself in a conversation and you begin to reflect on how you should respond to what you're hearing. Perhaps the Holy Spirit brings Ephesians 4:29 to mind for you to share: "Do not let any unwholesome talk come out of your mouths, but only what is helpful for building others up according to their needs, that it may benefit those who listen."

Or maybe you're talking to someone in your small group at church and you're thinking about shading the truth just a bit. At just the right moment, a verse guides your response: "Each of you must put off falsehood and speak truthfully to his neighbor, for we are all members of one body" (Eph. 4:25).

We could multiply these examples a thousand times. Of course, you might misunderstand the voice of the Holy Spirit or you might not be sure how to apply some principle in a specific situation. Yet when the Spirit brings texts we've memorized to our minds, God's guidance will never be clearer.

Memorization Stimulates Meditation

Perhaps one of the most underrated benefits of memorizing Scripture is that it fuels meditation. When you memorize a verse of Scripture, you can meditate on it anywhere and at anytime. If you value God's Word enough to memorize it, you can become like the writer of Psalm 119:97, who exclaimed, "Oh, how I love your law! I meditate on it all day long." Whether you're driving your car, riding the train, waiting at the airport, standing in line, rocking a baby, or sipping a latte, you can benefit from the spiritual discipline of meditation if you've previously stored up God's Word in your mind. As you meditate on God's Word, the Spirit can then help you apply God's wisdom in your life, prompting you to take action, enter into a time of personal praise and worship, or respond in other ways.

You Can Memorize Scripture

Most people think they have a bad memory, but it's not true. Memorizing mainly becomes a matter of motivation. If you know your birthday, phone number, Social Security number, home address, and e-mail address and you can remember the names of your friends, then you can memorize Scripture. Many people know the lyrics to dozens of songs. Others can recite the statistics of their favorite sports teams. People memorize sales presentations all the time. So when it comes to memorizing Scripture, you simply need to ask yourself if you're willing to discipline yourself to do it. Will you give yourself the opportunity to prove that the rewards of placing God's Word in your heart are worth the effort?

Have a Plan

You can develop the mental skill of memorization with a plan and some practice. While it might seem like an intimidating goal, you can succeed. If you want, you can even memorize entire books of the Bible. Here are some guidelines for developing your own plan:

Select a version of the Bible to memorize. This first step is mostly a matter of personal preference, but I suggest you select a translation that is more formally equivalent (for example, NIV, TNIV, NRSV, NASB, ESV) rather than a paraphrase. Of course, if you find a specific verse in a paraphrase that speaks clearly to you, you might want to commit it to memory too.

Select texts to memorize. You can choose from several excellent prepackaged Scripture memory plans available in Christian bookstores, or you might want to choose verses on a particular topic of interest or importance in your life right now. If you sense that your faith is weak, memorize verses on faith. If you struggle with a sinful habit, find verses that can help you experience victory over it, and commit them to memory. If you realize that pride is a persistent pitfall, use a concordance to find verses on humility and memorize those.

Beware of picking verses in isolation—taking them out of context—especially if it causes you to get the wrong ideas about their meaning. Because of the verse numbering in our Bibles, we can easily locate texts. However, this can also cause us to think of individual verses as isolated entries, like the entries in a phone book, where context is irrelevant. Literature isn't like that, and we need to understand verses in their contexts to grasp their meaning and significance. If you choose to memorize individual verses, make sure you still read them in context. Or you can memorize whole sections of Scripture—paragraphs, chapters, or even entire books—rather than isolated verses.

Write out the verses. The act of writing will help you memorize. Record the texts on a sheet of paper, or write each passage on a separate index card. You might decide to have an electronic file of passages to memorize on your laptop computer, or you might write the texts on your PDA or mobile phone so they'll be available to review.

Determine a schedule. Set reasonable goals for the passages you want to memorize. If you set your mind to it, you can easily memorize a verse in a day, a paragraph in a week, or a chapter in a month. At that rate, you could memorize a short book of the Bible in three to six months, or a longer one in a year.

As you work on your plan, break up the time into smaller units and set specific mini-goals along the way. For example, if you decide to memorize the epistle of James during the summer, you might set a goal to memorize half of a chapter every two weeks. You need to determine the system that works best for you as well as times during the day to devote to your memorization. But if you don't start with some kind of plan, you'll soon be tempted to give up.

Draw picture reminders. You might find that visualizing the meaning of texts helps fix them in your mind. You don't have to be a great artist because no one else will see your drawings. Just draw a few lines or stick figures—whatever makes sense to you—beside a verse or passage to make a verse "visual." This puts the "a picture is worth a thousand words" principle to work for you. A simple drawing can remind you of a couple dozen words, especially if your drawing illustrates an action described in the verse.

For example, with Psalm 119:11 you might make a crude drawing of a heart with a Bible inside to remind you of treasuring God's Word in your heart. For Ephesians 6:17, a sketch of a sword stands as an obvious reminder. You'll find this method particularly helpful when memorizing a section of consecutive verses.

Memorize the verses word-perfectly. As you begin the process of memorizing, these four steps will prove useful:

1. Read the verse aloud. Reread as many times as you need to until you can move on to step 2.
2. Recite the verse from memory.
3. Review the verse mentally (silently in your mind).
4. Recite the verse from memory again.

Repeat this cycle until you can recite a verse from memory easily and with consistent accuracy. Once you have that verse down, move on to the next one in the passage and repeat the cycle, verse by verse, until you achieve your goal.

Especially when you're first learning a verse, you might be tempted to lower your standards. Don't settle for just getting close or getting the main idea. Memorize the passage word for word and include the reference as well. Without this objective standard of measurement, you might continue to lower the standard until you quit completely. What's more, if you don't memorize a verse exactly, you won't be confident about using it in conversation or witnessing. Even though memorizing precisely seems harder in the beginning, it's easier and more productive in the long run. Incidentally, verses you know word-perfectly are easier to review than those you don't know accurately.

Find a method of accountability. Because most of us tend to get lazy or distracted, we need some kind of accountability to make sure we stick with memorizing Scripture. The busier we are, the more we excuse ourselves from this commitment. However, you'll be more consistent if you meet or talk regularly with someone else to review your verses. Perhaps you can find a partner or a small group of people who will commit to memorizing portions of Scripture together; you can meet regularly to review and to encourage each other.

Review and meditate every day. This might be the most important principle of Scripture memory. Without adequate review, you'll eventually lose most of what you've memorized. However, once you really learn a verse or passage, you can mentally review it in a fraction of the time it would take you to speak it. When you know a section well, you might need to review only once a week, once a month, or even once every three to six months to keep a sharp edge on it. Eventually, you'll reach a point where you spend most of your Scripture memory time in review. Don't begrudge devoting so much time to sharpening your swords. Instead, rejoice at having so many!

The time while you're falling asleep can actually be a great time to review verses you know best. You don't need a written copy of the verses in front of you, so you can repeat them and meditate on them while dozing off or even if you have trouble sleeping. If you can't sleep, you'll be putting the most profitable and peaceful information possible into your mind as well as making good use of the time.

Remember that memorizing Scripture isn't an end in itself. Your goal isn't to see how many verses you can memorize. The goal is godliness: memorizing the Word of God so it can transform your mind and your life. Dallas Willard wrote,

> As a pastor, teacher, and counselor I have repeatedly seen the transformation of inner and outer life that comes simply from memorization and meditation upon Scripture. Personally, I would never undertake to pastor a church or guide a program of Christian education that did not involve a continuous program of memorization of the choicest passages of Scripture for people of all ages.[3]

MEDITATING ON THE WORD

Sadly, many people in our modern culture identify meditation with non-Christian systems of thought rather than with biblical

Christianity. Some Christians even feel uncomfortable with the subject of meditation and look suspiciously at those who engage in it. They associate the practice of meditation with yoga, transcendental meditation, relaxation therapy, or New Age practices more than as a discipline that has a long history with God's people, both Israel and the NT church. In fact, as we'll see, God both commands and models meditation in Scripture.

If a cult used the cross as a symbol, the church shouldn't cease to use it. In the same way, we shouldn't discard or have fears about scriptural meditation simply because others have adapted it for their own purposes. In fact, others practice it precisely because of its benefits.

The kind of meditation that Scripture encourages differs from other kinds of meditation in several ways. Most other groups urge meditation as a way to empty your mind; Christian meditation involves filling your mind with God and truth. For the others, meditation attempts to achieve complete mental passivity; biblical meditation requires constructive mental activity.

Christian history has always had a place for the sanctified use of our God-given imagination in meditation. Our imagination serves to help us meditate on things that are true (see Phil. 4:8). However, instead of "creating our own reality" through visualization techniques (as other types of meditation urge), we link Christian meditation with prayer to God and responsible, Spirit-filled human action to effect changes.

In addition to these distinctives, you might most simply think of meditation as deep thinking on the truths and spiritual realities revealed in Scripture for the purposes of understanding, application, and prayer. Meditation goes beyond hearing, reading, studying, and even memorizing as a discipline for taking in God's Word.

The Bible speaks of four appropriate objects of our meditation:

1. Foremost, we meditate on God's Word (for example, see Josh. 1:8; Ps. 1:2; 119:15,23,48,78,97,99,148).
2. Creation is also a worthy object of our meditation (see Ps. 143:5).
3. We can also meditate on God's providential care through all he has made (see Ps. 77:12; 119:27; 145:5).
4. We should meditate on God's character (see Ps. 63:6; 145:5).

Of course, Scripture supplies God's perspective on all these areas, and that informs all our meditation.

However, meditation isn't always quiet introspection. The Hebrew words usually translated *meditation* in our English Bibles can sometimes mean "groan," "moan," or "mutter" as well as "ponder" or "muse." In other words, you can meditate out loud as you turn your full attention to your encounter with God in the Scriptures.

Finally, meditation differs from the analysis and interpretation we do in other dimensions of our Bible study. Meditation is interactive and expressive—a way of connecting the things God says to the joys and pains of our lives. It allows God's Word to connect with our lives in ways that enable application.

Joshua 1:8 — The Promise of Success

In the OT, we can find a fascinating connection between success and the practice of meditating on God's Word. As the Lord commissioned Joshua to succeed Moses as the leader of his people, God told Joshua, "Do not let this Book of the Law depart from your mouth; meditate on it day and night, so that you may be careful to do everything written in it. Then you will be prosperous and successful" (Josh. 1:8).

In this text, God promises true success to Joshua and, by extension, to all who meditate on God's Word—to those who think deeply on it, not just at one time each day but also at moments throughout the day and night. Those who meditate this much find that God's Word saturates their lives on every level. The fruit of their meditation is action—they do what they find written in God's Word. And God prospers their way and grants them success. Of course, the nature of prosperity and success is defined by God, not the world. It might be material, as it was for Israel in this text from the OT, but often God defines prosperity in terms of spiritual success, specifically how his wisdom influences all dimensions of life.

How does the discipline of meditation change us and place us in the path of God's blessing? David wrote, "My heart grew hot within me, and as I meditated, the fire burned; then I spoke with my tongue" (Ps. 39:3). The Hebrew word translated *meditated* here is related to *meditate* in Joshua 1:8. It means "to muse on something; to reflect deeply." For us, it means that when we meditate on God's Word, our meditation functions like a bellows. Then as the fire blazes more brightly, it gives off both more light (insight and understanding) and heat (passion for obedient action). "Then," says the Lord, "you will be prosperous and successful" (Josh. 1:8).

Psalm 1:1-3 — Meditation and Fruitfulness

Another important passage underscores other virtues of meditation. In Psalm 1, we find crucial words of wisdom that promise rich blessing on those who meditate on God's Word:

HAPPY [OR BLESSED] ARE THOSE WHO DO NOT
    FOLLOW THE ADVICE OF THE WICKED,
    OR TAKE THE PATH THAT SINNERS TREAD,
    OR SIT IN THE SEAT OF SCOFFERS;

> BUT THEIR DELIGHT IS IN THE LAW OF THE LORD,
>
> AND ON HIS LAW THEY MEDITATE DAY AND NIGHT.
>
> THEY ARE LIKE TREES PLANTED BY STREAMS OF
>
> WATER,
>
> WHICH YIELD THEIR FRUIT IN ITS SEASON,
>
> AND THEIR LEAVES DO NOT WITHER.
>
> IN ALL THAT THEY DO, THEY PROSPER. (PS. 1:1-3, NRSV)

We naturally think about those aspects of life that we delight in. For example, a couple that has found romantic delight in each other think about each other all day. A new baby delights his parents so much that they think about him even when someone else takes care of him. Some parents claim to sense that delightful smell of a baby even in her absence.

When we delight in God's Word, we think about it and meditate on it at times, all throughout the day and night. Its wonderful aroma fills our nostrils. Our meditation at this level brings stability, fruitfulness, perseverance, and prosperity.

If you can imagine your spiritual life as a tree, you can picture it thriving best when meditation helps you absorb the water of God's Word deep into your roots. Hearing or reading the Bible, for example, can be like a short rainfall on hard ground. While this can be refreshing, regardless of the amount or intensity of the rain, most runs off and little sinks in. In fact, you could encounter a torrential amount of God's truth—sermons, Bible studies, and the like—but without absorbing the truth, you'll be little better for the experience. Meditation enables absorption, opening the soil of the soul and allowing the water of God's Word to soak in deeply. As a result of this deep nourishment, we experience fruitfulness and spiritual prosperity.

The author of Psalm 119 expressed confidence that he was wiser than all his enemies (v. 98). Moreover, he said, "I have more insight than all my teachers" (v. 99). This was quite a boast! How could he make such claims? Is it because he heard or read or studied or memorized God's Word more than every one of his enemies and his teachers? Probably not. The psalmist knew he was wiser, not necessarily because of more input but because of more insight. How did he acquire more wisdom and insight than anyone else? His explanation follows his claims:

> YOUR COMMANDS MAKE ME WISER THAN MY ENEMIES,
>
> FOR THEY ARE EVER WITH ME.
>
> I HAVE MORE INSIGHT THAN ALL MY TEACHERS,
>
> *FOR I MEDITATE ON YOUR STATUTES.* (PS. 119:98-99,
>
> EMPHASIS ADDED)

Not only were God's commands always with the psalmist because he had memorized them, but he meditated on God's words and they made him wise.

Meditation could be more crucial in our day than it was in ancient Israel. Each day, we experience a flash flood of information and diversions the psalmist never could have imagined or experienced in a lifetime. Combine this rush of information with the complexities of modern life, and the resulting mental distractions and exhaustion can choke our absorption of Scripture.

Even as recently as a hundred years ago, a person didn't even need to answer a telephone, much less have a phone in his pocket wherever he went! The psalmist didn't face the distractions of instant world news, television, radio, MP3 players, cell phones, rapid transportation, junk mail, e-mails, spam, and so on. Because of these diversions, we find concentrating on our thoughts more challenging than it has ever been. This rings especially true of God and his Word.

The Method of Meditation

So what do we do? Even if we wanted to, we can't return to the days of simpler lives. Besides, most of us like our gadgets; we like getting more done with less effort. However, we can restore an order to our thinking and recapture some of the ability to concentrate—especially on spiritual truth—through biblical meditation. While we face challenges to godly living that differ from our ancestors in the faith, we also need to be transformed by the renewing of our minds (see Ro. 12:2) through disciplined meditation upon Scripture. As you approach meditating on God's Word, you might find the following guidelines useful.

SELECT AN APPROPRIATE PASSAGE

Deciding what to meditate on is easy. Simply choose the verses, phrases, and words that impress you most during your encounter with Scripture. Of course, this is a subjective approach, but any approach will be somewhat personal. Besides, meditation is essentially a subjective and self-centered activity, a fact that stresses the importance of basing meditation on Scripture.

The Holy Spirit, as the Author of Scripture, might impress you with a certain text or passage because God wants you to meditate on that very portion of Scripture that day. In addition, be sure to meditate often on Jesus and his ministry as well as on the great themes of the Bible. Verses that clearly relate to your concerns and personal needs also provide good texts for meditation. Although the Bible isn't meant to be a digest of wise advice, a collection of promises, or an "answer book," God certainly wants us to give our attention to the words of Scripture that directly pertain to our circumstances.

For example, if you've been struggling with sinful thoughts and you read Philippians, then the Holy Spirit is likely guiding you to meditate on the implications of 4:8: "Fix your thoughts on what is true, and honorable, and right, and pure, and lovely, and admirable.

Think about things that are excellent and worthy of praise" (NLT). Or if the salvation of a friend or family member is on your mind and you read John 3–4, you can meditate on the ways Jesus communicated and draw parallels to your own situation. Or maybe you sense distance from God or a dryness in your spiritual condition; looking for passages about God's character and meditating on them is a good choice.

Consistently try to discern the main message emerging from your times of engaging in a passage of Scripture, and then meditate on its meaning and application. This might grow out of your hearing, reading, studying, or memorizing of Scripture. For example, when reading Luke 11:1-13, you find Jesus' teaching on prayer. You can then meditate on what this means in your life, especially about the need to keep asking, seeking, and knocking (see vv. 9-10).

Repeat the Passage in Different Ways

Sometimes meditation involves taking a verse or phrase of Scripture and turning it like a diamond to examine every facet. This can be part of the practice of *lectio divina*, which we'll explore in chapter 6. For example, meditating this way on Jesus' words at the beginning of John 11:25 would look like this (the italics indicate emphasis):

> "*I* am the resurrection and the life." "I *am* the resurrection and the life." "I am *the resurrection* and the life." "I am the resurrection *and* the life." "I am the resurrection and *the life.*" "*I am the resurrection* and the life." "*I am* the resurrection and *the life.*"

Of course, the point isn't simply to repeat each word of the verse thoughtlessly until you emphasize each one. Instead, meditate deeply on the light (truth) that flashes into your mind each time you "turn" the verse in one direction and then another. This method is simple but effective, especially when you have trouble concentrating on a passage or when insights seem to come slowly.

Rewrite the Passage in Your Own Words

Writing helps you focus your attention on the text while stimulating your thinking. Paraphrasing the verses also offers a good way to make sure you understand their significance to you. Read a passage from *The Message* to get a sense of what this paraphrasing can look like, and then take a more dynamically equivalent version and put it in your own words. The act of thinking of synonyms and other ways to restate the inspired meaning of God's Word is an excellent way to meditate.

Keep a Journal

Journaling in response to your interaction with Scripture is another way of meditating—musing, reflecting, and muttering what you experience. To help you journal, these steps might be useful:

- List several issues or concerns you're facing in your life.
- Address God personally as you write about these issues in response to your meditation on God's Word. Recall how the psalmists often addressed God personally.
- Select a portion of Scripture that you think speaks to these issues. You might want to write out the verses in your journal.
- Reflect on the possible implications of the passage for your situation. What is God trying to teach you through the passage?
- If God speaks to you through his Word, reflect on this in your journaling.
- Tell God how you feel in your writing. Listen for and record in your journal how he might respond to you.
- Write out a prayer in response to God.

LOOK FOR APPLICATIONS OF THE TEXT

The discipline of journaling underscores an important element in meditation: Ask yourself, *How am I to respond to this text? What action would God have me take as a result of my encounter with this part of his Word?* The outcome of meditation should be application. Just like chewing without swallowing, meditation is incomplete without some type of application.

PRAY THROUGH THE TEXT

This is the spirit of Psalm 119:18: "Open my eyes that I may see wonderful things in your law." The Holy Spirit serves as our guide into the truth (see Jn. 14:26). Remember that meditation on God's Word is more than just riveted human concentration or creative mental energy. When you pray your way through a portion of Scripture, you submit your mind to the Holy Spirit's illumination of the text. He reveals not just what it means but also what it means to *you*. Ask the Spirit to intensify your spiritual perception.

Let's consider an example. Perhaps some circumstance in your life causes a time of distress. You might prayerfully meditate on Psalm 22:24: "He did not despise or abhor the affliction of the afflicted; he did not hide his face from me, but heard when I cried to him" (NRSV). In response, you might pray through the text along these lines:

> Lord, you know the stress I'm experiencing right now. Your Word assures me that you know all about my trouble and that you hear my cries to you for help. Your Word can revive me in my suffering. I really believe that's true because your Word has revived me in difficult times in the past. So in faith, I trust that you will revive me in this experience. I pray that you will renew me now through the comfort of your listening presence. May this truth fill my

mind and heart so I cling more firmly to you and learn to draw my encouragement from your Spirit.

In prayerful meditation on this text, the Holy Spirit might bring to your mind other truths from Scripture about God's sovereignty over his people, his providence over the circumstances in life, his power, his constant presence and love, and so on. In this extended time of meditation and prayer, your soul will be revived and you'll experience the comfort of the Comforter.

Meditation must always involve two individuals: the Christian and the Holy Spirit. When you pray through a text, you invite the Holy Spirit to hold his divine light over the words of Scripture to show you what you can't see without him.

DON'T RUSH!

What value comes from reading one, three, or more chapters of Scripture only to find that after you've finished, you can't recall a thing you've read? Choose a small portion of Scripture and meditate on it instead of reading an extensive section without meditation. If necessary, read less in order to meditate more. Even though you might use moments throughout the day to meditate on God's Word (see Ps. 119:97)—a process made easier because you've hidden his Word in your heart—the best meditation generally occurs when you make it part of your main daily encounter with the Bible.

CONTEMPLATING THE WORD

Studying the Bible should lead to a final stage, called contemplation. Let's look at this step from two perspectives. One way is to contemplate how the Word needs to move from the study to the world. Contemplation takes what God's Spirit reveals to you into life. The life of holiness isn't lived in isolation but outwardly as we demonstrate in tangible ways what it means for us to love God and our neighbors. Contemplation is the step where we link who we are in Christ with how we live in the world.

At the same time, don't view contemplation as something more to do. As the label "contemplation" suggests, in this stage we reflect on God's Word to us. We receive his gifts, rest in his presence, and wait expectantly before him in order to move out into our daily activities as vessels for God to fill and use. The hearing, reading, study, memorizing, and meditating are behind us. And in contemplation, we stand ready before God. In this place, we allow him to infuse us with whatever it is he wishes us to have. We rest in his presence. Contemplation is the culmination of Bible study.

Most of us need to find time to increase our Bible intake. We've explored several practices we can use to accomplish this important discipline: hearing the Word, reading the Word, studying the Word, memorizing the Word, meditating on the Word, and contemplating the Word. We've explored how performing this spiritual discipline takes practice, preparation, perseverance, and discipline. My hope is that you'll see beyond the mere steps and methods of practicing the discipline of Bible intake and understand the benefits that will come from it.

FOR FURTHER STUDY

Baker, H. *Soul Keeping: Ancient Paths of Spiritual Direction.* Colorado Springs, CO: NavPress, 1998.

Bonhoeffer, D. *Meditating on the Word.* Cambridge, MA: Cowley, 1986.

Demarest, B. *Satisfy Your Soul: Restoring the Heart of Christian Spirituality.* Colorado Springs, CO: NavPress, 1999.

Foster, R. J. *Celebration of Discipline.* 3rd ed. New York: Harper and Row, 1988.

Longman III, T. *Reading the Bible with Heart and Mind.* Colorado Springs, CO: NavPress, 1997.

Mulholland Jr., M. R. *Shaped by the Word: The Power of Scripture in Spiritual Formation.* Rev. ed. Nashville: The Upper Room, 2001.

Peterson, E. H. *Eat This Book: A Conversation in the Art of Spiritual Reading.* Grand Rapids, MI: Eerdmans, 2006.

Thompson, M. J. *Soul Feast: An Invitation to the Christian Spiritual Life.* Louisville, KY: Westminster John Knox, 1995.

Toon, P. *Meditating as a Christian.* London: Collins, 1991.

Whitney, D. S. *Spiritual Disciplines for the Christian Life.* Colorado Springs, CO: NavPress, 1991.

CHAPTER 5

INTERPRETING THE BIBLE

If you've ever parented a teenager or if you've been through those years yourself (one of those situations applies to just about everyone reading these words), you know that when parents and teenagers talk to each other, what they communicate often has two very different meanings. A new teen driver might tell her dad that she's "just going to drive over to Amy's house." But when Dad calls Amy's house a half hour later to remind his daughter to be home by six, she's not there. That's because his teenage daughter meant she was "going to pick up Sarah and Jessica on the way, stop at the mall to do some shopping, hang out for awhile at a coffee shop, give Ben a ride to work and Josh a ride to school and then 'just drive over to Amy's house.'"

If family members struggle to understand each other when we all speak everyday English and we all live in the same century, we can understand why Christians have a hard time agreeing on what part of the Bible means, even when we agree that the Bible has authority as the Word of God. All we have to do is look at the number of denominations and fellowships and branches of faith that fall under the umbrella "Christian," and we get a pretty clear picture of how difficult it is to interpret and agree on what Scripture means.

In chapter 3, as we discussed the importance of establishing the goal of Bible study, we concluded that we treat the Bible most respectfully and faithfully when we understand it the way the authors intended their readers to understand it — the way we normally treat all communication.

Three questions can help us think about the goal of interpreting the Bible:

1. What were the biblical authors seeking to do when they wrote? In other words, what were their motives and purposes in writing?
2. What meaning did they want to convey through their writings?
3. What can we do to understand what the writings mean?

If we can agree on the goal, then we need to ask the next question: What will help us discover the meaning the authors intended through the texts they wrote? That's our objective in this chapter. But first we need a bit of historical perspective.

A BRIEF HISTORY OF BIBLICAL INTERPRETATION

Let's start by taking a brief journey back in time to see how our ancestors — both Jewish and Christian — interpreted the Bible. We're not the first to attempt to make sense of God's revelation, and it seems logical to learn from those who've done this before us. How did they treat the Bible?

We also want to avoid the mistakes those before us made. For example, we'll see what can happen when we don't try to determine the intention of the authors, such as when interpreters do whatever they wish with a text. If interpretations are at the whim of the interpreters, any view is as good as any other one.

Jewish Interpretation

The first "Christian" interpreters were Jews who believed that Jesus was the long-awaited Messiah and were familiar with the methods Jewish rabbis used to interpret OT Scripture. The rabbis used several methods for interpreting the Hebrew Bible that allowed them to find ongoing significance in their ancient texts. These methods included:

- *Midrash* (which means "interpretation") — to find meanings in texts below the surface meaning
- *Pesher* (which also means "interpretation," but in the sense of bringing out the full significance of texts that were previously only partly known) — used especially at Qumran (a monastic community on the shores of the Dead Sea) to explain the mysteries in the texts that accounted for their own experiences
- Allegory — to extract deeper and often multiple senses in texts
- Typology — to draw out from texts what they saw as patterns of God's working in history

New Testament Interpretation of the Old Testament

Some of the rabbis' methods likely influenced various writers of the NT. But as these early disciples tried to understand and explain the significance of Jesus in light of their Scriptures and traditions, they took their lead from Jesus. Luke said of Jesus: "Beginning with Moses and all the Prophets, he *explained* to them what was said in *all the Scriptures* concerning himself" (Lk. 24:27, emphasis added).

Jesus set the stage for Christian interpretation of the OT.

The first Christians believed that Jesus had fulfilled the Scriptures (see Mt. 5:17-19; Ro. 10:4). They had clear ideas about the function of the OT, which they used to support and explain Jesus' significance and their own experiences as members of his community.

While the first Christian interpreters defended the importance of Jesus, they didn't always explain the OT in what we might call a literal or historical sense. For example, Jesus' parents' taking refuge in Egypt when Herod tried to murder Jesus was seen as a fulfillment of Hosea's words, "Out of Egypt I called my son" (Hos. 11:1; see Mt. 2:15). For Hosea, God's "son" was the nation Israel, whom God protected in Egypt. But as Matthew read Hosea, he concluded that God's protection of Israel suggested a pattern: God protects his "sons." So when Mary and Joseph hid Jesus in Egypt, God was acting to protect another "Son."

This example probably best falls under the method of typology. The prophecy is fulfilled, but not in the more straightforward way such as when Matthew (2:6) cites the prophet Micah (5:2), who predicted Bethlehem as the site of the Messiah's birth. In these and many other ways, NT writers mined the OT for evidence of Jesus' significance and mission.

Early and Medieval Christian Interpretation

After the time of the apostles, the next generations of Christians continued these same tactics. Once the Canon consisting of both the Hebrew Scriptures and what came to be the NT had been adopted, Christians searched the Bible to establish their beliefs and instructions for the church. As heresies and other threats to the church became increasingly severe, these Christians became concerned about explaining and defending an emerging "orthodoxy" — that is, what they believed to be the true understanding of the Christian faith.

During these centuries following the apostles and then into the Middle Ages, church scholars interpreted the Bible in a variety of ways. Some interpreted the Bible in light of the historical (what the author intended) meaning of its texts. Others, such as Origen (an early church father and philosopher, about AD 185–250), detected two or more levels of meaning in biblical texts. One fourth-century scholar and theologian, John Cassian, believed that each biblical text had four levels of meaning: literal, allegorical (doctrinal), moral (tropological), and anagogical (eschatological—its significance for the future). These interpreters believed that the Holy Spirit placed meanings in texts beyond what the original writers intended.

Church doctrine often led to interpretations that weren't literal, as church scholars defended practices and views they couldn't support from the literal meanings of texts. They found the arguments they needed in meanings below the surface. And when the church required interpretations that couldn't be based on the Bible, it had the Magisterium (the church's teaching authority) make official pronouncements about orthodox beliefs and practice.

The Protestant Reformation

The Protestant Reformation, coupled with the Renaissance, began the shift toward a more literal interpretation of Scripture. The Reformers believed that some of the excesses and beliefs of the church couldn't be defended from Scripture and, as a result, were suspect and misguided.

Martin Luther differed from the Catholic Church on the fundamental location of authority. He insisted on appealing to Scripture alone (*sola Scriptura*) as the channel of God's Word and will for the church, not Scripture plus tradition as the church insisted. To emphasize the importance of the texts' original meanings, he translated the Bible into German and no longer relied on the Latin Vulgate (a fifth-century Bible version) as interpreted by Rome's

Magisterium. This spurred others to seek the historical meaning of biblical texts. About the same time, the Renaissance created a new interest in the classics, igniting an interest in the original Hebrew and Greek manuscripts of the Bible.

After Luther, William Tyndale and King James of England brought the Bible into everyday English—everyday in the sense that it was the language of the people of that day. Other languages followed. As Bibles came off printing presses and became accessible to more people, individual Christians, for the first time, could own and read the Bible for themselves. This development took interpretation out of the hands of scholars and church leaders alone and put it into the hands of anyone who wanted to read the Bible.

Common people read the Bible devotionally, often not having the desire or qualifications to discover the historical sense of some of its content. This had both positive and negative consequences. Anyone—with or without theological education or credentials—could "interpret" the Bible and even start or lead a church. As various leaders claimed the Holy Spirit's illumination about the meaning of the Bible, movements emerged and gained followers. New churches and denominations began, and new groups broke off from existing church groups. Many claimed that they alone were interpreting the Bible correctly.

Rationalism and Modernity

Still, reading the Bible in a "reasonable" manner was the central contribution of the post-Reformation period. In the 1800s and beyond, "rationalism" led to many other critical methods for studying the Bible, as the church no longer controlled the outcomes of scholarly use of the Bible. The rise of scientific thinking led many to question the Bible's record of supernatural phenomena. As a result, many scholars and common people began to view the miracles of the Bible as myths.

Some saw the Bible as just a collection of religious writings, like the "sacred texts" of other religions. Emerging scientific methods gave scholars access to facts and evidence of the history and culture of the era when Scripture was written, independent of the Bible's statements. Some called the historical reliability of the Bible into question. For many, the Bible became a good source for moral or ethical values, but not for theological or historical truths.

Not all scholars agreed with these trends. In Germany, the British Isles, and North America, prominent scholars resisted many of these trends, insisted on the reliability of the biblical documents, and argued against some of the critical conclusions of the strict rationalists and anti-supernaturalists.

Postmodernity

In the 1900s, some Bible interpreters began shifting the focus from the biblical text as the object of study to the reader as the one who "produces" meaning. Embracing the values of postmodernism emerging in the rest of the culture, other interpreters insisted that readers abandon all attempts to discover objective meanings in biblical texts. Many scholars viewed historical methods as too restricting and began employing other ways to scrutinize biblical texts: literary and rhetorical criticism, psychological exegesis (explanation), deconstruction, various advocacy criticisms (such as feminist, liberationist, Marxist, "Queer," or other types of criticism), and social-scientific analyses, among others.

The biblical text was no longer central; readers now ruled and could do anything they wanted to with texts. As a result, many churches and denominations no longer felt that the historical meanings of the texts should determine their structures or values. In effect, they said, "We know better than the original writers."

At the same time, many conservative readers welcomed the new tactics for understanding the ways texts work (such as literary and rhetorical criticism), but they didn't abandon the goal of seeking the text's and author's intentions. If new methods help uncover what texts mean, we can use them, but in a careful way.

Interpretive Communities

By now, we should realize that what we might call an "interpretive community" determines how its members will interpret the Bible. A community of biblical scholars exists, but within that group, many subsets span the spectrum from conservative to liberal. Each sets its research agenda and determines acceptable findings.

Another important group is the community of believers. Believers have faith that the Bible holds divine revelation (believing the Bible teaches authoritatively), although subsets of believers also exist who feel more or less limited by the historical meaning of the texts.

Of course, the community of society also exists. Some of these people read the Bible, but they aren't scholars or believers. The Bible is simply "there," and people decide what they'll believe about it and what they'll do with it, if anything.

I assume that readers of this *Handbook* study the Bible as believers. We read the Bible as a "sacred text" that embodies God's revelation. I also presume that this "believing community" occupies the best position to understand the Bible on its own terms—the way, in fact, that most communication is designed and intended to be understood. I believe that this approach best matches the purpose of the Bible, the intention of the Bible's authors, and the historical view of the church.

Along with many scholars, I disagree with the postmodern claim that no interpretation can ever be correct. In fact, I believe that by following the methods from these next pages, we put ourselves in the best possible position to understand correctly what the original authors meant by the words they wrote. As most Christians do, I read the Bible with a desire to understand its meaning for myself. As believers, we approach Scripture positively and openly, with a desire to learn and grow by engaging with its message. My goal is to help us do that successfully.

GENERAL PRINCIPLES OF INTERPRETATION

The Bible comes to us as literature: a written document or collection of documents. Because it is literature, we have a framework and agenda for how we interpret it. If we want to understand a piece of literature, we use an approach and specific methods that allow us to determine its meaning. We can divide this approach into two categories: general steps that apply to understanding all literature, and methods that more specifically relate to the kind of literature we're studying.

To take a simple example, we can easily understand the statement "Those girls are clapping their hands." However, the statement "Those trees are clapping their hands" (see Is. 55:12) requires a different method to interpret its meaning.

First, we'll cover general principles used to interpret all types of literature before we then move on to tactics for understanding the specific genres in the Bible. These principles seek to answer the question "What do we need to consider if we want to make sense of the words?" Pursuing a text's historical meaning or interpretation involves examining:

- The literary context in which the text occurs
- The proper understanding of the historical and cultural features reflected in the text
- The correct meanings of the words of the text
- The proper understanding of the grammar employed in the text

Let's look at each of these four principles.

Literary Context

You've probably heard the adage that realtors give when selling a home: "Location, location, location." In a similar way, "context, context, context" summarizes the essential principle of interpretation. Taking words out of context keeps us from knowing whether we understand them correctly. For example, no matter how much we think about it, we can't be certain of the meaning a writer intended in the sentence "Those were the largest trunks I've ever seen" unless we also consider the sentences that precede or follow the statement. Is this a reference to automobiles, luggage, elephants, trees, or swimwear? Only the context can tell us.

Biblical texts are no different. Whether a sentence, a paragraph, or a larger section, all literature functions in a context that flows from one portion to the next. Consider these words from Paul: "I can do everything through him who gives me strength" (Phil. 4:13). Do we conclude that Paul thought he could jump from a high cliff and not suffer the effects of gravity when he hit the ground? And from that, do we reason that we also can do anything because God provides the strength? What things are included within "all things"?

The context of the previous verses (4:11-12) makes clear what Paul really meant. He was affirming that he could do all the things God called him to do and be content no matter what his circumstances.

Interpreting a text apart from its context runs the risk of misunderstanding its meaning, and this can lead to applying incorrect interpretation. A study of the literary context helps us avoid that. The literary context supplies the theme or topic of the discussion, gives the likely meanings of the words, and allows us to follow the flow of the argument or story. In other words, the correct meaning of a passage is the meaning that best fits the literary context it occurs within.

Literary context study also requires moving beyond the immediate context of a biblical text to its place within a larger section of the book and to the context of the entire biblical book where it occurs. If possible, we also want to consider other books written by the same author (for example, Luke and Acts). We should also consult other books that might parallel the content we're studying (Matthew, Mark, and Luke; Kings and Chronicles). Ultimately, the entire Bible itself occupies the largest literary context that sheds light on a text. Obviously, the further away we get from the text we're reading, the less insight we'll have about its precise meaning.

A study of literary context also prevents us from importing meanings from other contexts into a specific passage we're studying. You might have come across Bible study methods that direct you to a concordance to look up other locations where a specific word occurs. While this method works sometimes, it works only if both verses are truly about the same subject matter.

Imagine how misguided that could be in deciphering the sentence "Those were the largest trunks I've ever seen." If you're reading a story about elephants in the zoo, the fact that "trunk" also refers to the storage compartment of a car is irrelevant. How silly to import the meanings of "trunk" from other uses into the specific context you're reading.

In the same way, if you're studying "What good is it, my brothers and sisters, if you say you have faith but do not have works? Can faith save you?" (Jas. 2:14, NRSV), you need to be sure you know how James is using the terms *faith* and *works* in his context and not import what Paul means when he uses those words.

Historical-Cultural Background

The texts of the Bible were written long ago, composed in many different lands and in different languages—some by Semites living in Palestine centuries before Christ, and others by Greek-speaking inhabitants of the Roman world in the first century AD. The texts are distant from us in many ways. The cultures, as varied as they were from each other, also differ from ours. Trying to understand their meanings requires research into their worlds.

BOOK CONTEXT

Initially, we must put a biblical book into its historical context. For example, if we want to understand the OT book of Ruth, we need to place ourselves back in the time when the events occurred. We also need to be aware that some books, such as Ruth, were written years after the events occurred. To make sense of a book's message, we must try to understand the setting, the author and his or her circumstances, the situation of the original readers, the time of the writing, and the circumstances that brought about the writing.

Some books in the OT present great challenges to our understanding of their backgrounds. This knowledge isn't always available, but when it is, it greatly helps us as we interpret and study a passage. For example, we can read Psalm 51 as an admission of the author's guilt and his recognition of the gravity of his sin. But in this case, the prescript (the words introducing the Psalm) tells us an important detail behind the psalm: "To the leader. A Psalm of David, when the prophet Nathan came to him, after he had gone in to Bathsheba" (from NRSV). With a little effort, we can turn to the account of David's adultery, his murder of Uriah, and the prophet Nathan's confrontation of David in 2 Samuel 11–12. This historical background sheds important light on Psalm 51, allowing us to read the psalm with new insight.

Some OT prophetic books also explain their historical setting at the beginning or within the book. Isaiah starts with these words: "The vision concerning Judah and Jerusalem that Isaiah son of Amoz saw during the reigns of Uzziah, Jotham, Ahaz and Hezekiah, kings of Judah . . ." (1:1). Hosea is equally helpful: "The word of the

Lord that came to Hosea son of Beeri during the reigns of Uzziah, Jotham, Ahaz and Hezekiah, kings of Judah, and during the reign of Jeroboam son of Jehoash king of Israel . . ." (1:1). From these initial verses, we discover that the ministries of these prophets overlapped, and we can use them to interpret each other where appropriate.

We usually have more information about the background of NT books, at least after we leave the Gospels and Acts. Information within Paul's letter to the Romans sheds some light on the circumstances behind the apostle's reasons for writing the letter (for a few insights see Ro. 1:1,7-15; 15:22-29; 16:21-23). Often we can know a lot about the specific authors, recipients, dates, and other historical details that help us put a verse or a passage into a context.

In other places, we lack this kind of helpful information. Study Bibles, Bible dictionaries, and encyclopedias, as well as the beginnings of commentaries on specific books spell out the historical background and circumstances behind biblical texts. We need to interpret the Bible's messages in light of this kind of background information.

PASSAGE CONTEXT

In addition to the overall setting of a biblical book, we should investigate specific historical and cultural details within the book itself and the particular passage we're studying. As you study the Bible, you might encounter unfamiliar references; in those cases, you'll need to do some research.

Let's say you encounter this text while reading: "The scribes and the Pharisees sit on Moses' seat" (Mt. 23:2, NRSV). Unless you do some research into the historical background of "Moses' seat," you won't grasp Jesus' meaning.

At other times, you might not realize that you're unaware of what something means. For instance, imagine you're reading your Bible and come to Mark 7:1-4:

The Pharisees and some of the teachers of the law who had come from Jerusalem gathered around Jesus and saw some of his disciples eating food with hands that were "unclean," that is, unwashed. (The Pharisees and all the Jews do not eat unless they give their hands a ceremonial washing, holding to the tradition of the elders. When they come from the marketplace they do not eat unless they wash. And they observe many other traditions, such as the washing of cups, pitchers and kettles.)

Naturally, we might read this passage with our own culture in mind, thinking about why we wash hands, cups, pots, and kettles. We value cleanliness. We know about germs and impurities, so we scrub our hands and the items we use to prepare and eat food. We don't want last night's spaghetti sauce to spoil tonight's cauliflower, so we wash the pot.

However, the reasons we wash our hands and utensils don't help us understand why the Jews in this passage washed these items. In addition to washing away dirt, they were concerned about ritual defilement. We need to engage in some historical-cultural background research if we want to understand the important nuances in Jesus' subsequent confrontation with these Jews (see Mk. 7:6-15).

In this case, it might be helpful to know the definition of ritual defilement according to regulations spelled out in the OT. For example, if your cat died and you put its remains in a box for burial, you would be ritually unclean until that evening: "Of all the animals that walk on all fours, those that walk on their paws are unclean for you; whoever touches their carcasses will be unclean till evening" (Lev. 11:27). Ritually, you'd be "unclean" and need to take appropriate steps throughout the day.

To interpret Mark 7, however, you'd also need to understand how ritual defilement was understood and managed under the jurisdiction of the Pharisees at the time of Jesus. The Pharisees expanded the specific regulations found in the Torah to cover circumstances the OT Law did not envision. While this was a laudable practice, these extensions of OT regulations sometimes undermined the original intentions of the Law (see the example Jesus exposed in Mk. 7:9-13).

Most of us have experienced misunderstandings due to cultural expressions. For example, you might use a familiar hand gesture that everyone in your culture (or subculture) knows the meaning of. Yet outside of your circle—or in another country's culture—your innocent gesture might mean something different and could even be rude or obscene. Your instincts can't guide you; you need to know what specific features mean in another culture.

These misunderstandings even exist in churches. If you attend certain churches on Sunday morning, most of the women will be wearing dresses and most of the men will have on neckties. In other churches, dresses and ties will be nonexistent or worn just by visitors who don't know the dress code. In either instance, if you don't know the dress code of a congregation, you risk being different. Likewise, you might think you know what a feature of a biblical text means—as with washing hands and pots—and find that you're mistaken.

Historical and cultural details include a variety of areas or topics. Among other things, we should be alert for:

- The worldview, values, and mind-set of people
- Societal structures of the time, such as marriage, family patterns, and roles of men and women
- Physical and geographical features, such as climate, means of transportation, and elevations
- Economic structures, such as wealth, poverty, and slavery
- The political climate, including structures and loyalties

- Behavioral patterns and customs
- Dress
- Religious practices, such as power centers, rituals, and affiliations

If you don't know these things, you risk misusing the Bible. If you think the Jews were mainly concerned that people wash before eating to avoid germs (and conclude that apparently Jesus wasn't), you've missed the point. We need to be diligent and careful readers who do necessary research to assure we understand obscure meanings of texts that are distant from us in time and culture. That means being willing to do careful study, even when we think we know what all the features in a text mean.

Word Meanings

Words are the basic building blocks of oral and written communication. Yet as important as words are, we often arbitrarily assign certain meanings to specific words. Why do English speakers call a certain plant *tree* while the Germans call it *Baum* and the French *arbre*? None makes more sense than the others.

In reality, words are sounds or symbols in writing that certain people associate with a specific meaning or meanings. Native speakers of a language agree on what the words mean. If a speaker and hearer agree what a word means by using it to mean that, communication works. As we study the Bible, we need to know what its words mean in order to understand a given text.

BASIC FACTS ABOUT WORDS

The study of words is fraught with pitfalls for several significant reasons. Let's look at a few.

The Bible's words require translation. We're in debt to many committed scholars who've worked for years to understand and translate the ancient languages of biblical texts into modern languages. But even if we have a good translation in our hands, we still face several challenges. That's because the translators themselves faced challenges and might solve them in different ways. In chapter 1 of this *Handbook*, we used 1 Corinthians 7:1 as an example of the problem facing translators. Here are some of the options for translating the Greek verb *haptesthai* ("to touch"; see Lk. 6:19):

> Now concerning the matters about which you wrote: "It is well for a man not *to touch* a woman." (NRSV)

> Now for the matters you wrote about: It is good for a man not *to marry*. (NIV)

> Now concerning the matters about which you wrote: "It is good for a man not *to have sexual relations* with a woman." (ESV)

> Now concerning the things about which you wrote, it is good for a man not *to touch* a woman. (NASB)

> Now regarding the questions you asked in your letter. Yes, it is good *to live a celibate life.* (NLT)

> Now concerning the things whereof ye wrote unto me: It is good for a man not *to touch* a woman. (KJV)

Which is the correct translation? What does the word *touch* mean?

Word meanings change over time. For example, when the KJV appeared in AD 1611, *prevent* was the correct way to translate the

Greek verb *phthanō* in 1 Thessalonians 4:14: "We which are alive and remain unto the coming of the Lord shall not prevent them which are asleep." The English word *prevent* might have meant "to go before" in 1611, but it no longer does. Because this word has changed its meaning over the centuries, many modern versions use *precede* to capture the meaning of the Greek word. No matter how much we might insist on using a word in its "original" sense, communication will break down. Good translations today must translate *phthanō* as *precede*.

Words add meanings over time. The adjective *gay* still means "happy," but in American English, the meaning "homosexual" has been added in recent decades. So most speakers will avoid calling a "happy man" a "gay man" to avoid misunderstanding. Using earlier or later meanings of words could be incorrect. We can't interpret a reference to a gay man in a letter written in the 1800s to mean he was a homosexual.

Here's another example. The English word *dynamite* is based on the Greek word *dynamis*, which means "power." Does this allow us to interpret Paul's statement about the gospel being the "power of God for salvation" (Ro. 1:15) to mean that the message of salvation is explosive? Such a conclusion would be nonsense. Paul couldn't envision dynamite, so he couldn't have intended his readers to understand the gospel as explosive in what we mean by that term.

Words sometimes take on meanings beyond their literal meanings. One way this occurs is by using euphemisms. For example, because death can be unpleasant to speak about, we might use "sleep" in its place. When Paul spoke of the death of believers, he referred to them as having fallen asleep (see 1 Thess. 4:13). Although Paul clearly referred to death, most versions translate the verb as "sleep" (NIV), while others translate it as "die" (NRSV; NLT). Which is the better translation? Or more precisely, what does the word *sleep* mean in this context?

Words can also take on connotations or figurative senses. When Jesus calls Herod Antipas a "fox," he uses a figure, probably to signify treachery (see Lk. 13:32). So we can't trust the literal meaning of *fox* in English to inform what Jesus intended. Similarly, we can't trust a modern connotation of *fox*, such as when someone says, "He is such a fox!"

Figures of speech constitute a special use of words and language where their meanings go beyond what they appear to say. While poetry makes special uses of such figures, we encounter them in virtually all kinds of writing. Images make writing colorful and invoke powerful mental images that appeal to our emotions.

Note what comes to your mind when you read of "the lake of fire" (Rev. 19:20; 20:10,14-15). This way of portraying the final state of sinners is vivid and arresting. In other places sinners are cast into outer darkness (see Mt. 8:12; 22:13; 25:30). Can it be both? Yes, because these are metaphors that help readers grasp the horror of exclusion from God's presence.

Consider another example of a figure of speech in Scripture: Jesus could have said to his followers, "You obtain salvation through me, and don't worry, I'll take care of you." But how more arresting to say, "I tell you the truth, I am the gate for the sheep" (Jn. 10:7). Why is Jesus a gate? What does a gate do? What do we picture when we think of a gate?

The biblical writers use many different figures of speech, and as we study Scripture, we must know how they work and how to interpret them correctly. Here's a list of the most common devices of figurative language:

- **Simile.** A simile makes a comparison between two items by using *like* or *as*. God warns, "I will crush you *as* a cart crushes when loaded with grain" (Amos 2:13, emphasis added). Or the kingdom of God "is *like* yeast that a woman took and mixed in with three measure of flour" (Lk. 13:20-21, emphasis added). The comparison between one item that we understand and the other enables us to grasp the point.

- **Metaphor.** A metaphor also compares two items but does so directly by equating the two, as in the previous example — "I am the gate" — or "Your word *is* a lamp to my feet and a light for my path" (Ps. 119:105). Understanding the roles of a lamp and a light helps us understand the point the author was trying to make about the nature of God's Word. Without a light we stumble around in the dark. That's a vivid picture of what occurs when we try to navigate life apart from God's Word. Psalm 23 makes extended use of metaphors.

- **Personification.** With this device, the writer speaks of an inanimate object as human or as having human abilities or traits. When the psalmist writes, "Lift up your heads, O you gates; be lifted up, you ancient doors, that the King of glory may come in" (Ps. 24:7), he treats the gates and doors as if they were people who could respond and raise their heads.

- **Hyperbole.** With this figure, a writer exaggerates to make a point, such as when we say, "I told you *a thousand times* to shut that door." Jesus used this tactic when he urged his followers, "If your right hand causes you to sin, cut it off and throw it away" (Mt. 5:30). Jesus used this graphic figure not to encourage self-mutilation but to urge disciples to take radical steps to remove causes of sin in their lives.

- **Metonymy.** This common device occurs when a writer substitutes one idea with something closely related to it. For example, we might read in a newspaper, "The White House issued a statement" or that "Moscow has agreed to the treaty." In these cases, "White House" and "Moscow" stand for the U.S. president or the Russian government, respectively. In Psalm 23 we read, "You prepare a *table* before me" (v. 5, emphasis added). Table is a metonymy for a meal or even sustenance in a larger sense. In other words, "Lord, you take care of all my needs."

- **Irony.** With this device, a writer or speaker uses words that on the surface say the opposite of what he or she really means. It sometimes turns into sarcasm. If said ironically, "Wow, that's a nice tie" really means, "That's an ugly tie." Elijah used irony to refer to the priests of Baal: "At noon Elijah mocked them, saying, 'Cry aloud, for he is a god. Either he is musing, or he is relieving himself, or he is on a journey, or perhaps he is asleep and must be awakened'" (1 K. 18:27, ESV).

When interpreting these and other figures of speech, take the following steps to assure that you understand what the writer meant:

1. Identify a word used in a figurative way.
2. Interpret the meaning by digging deeper into what the figure is. If Jesus is a "gate," seek to find the literal meaning inherent in a gate that the writer is drawing attention to. If a writer equates a person's tongue with swords (see Ps. 57:4), then what about swords (sharp, cutting, injurious, hurtful) helps us understand what a tongue can do?
3. Explain the function of the figure in its context. Seek to understand why the writer used the figure.

Be aware that the etymology of a word won't always help you understand the current meaning of a word. Etymology refers to a word's history, particularly its root or component parts. Sometimes, of course, etymology helps. The word *joyful* in English does convey the sense of "full of joy." But does *careful* mean "full of care"? In this case, the components aren't helpful in the sentence "He wasn't very careful" (he wasn't full of care).

Knowing the meanings of the parts of the word *butterfly* gives no clues to understanding the nature of that specific insect. Knowing that *prescribe* derives from the Latin roots *pre* (*prae* meaning "before") and *scribe* (*scribere* meaning "write") provides no insight into its current meaning in English. We don't use it in its Latin sense of "to write at the beginning."

If interpreters aren't careful, they can fall into this trap with the etymology of Greek words. Often we hear that the church means the "called out ones" since *ekklēsia* (the Greek word translated *church*) comes from the Greek preposition *ek* (out of) and the verb *kaleō* (call or invite). However, such a conclusion is no more valid in Greek than it is in English. The word *ekklēsia* means "assembly" or "congregation" and is used this way many times in the Greek OT. It does not mean "called-out ones," despite what some preachers or books might say.

Many words cover a range of meaning; that is, they have multiple senses. With words such as our "large trunk" example, it makes no sense to speak about their basic meaning. But we might hear in sermons or read in books that some word has a central meaning that must be carried over to interpret a specific biblical text. We need to be extremely careful here, for this isn't always true. We can't assume that because a word bears a certain sense in one location that it carries that sense over into another location. It might be no more valid than carrying the meaning of trunk from one location into another context. We must determine what meaning *trunk* has in each context.

PERFORMING WORD STUDIES

Word studies begin with discovering the possible meanings of a word at the time a passage was written. If possible, we start by trying to discover the history of the word's uses. For texts in the ancient worlds—whether in OT Hebrew and Aramaic or in NT Greek—we must access the best dictionaries and other historical research tools to help us settle on the most likely sense for biblical words in the specific contexts under study. In the case of the OT, words might have roots in other ancient Near Eastern languages that can shed light on their meanings.

In the case of the NT, we want to know whether the word also occurs in the Greek translation of the OT that the Jews produced in the second century BC (the Septuagint or LXX). If so, what Hebrew word(s) did it translate, and what light does that shed on its use by the Jews and potentially the Christians who wrote the NT? How was the word used in literary sources at the time? How did people use it in nonliterary sources—such as in inscriptions, letters, tombstones, business receipts, and so forth? The study of words in the NT is enriched by the availability of many contemporary written materials. On the other hand, some words occur in the NT and nowhere else.

Once we determine the possible meanings of a given word (such as with the different meanings of *trunk*), we're ready to decide on the likely sense in a specific context. We must be careful not to settle on a sense that fits what we already believe the passage means. As always, the context provides the most important guidance, and both the literary and historical contexts are crucial. Which meaning fits the literary flow, both thematically and structurally? Which fits the argument of the narrative or the poetic structure most appropriately? Also, which meaning fits the cultural situation when the passage was written? What's this passage about? Though words have a range of meaning, the author intended some specific sense in a given context. The goal of a word study is to discover that sense.

Grammatical-Structural Relationships

Because written languages communicate by combining words into larger units—sentences, paragraphs, sections, discourses, books—a correct understanding of the meaning of a text will account for the grammatical and structural features in the biblical passage we're studying. We communicate meaning to each other not merely by listing words but by putting together words in combinations appropriate to the language we're speaking or writing.

In English, "The ball hit the batter" has a different meaning than "The batter hit the ball," even though the two sentences use the same words. Still different meanings result when we put the letter *s* on the end of nouns. These are matters of grammar and syntax—how a language manipulates words and puts them together to produce meaning.

When it comes to interpreting a biblical text, those in the best position to evaluate grammatical and structural relationships have learned the biblical languages. They're better equipped to explain how things "work" within the requirements of that language, whether Hebrew, Aramaic, or Greek. Many critical commentaries give the best insights of grammatical analysis to readers. Other resource tools also explain grammatical features to those who either haven't or can't acquire competence in biblical languages. Use these tools.

The number of good translations of the Bible also enables most readers to study and analyze the basic structure of a biblical passage. It takes commitment, motivation, and an eye for detail. Try opening multiple Bible versions in front of you and then follow this exercise:

- Identify the natural divisions in a section.
- Trace the organization and development of the author's argument.
- Identify the function of the connectives (words such as *if, for, because, in order that, so that, while, when,* and so on).

- Explain how the author conveys meaning through the phrases, clauses, and sentences in a paragraph.
- Observe the impact of the key verbs, including the tense, voice, and mood they convey.
- Identify any other features of the grammar and structure that shed light on the meaning of a passage.

For example, let's look at a few features in James 1:2-5 (TNIV, emphasis added). I'll comment on the words in italics.

> [2]*Consider* it pure joy, my brothers and sisters, *whenever* you face trials of many kinds, [3]*because* you *know* that the testing of your faith produces perseverance. [4]*Let* perseverance *finish* its work *so that* you may be mature and complete, not lacking anything. [5]*If* any of you lacks wisdom, you *should ask* God, who gives generously to all without finding fault, and it *will be given* to you. (TNIV)

In verse 2, by using the imperative mood of the verb *consider*, James appeals to his readers to ponder the following course of action. The conjunction *whenever* tells readers the times they should be joyful: whenever they face trials. *Because* (v. 3) introduces the reason for James' outrageous appeal. By using the present tense for the verb *know*, James alerts his readers they should continually keep this thought in mind.

In verse 4, James employs another imperative mood with the verb *let . . . finish*, telling readers they must engage the process to be sure that perseverance accomplishes its purpose of maturity, because that's the result ("so that") God has in mind. In verse 5, James assumes that some of his readers will encounter difficulties, so he says "if" you lack wisdom, then you "should ask." This is another appeal using the imperative mood. Finally, James assures his readers that when they pray to God, wisdom "will be given." Here he uses a future tense of the verb—in effect, predicting this result when people pray to God for wisdom in the midst of trials.

SPECIAL INTERPRETIVE PRINCIPLES: GENRES

While we usually think of the Bible as one book, it includes many books of distinct literary types or genres written over a period of more than a thousand years. Genre means a work of literature distinguished by a particular style, structure, or content. As you become more competent in your study of the Bible, you'll want to pay attention to the ways various genres convey messages. In the OT, you'll find the following genres: narratives of various kinds, legal writings, poetry, prophecy, apocalyptic writing, and wisdom literature—along with various subcategories, such as proverbs, riddles, parables, songs, and lists. In the NT, you'll find gospels (theological biographies of Jesus), epistles (letters), narrative (Acts, sometimes termed "theological history"), and apocalyptic (Revelation).

Of course, within some of these categories, you'll also find subtypes such as parables, miracle stories, hymns, vice and virtue lists, and household codes. Each genre or subtype has its own rules of interpretation, and we need to treat each with the integrity and tactics that its form requires. Next we'll explore the nature and give examples of each genre and suggest various "insights for interpretation" in light of what we discover about each genre.

Genres of the Old Testament

Let's look at the essential features of how each literary genre works so that we can think "literarily" in our study of the Bible. I'll give a description of each genre to help you better understand what God has revealed through it. You'll also see the diversity of the Bible and the many dimensions God has used to convey his message over the centuries.

NARRATIVES

Narratives are stories. The beauty of stories is that they have universal appeal. Open a Bible storybook for children and you'll typically find illustrated exploits of famous characters from the OT. You can read the stories of the first couple in Eden, Noah and the animals in the Ark, Abraham's trek to the Promised Land and later his close call in sacrificing his son Isaac, Joseph and his multicolored coat (the dreamer sold into slavery who became second in command in Egypt). Think of Moses and the Red Sea, the conquest of Canaan, all those Judges who rescued the Jews, the prophet Samuel, King Saul, David and Jonathan, and the list goes on and on. No wonder storybooks and even Broadway employ stories from the Bible — it has so many good tales to tell.

Why does the Bible contain stories, and how can you learn to read and profit from them? Let me clarify two points. First, by stories I don't mean fiction. While stories show a storyteller's craft in how to tell a narrative well to communicate a message, these Bible stories come from historical events. Second, as a specific genre, narratives convey their messages through such elements as the characters, the plot, and where the climax of the story occurs. In other words, writing a story involves creativity — it's not stating "just the facts."

In a biblical narrative, a writer paints a picture to instruct readers about the kind of conduct that honors (or dishonors) God. Of course, not all stories are as complex and lengthy as the Joseph narrative (see Gen. 37,39–50). Some might be just a few verses, such as the incident involving Abraham and Melchizedek (see Gen. 14:18-20). Some narratives are reports (see Ex. 3:2-12). Others give episodes in the life of one of Israel's heroes (see the story of Deborah in Jdg. 4–5 or the other judges).

The OT also includes stories of the prophets such as Daniel (1–6), Elijah, and Elisha (see 1 K. 17–2 K. 9). Jonah is an entire biblical book with a single narrative. Other examples are Ruth and Esther, narratives we can also classify as examples of a comedy — that is, a story in which the plot moves from tragedy to triumph, ending happily. You can categorize Joseph's life-story as a comedy as well.

Insights for interpretation. How can you profit from your study of the Bible's narratives? As you come to a story, you need to understand the function of the story in its context and appreciate its historical content and literary form. Then you need to see how function, content, and form point the way to the significance of the story for the original readers and for present-day readers. Employ the tools we explored earlier about literary context, historical and cultural features, words, and grammar to shed light on the details of the story.

For short stories, such as reports or anecdotes, focus your attention on the main topic of the story and what it contributes to the theme of the section where it occurs. Often a short story makes its point indirectly, and you might need to keep track of a series of such stories to see an overall pattern. You can see evidence of this in the collection of stories in the book of Judges. What common themes emerge? What did the author expect the readers to see? After you've answered those questions, you can ask about these narratives' implications for present-day situations. Where do we fall prey to similar sins or errors that plagued these ancient Israelites?

In longer stories, such as heroic narratives or the stories of prophets, you should focus your study on the main character: Joseph, Elijah, Esther, Ruth. What does the author tell you about this person's life with God? What noteworthy traits stand out regarding this hero's relationships with other people? What about this person should you admire, and what should you avoid? What roles do other characters in the story play, and what can you learn from their parts in the story? What themes emerge?

In the Joseph story, you might learn about God's sovereign purposes, the rewards of faithfulness, and the values of family (portrayed both positively and negatively). Esther might teach you courage in the face of opposition. Where does God call you to stand up for truth when the cost is great? Esther's story also shows God's faithfulness to his people even in the face of great opposition.

Some stories of the OT contain shorter, embedded genres. These include features such as popular proverbs, riddles, fables, parables, songs, and lists. Including such features makes a story more interesting and lifelike. These embedded genres might appear in other places within the Bible as well, but they're common in narratives.

For example, Nathan shows the cunning of a prophet who gets his point across to the king through a parable (see 2 Sam. 12:1-4). Samson is famous for his riddles (for example, Jdg. 14:14,18). Genealogy lists are important to a culture that values ancestors, and they demonstrate God's faithfulness to his promises (for example, Gen. 10; Ruth 4:18-21). People employ these kinds of tactics in their interactions with each other, so when you encounter one of these features, you need to understand what it means and how it contributes to the larger story.

This is a good place to mention, briefly, a crucial point as we study narratives, and it has implications for studying the Bible elsewhere as well. We must understand the distinction between descriptive and prescriptive (or normative). Simply because the Bible relates a story of what happened to people in the past, it doesn't necessarily imply that what occurred back then is how things will or should operate either for us or for others in the future. For example, we learn from the stories in Genesis that God overcame infertility to keep the line of the patriarchs intact (see Gen. 21; 29–30). But we can't presume from these stories that God will always overcome problems of infertility for his children. These stories are descriptive of what happened in the past, but it's not how God will always work in our lives.

Consider another example: In Genesis we learn that because Joseph was faithful, God rescued him from unjust imprisonment. But we can't presume that God will rescue all faithful Christians from unjust imprisonments. That's not the point of the Joseph story. Faithfulness pays off, but not always in the ways it did for Joseph.

Narratives primarily tell us what happened. They teach lessons, values, principles, and what relationship with God involves. But stories don't assure us that because God did specific things for people in the past, he'll repeat those same feats for us today.

Not all teachers and preachers understand this principle. We often hear stories lifted from the OT and explained as if what God did then he wants to do today. While this might be true sometimes, we need further explanation and assurance that this was the intention of the text and its author. Otherwise, we have no basis for such claims. Stories tell us what happened, and we should learn the lessons in them for our lives and churches. But stories don't guarantee that the same events will happen in our lives.

LAW

For many of us, *law* initially strikes us in a negative way; we might think of legalism. However, we can appreciate and embrace the importance of the rule of law. We know of situations and cultures where anarchy reigns. When people aren't subject to law, they become a law unto themselves and to each other. As a result, the powerful often flourish while the poor suffer.

When it comes to the Bible, we find that law plays a major role in the religion of ancient Israel. First we discover four major collections of laws: the Covenant Code (see Ex. 20:22–23:33), the Deuteronomic Code (see Dt. 12–26), the Holiness Code (see Lev. 17–26), and the Priestly Code (see Ex. 25–31; 34:29; Lev. 16). Sometimes Christians today look askance at ancient Israel's legal system, describing it as a system of legalism, and they rejoice that Christians are under grace instead of law. But such a view includes a number of misconceptions, including the disparaging of God, who prescribed Israel's legal codes.

Think about this important text from Deuteronomy 4:5-9:

> See, I have taught you decrees and laws as the LORD my God commanded me, so that you may follow them in the land you are entering to take possession of it. Observe them carefully, for this will show your wisdom and understanding to the nations, who will hear about all these decrees and say, "Surely this great nation is a wise and understanding people." What other nation is so great as to have their gods near them the way the LORD our God is near us whenever we pray to him? And what other nation is so great as to have such righteous decrees and laws as this body of laws I am setting before you today? Only be careful, and watch yourselves closely so that you do not forget the things your eyes have seen or let them slip from your heart as long as you live. Teach them to your children and to their children after them.

In Moses' speech to the Israelites as they were about to enter the Promised Land, he reminded them of God's presence and past protection. As they took possession of their new land, God wanted to construct a new social and religious reality in stark contrast to oppressive ways of Egypt. The laws were meant to create and assure that new reality.

This new life in Canaan would give obedient Israel the opportunity to witness to the nations about the superiority of Israel's God. By following God's laws and decrees, they could demonstrate to the nations around them the wisdom of a superior life, one designed to attract those nations to Israel's God. Israel would then fulfill her destiny to be a light to the nations (see Is. 42:6; 49:6).

Moses didn't envision the laws as oppressive and imposing. This "rule of law" would enable God's people to flourish because they would be living in obedience to the God who loves them, and they would enjoy God's manifold blessings (see Dt. 28:1-14). Further, unless God's people succeeded in passing on this way of life to their children, they would forfeit the blessings and receive God's curses (see Dt. 28:15-68).

Psalm 119 shows us the heart of someone who grasped the significance and value of following God's laws and statutes. Virtually every verse of this lengthy psalm extols the virtues of life lived under God's Law.

So what kinds of laws do we find in the OT? After listing the types, we'll try to draw out insights for Christians today for our study of the OT laws.

- **Casuistic law.** We sometimes hear this kind of legal material referred to as "case law" because it refers to specific cases and what to do when those situations occur. They take the form of "if/then." Exodus is full of case law: If a condition occurs, then the penalty or appropriate action must follow. For example, "If anyone of your kin falls into difficulty and sells a piece of property, then the next of kin shall come and redeem what the relative has sold" (Lev. 25:25, NRSV).

- **Apodictic law.** This is absolute law of the "you shall" and "you shall not" variety, though this precise wording doesn't always occur. The Ten Commandments are examples of these: "You shall not murder" and "Honor your father and mother" (Ex. 20:12-13). The Ten Commandments, also known as the Decalogue, also points to another feature of law in the OT: Laws often occur in lists.

- **Legal instruction.** The book of Leviticus contains two kinds of lengthy instructions—one for priests conducting their duties and remaining pure (Lev. 6–7; 21), and the other for laypeople performing the various rituals required of them (see Lev. 1–5).

Insights for interpretation. Even if the OT Law laid out life-giving prescriptions for how the ancient Israelites should live, what do we, as Christians, make of these laws now? We don't live in Israel under the terms laid out in the Pentateuch. We don't know what to make of such bizarre rules as "You shall not boil a kid in its mother's milk" (see Ex. 23:19; 34:26; Dt. 14:21). However, if we reflect on the purposes for the Law, we can gain insight into the ongoing relevance of the OT Law, even for Christians today.

By giving the Law, God wanted to establish a new worldview with fundamental values that reflect his will. The Law supervised the identity of God's people—what it meant to live life under obedience to his ways. We hit the mark when we realize the point of the Law was to instruct God's people in holy living, not to prescribe specific regulations about every detail of life. It did some of that for Israel, but that wasn't its primary intention. It taught the virtues of moral living. The laws against murder and stealing and in favor of honoring parents express God's will for people made in his image. The Law teaches us about right and wrong, and Christians should think through OT laws to see where they express God's moral categories for life.

Beyond these moral categories, God also gave the Law to construct a life in relationship to him and to create a distinctive people who love God and serve others. When people obey God, their lives go well; when they disobey (the Garden of Eden provides a prime example), life goes dreadfully wrong. Because the original instructions fit the circumstances of the original Israelites and not us, many specific prescriptions of the OT Law have little relevance for modern life. Therefore, we must seek the intention of the rule in its own time and ask whether we can apply the principle today, even if its specific application takes a radically different form.

Jesus made an important statement: "Do not think that I have come to abolish the law or the prophets; I have come not to abolish but to fulfill" (Mt. 5:17, NRSV). Jesus didn't come to terminate the significance of the Law (or the rest of the OT for that matter); he came to fulfill the Law. The significance of the OT remains, but it doesn't continue as it did prior to Christ's advent because he "fulfilled" it.

Although *fulfill* has an expansive meaning, several points are clear. First, the Law of Israel (and the Old Covenant, more generally) established the people of God before Christ. It pointed to the need for an ultimate solution to the sin problem: people's rebellion against God and their spiritual death. Jesus fulfilled that trajectory. He brings the solution: the atonement that the sacrificial system could only dimly portray. Now Christ constitutes God's people.

Only "in Christ" do people attain salvation and forgiveness from sin. To be "in Christ" requires faith in him alone; those "in Christ" are no longer required to keep the OT Law to be part of God's people. In Paul's words, "Christ is the end of the law so that there may be righteousness for everyone who believes" (Ro. 10:4). Paul's use of the word *end* probably conveys two nuances: Christ terminates the role of the Law in defining the structure of reality for the people of God, and Christ is the goal that the entire Old Covenant pointed toward.

Christians need to heed the message of OT laws, but only as they apply in light of Christ's fulfillment of them. As Paul pointedly said about the OT in general, it's "useful for teaching, rebuking, correcting, and training in righteousness" (2 Tim. 3:16). The NT itself shows how Christ has fulfilled some of the OT regulations (for example, the sacrifices: see Heb. 9:1–10:25). Food laws no longer apply (see Mk. 7:19).

Still, some laws remain intact. We still must love God and our neighbors (see Mt. 22:40; see Dt. 6:5). Wherever the NT invokes an OT law, we must obey it (for example, see 1 Tim. 5:19; Dt. 17:6). We must also follow the NT where it clarifies an OT law, as in the case of marriage; while the OT permitted divorce and remarriage (see Dt. 24:1-4), Jesus tightened the requirements (see Mt. 19:3-12).

In other cases, we should try to understand what the Law sought to accomplish for ancient Israel and ask how it might guide us as God's people today. For example, we can learn from the Law how seriously God regards sin and disobedience. We must refrain from copying the practices of pagans and falling into their rebellious ways. As God's children, we should pursue lives that please God.

At the same time, we have the Holy Spirit to produce within us the kind of life that pleases God and that he requires. While we still study the OT to understand the implications of serving God and what a relationship with him entails, now God's Spirit instructs his people in constructing their new reality. Here are several of the apostle Paul's reflections on the Holy Spirit's role from Galatians 5 (NRSV):

- "Live by the Spirit, I say, and do not gratify the desires of the flesh." (5:16)
- "If you are led by the Spirit, you are not subject to the law." (5:18)
- "The fruit of the Spirit is love, joy, peace, patience, kindness, generosity, faithfulness, gentleness, and self-control. There is no law against such things." (5:22-23)
- "If we live by the Spirit, let us also be guided by the Spirit." (5:25)

POETRY

Poetry occupies an important place in the OT: in the book of Psalms, as well as in Job, Songs of Songs, and Lamentations. Even books we consider historical or narrative often contain sections of poetry (see 1 Sam. 2:1-10; 2 Sam. 23:1-7). Many modern versions of the Bible print its poetical sections in stanzas so we can see how the parallel lines and other features work. In additional to poems themselves, both Testaments employ many poetic features, such as figures of speech. While a complete analysis of OT poetry would need to take into account the original Hebrew language letters and sounds, even by using just our English Bibles we can learn some essential elements to enhance our reading of the OT.

The nature of poetry. Through the use of sounds, rhythm (meter), and special arrangements of the words—often in parallel lines—poetry uses highly concentrated and figurative language to create its intended response. It often appeals to the emotions. To see all these features in the Psalms, such as rhyme and meter, we'd need to read them in Hebrew. But while our English versions rarely can capture all their original beauty, much about these passages as poetry can enrich our reading of them.

Parallelism. Biblical poetry combines two or more lines together to produce the author's desired effect. Let's look at Psalm 1. I've numbered the lines for clarity; verse numbers are superscripted.

1. [1] Happy are those
2. who do not follow the advice of the wicked,
3. or take the path that sinners tread,
4. or sit in the seat of scoffers;
5. [2] but their delight is in the law of the Lord,
6. and on his law they meditate day and night.
7. [3] They are like trees
8. planted by streams of water,

9. which yield their fruit in its season,

10. and their leaves do not wither.

11. In all that they do, they prosper.

12. [4] The wicked are not so,

13. but are like chaff that the wind drives away.

14. [5] Therefore the wicked will not stand in the judgment,

15. nor sinners in the congregation of the righteous;

16. [6] for the Lord watches over the way of the righteous,

17. but the way of the wicked will perish. (NRSV)

Note that verse 1 consists of four lines. Line 1 identifies a group the author terms "happy" or "blessed." The next three lines capture activities these blessed people don't engage in, arranged in parallel lines. Lines 3 and 4 continue the thought of the second. Verse 2 consists of two parallel lines. In contrast to the three avoided behaviors (verse 2 starts with "but"), the blessed people engage in two pursuits: delighting and meditating on God's Law (lines 5 and 6). Again, line 6 continues the thought of line 5 — they're connected by "and." Verse 3 compares the happy ones to trees, again described in four parallel lines (7-10) followed by a summary statement: They prosper in all things (line 11). The remaining verses consist of two parallel lines. In verses 4 and 6, the second line provides a contrast to the first. In verse 5 the second line continues the thought of the first line.

As we analyze lines of poetry, our first goal is to uncover relationships between the lines. Essentially, Hebrew poetic lines can function in the following ways:

- The second line *echoes* the previous line or provides a *contrast* to it.
- The second line is *subordinate* to what precedes it, providing the means, reason, or time of the first line.
- The second line *continues* the prior thought.

- The second line gives a *comparison* to the previous line.
- The second line makes the previous line more *specific*.
- The second line *intensifies* in some way the idea of the prior line.

As you encounter the Bible's poetry, try to identify lines that are parallel and then, using the possible relationships between the lines, seek to uncover how the author puts the ideas together to develop the poem.

Structure. In addition to parallel lines, poems have structure. To understand poetry we need to think in larger units to see how the meaning of the poem progresses. Read Psalm 1 again and see if you can make out its structure—how it moves from section to section.

You probably identified three sections. In verses 1-3, we learn about the conduct of God's righteous people. They avoid the infectious ways of the wicked but take their cues from God's laws. The result is a solid and fruitful life. In the second section, verses 4-5, we learn about the wicked, the counterpart to those who are righteous. The wicked aren't rooted at all, and on the day of judgment they'll be condemned. The final section, verse 6, sums up outcomes of the two kinds of people: The righteous enjoy God's protection, while the wicked will perish.

After identifying the basic structure, you should look at why the poem progresses the way it does. How is it organized? Sometimes the structure is thematic, or it might progress logically or liturgically. What themes does the poem contain? What did the poet want to accomplish? What lessons can we learn from it? Why was it included in the canon of Scripture?

Figures of speech. In addition to structural features, poetry works by employing a dizzying variety of figurative language that adds incredible richness. In Psalm 1, note the use of walking, sitting, trees with leaves and fruit, and the wind-driven chaff. These figures paint pictures in the reader's mind that point to a different message than more straightforward prose. Try putting verse 3 into concrete words that avoid all the poignant imagery. Do you see how much is lost in the process?

It's not important to correctly name the devices we encounter in the Bible's poetry. However, it's important to recognize that such features play a huge role in poetry (and the rest of the Bible) and that we interpret them correctly. What must we do to interpret figures of speech properly?

The steps might appear obvious, but they're worth repeating. First, identify when you encounter a figure of speech. Second, describe the "literal" sense of the figure. For example, when the psalmist calls the righteous "trees," we should think about what trees do: They provide shade from the sun, and they produce olives or other kinds of fruit. Third, what idea does the author or speaker want to convey by using the figure of speech? In other words, what's the "figurative" meaning? In what ways are righteous people like trees laden with luscious fruit? Try to determine why the author used this figure in this context. What pictures and emotions emerge?

Types of poetry in the OT. To assure that we interpret and apply the poetry of the OT correctly, we need to have a grasp on the various kinds of poetry we might encounter. Some of the psalms are prayers in the form of complaints (individually or corporately) for the misery the writer feels. This misery might be because of illness, enemy attacks, plagues, or other misfortunes. For example, sense the cry of anguish found in these words:

My God, my God, why have you forsaken me?
Why are you so far from helping me, from the words of my
groaning?
O my God, I cry by day, but you do not answer;
and by night, but find no rest. (Ps. 22:1-2, NRSV)

Sometimes these complaints lead the writer to cry to God to rain down misery and destruction on his enemies. These are often called imprecatory psalms. For example:

Let them vanish like water that runs away;
like grass let them be trodden down and wither.
Let them be like the snail that dissolves into slime;
like the untimely birth that never sees the sun. (Ps. 58:7-8,
NRSV)

On the other hand, many psalms are individual or corporate songs of praise to God. Often the writer intends for these to be sung in worship to extol God's splendor, his holy character, and his wonderful deeds toward Israel. In the psalms, we find songs of thanksgiving, praise, and love. Of course, the Song of Songs is a prime example of love songs in the OT, but some exist in the psalms as well (for example, Ps. 45).

Some psalms embody liturgies. Often they involve several participants—perhaps the worship leader and the congregation, or two groups within the congregation. Psalms 20 and 136 are good examples.

We might call other examples of Hebrew poetry "wisdom psalms." These were employed not in worship but for the instruction of God's people. Psalm 1 probably fits in this category: Study God's Word if you want to flourish and to be approved on the day of judgment. Psalm 19 recounts the ways God has revealed himself, both in nature and through his word. Psalm 33 contains a wealth of wise counsel for the person who wishes to thrive.

Insights for interpretation. First, give yourself the time and attention necessary to engage these poems. Unlike narratives, poetry requires more concentration, reflection, and rereading to profit from its insights.

Second, you must engage the entire poem as a unit. A quick eyeballing to find a nugget or verse to extract is not a good way to handle a poem. That violates the principle of context. See how the entire poem works and the overall impression it leaves.

Third, consider the setting of the poem when you interpret it. If it's written by an individual, see how the message applies to you personally. If written for corporate worship, look for the central message in the corporate worship of God's people today. Obviously, complaints, curses, worship, or praises point the way to application. Be alert for evidence of how King David sets the stage for his successor, the Messiah. Some of the royal psalms point to the kingly role that the NT applies to Jesus as Lord. Examples include Psalms 2, 45, 89, and 110.

Fourth, seek to apply poetry in ways that respect the spirit of the poet. If the poem expresses a complaint, allow it to help you articulate your own complaints, either the specific ones the poet mentions or others that you feel. If you don't have a complaint that corresponds to what the poet expresses, perhaps you can use the poem to express the anguish of other people who might be in agony and feeling angry. Give voice to their pain.

Or if the poem expresses praise to God for his wonderful works, use it praise him similarly for his mighty deeds. The poetry of the Bible gives us patterns and permission to express the full range of human emotion that we feel in our world—a world full of beauty and blessing as well as of tragedy, pain, and defeat.

One important word of caution: It's one thing to have the freedom to express our anguish to God; it's another thing to act on our feelings. We must filter all our actions through the lens of our commitment to Christ and God's will for our lives. So while a psalm might express a desire to kill an enemy—and we might well feel that way ourselves as we pray with the psalmist—Jesus calls us to pray for our enemies. A psalm might give voice to the anger in our hearts, but Paul reminds us that we must not allow our anger to lead to sin (see Eph. 4:26).

Prophecy

God called prophets to speak his message to his people, and we give the name "prophecy" to those messages. At times, these prophetic messages announced God's future plans, resulting in predictions or what we might call "foretelling." Far more often, however, prophecy consisted of "forthtelling" — that is, delivering God's messages to his people (what he thinks about them and their behavior, and what actions he plans to take as a result).

The OT books in the genre of prophecy record some of the actions of the prophets as well as the messages they proclaimed. They might be the literary creations of the prophets themselves or of followers who compiled the prophets' works and words. As a result, these OT books contain narrative sections, some poetry, and prophecies.

Types of prophecy. We begin studying the prophecy genre by identifying the types of prophetic messages we find in the OT. Knowing how these messages functioned for Israel help us interpret and apply them correctly. Essentially, just two types of prophecy exist: announcements of disaster, and announcements of salvation. On the negative side, prophecies pronounce disaster about to fall on people for their sins or disobedience to God. Note how the prophet Micah outlines the following situation and announces how God will act:

HEAR, O PEOPLES, ALL OF YOU,

LISTEN, O EARTH AND ALL WHO ARE IN IT,

THAT THE SOVEREIGN Lord MAY WITNESS AGAINST YOU,

THE Lord FROM HIS HOLY TEMPLE.

LOOK! THE LORD IS COMING FROM HIS DWELLING PLACE;

HE COMES DOWN AND TREADS THE HIGH PLACES OF

THE EARTH.

THE MOUNTAINS MELT BENEATH HIM

AND THE VALLEYS SPLIT APART,

LIKE WAX BEFORE THE FIRE,

LIKE WATER RUSHING DOWN A SLOPE.

ALL THIS IS BECAUSE OF JACOB'S TRANSGRESSION,

BECAUSE OF THE SINS OF THE HOUSE OF ISRAEL.

WHAT IS JACOB'S TRANSGRESSION?

IS IT NOT SAMARIA?

WHAT IS JUDAH'S HIGH PLACE?

IS IT NOT JERUSALEM?

THEREFORE I WILL MAKE SAMARIA A HEAP OF RUBBLE,

A PLACE FOR PLANTING VINEYARDS.

I WILL POUR HER STONES INTO THE VALLEY

AND LAY BARE HER FOUNDATIONS.

ALL HER IDOLS WILL BE BROKEN TO PIECES;

ALL HER TEMPLE GIFTS WILL BE BURNED WITH FIRE;

I WILL DESTROY ALL HER IMAGES.

SINCE SHE GATHERED HER GIFTS FROM THE WAGES OF

PROSTITUTES,

AS THE WAGES OF PROSTITUTES THEY WILL AGAIN BE

USED. (1:2-7)

On the positive side, we find salvation prophecies that announce rescue or the coming of blessing. Note this example from the prophet Amos that promises restoration:

"IN THAT DAY I WILL RESTORE

DAVID'S FALLEN TENT.

I WILL REPAIR ITS BROKEN PLACES,

    RESTORE ITS RUINS,

    AND BUILD IT AS IT USED TO BE,

SO THAT THEY MAY POSSESS THE REMNANT OF EDOM

AND ALL THE NATIONS THAT BEAR MY NAME,"

    DECLARES THE LORD,

    WHO WILL DO THESE THINGS.

"THE DAYS ARE COMING," DECLARES THE LORD,

"WHEN THE REAPER WILL BE OVERTAKEN BY THE

    PLOWMAN

AND THE PLANTER BY THE ONE TREADING GRAPES.

NEW WINE WILL DRIP FROM THE MOUNTAINS

    AND FLOW FROM ALL THE HILLS.

I WILL BRING BACK MY EXILED PEOPLE ISRAEL;

    THEY WILL REBUILD THE RUINED CITIES AND LIVE IN

    THEM.

THEY WILL PLANT VINEYARDS AND DRINK THEIR WINE;

    THEY WILL MAKE GARDENS AND EAT THEIR FRUIT.

I WILL PLANT ISRAEL IN THEIR OWN LAND,

    NEVER AGAIN TO BE UPROOTED

    FROM THE LAND I HAVE GIVEN THEM,"

    SAYS THE LORD YOUR GOD. (9:11-15)

A disaster prophecy might be conveyed through a woe speech, a declaration of impending doom that uses the special formula "woe" or "alas" (see Num. 21:29; Is. 3:11; 45:9; Jer. 13:27). Or disasters may take the form of a dirge, a funeral lament as if the nation is dead and ready to be buried (see Jer. 4:8; 49:3; Ezk. 27).

Within the prophetic books, we find other specific types or ways of announcing God's messages. Some prophecies take the form of hymns (see Is. 25:1-8; 42:10-13; Amos 5:8-9; 9:5-6), while others are liturgies (see Joel 1–2). Hymns and liturgies can prophesy either disaster or salvation. We also encounter disputes, where the prophet engages the readers by making God's case against them (see Mal. 1:1-14). Sometimes God brings a lawsuit or indictment against his people (see Hos. 4:1-3).

Insights for interpretation. How much better to be the recipient of God's blessings than his punishments! That's the key lesson of prophecy. Faithfulness and obedience bring blessing, while disobedience to God's ways results in his judgments. Fortunately, God tempers his punishments with grace so salvation might follow disaster for those who learn God's lessons.

When it comes to God's message, the prophets "tell it like it is" so God's people will clearly know what he thinks of their behavior and their faith. In fact, that describes the crucial role of prophecy for us: What does God think of our behavior and faith?

Of course, the writings of the prophets can be among the most confusing parts of the OT and are often the objects of the most disagreement and—dare we say it—abuse at the hands of those who try to interpret these texts. It's one thing to see these various types of prophecies on the pages of the OT; it's quite another to know how to apply their words of disaster and salvation, whether they occur as forthtelling or foretelling. Several steps can help us navigate through the mysterious and frustrating writings of the OT prophets:

1. Aim to understand the historical situation the prophecy emerges from. Chapter 2 of this *Handbook* outlined a general history of OT times, but that might be too general for this purpose. You need to know the circumstances that prompted a prophet's message of disaster or salvation. Was it a time of prosperity or was Israel under siege? Were the kings faithful or prone to idolatry? Is the prophecy directed at Israel or a foreign nation? Answers to these

kinds of questions can help us understand what the
prophet intended and can point to possible ways we can
apply the message.

2. Determine the nature of the judgment or blessing the
prophet announced. Was it military defeat or natural
disasters? Will it involve a return to the land and renewed
prosperity? Would the readers view the outcome as a
blessing or curse?

3. Discover the reasons for the Lord's actions for or against
the recipients. Typically, a prophet will clearly state why
God is sending judgment on his people or against other
nations (see Amos 2:6-12; Micah 3:2-3). What's at stake?
Why is God upset? What attribute of God causes him to
utter the word of prophecy?

Understanding the reasons for God's judgments often points the
way to application for us. When we see the types of sins and rebellion that caused God to judge, we learn to avoid those sins ourselves.
If God judged Israel for cursing, lying, murder, stealing, adultery,
and bloodshed (see Hosea 4:1-2), can we engage in those and expect
that he won't be displeased with us?

For example, consider Haggai 1:4: "Is it a time for you yourselves
to live in your paneled houses, while this house lies in ruins?" After
returning from exile, the Israelites were careful to rebuild (luxu-
riously) their own houses, while the "house" of God (the temple)
remained a wreck. So we might ask whether we care as much about
our churches as we do about the houses we remodel to be as comfortable as possible.

Similarly, we should listen to the words of Amos: "Hear this
word, you cows of Bashan who are on Mount Samaria, who oppress
the poor, who crush the needy, who say to their husbands, 'Bring
something to drink!'" (4:1, NRSV). In this case, we might ask if we

enjoy our cool drinks in the summer yet neglect the poor.

In other words, we should carefully observe the causes of God's judgments against his people. What did God hope to achieve by those judgments? Were those results achieved? What did God do in response? These important questions can pave the way for a rich application of the prophets' messages to our own lives.

Prophecies of salvation can encourage us to persevere in the ways of righteousness, even when we experience times of "exile." Israel feared that God's judgments might be final—that God would abandon his covenant people who had failed to keep his laws. However, the promises of the return and of a better future for Israel (for example, Micah 4) should assure God's people today of his faithfulness to his promises, even when times or circumstances are unpleasant.

Insights for interpreting predictive prophecy. One issue still remains: What about prophecies we identify as "foretelling," where there seem to be predictions of the future that point to a time beyond the circumstances of the OT writers? At this point, experts who interpret these texts diverge greatly. Some think prophecies about Israel in the OT apply to the reconstituted nation of Israel, often the political entity that came into existence in AD 1948. Others apply such prophecies to "spiritual Israel," the church. And some variations combine both ideas.

Without going into great detail, allow me to provide several suggestions to keep you on track. Foremost, because Jesus (and the message about Jesus contained in the NT) constitutes God's revelation following the OT, we should interpret predictive prophecies in light of what the NT reveals and explains. Jesus said in the clearest of terms, "Do not think that I have come to abolish the law or the prophets; I have come not to abolish but to fulfill" (Mt. 5:17, NRSV). Jesus fulfilled the message of the prophets. What does that include?

We don't have to wonder about the significance of some

prophecies, such as the prophecy about Bethlehem (see Mic. 5:2) and what its fulfillment involved. The Messiah's birthplace would be Bethlehem. In addition, in citing this text from Micah, Matthew informs us that the one "who is to rule in Israel, whose origin is from of old, from ancient days" is none other than Jesus (see Mt. 2:6).

Of course, even with such clear fulfillment, Jesus isn't currently ruling Israel in some "literal" sense. How, then, was the prophecy fulfilled? In light of further revelation in the NT, we understand that the full realization of Messiah's rule will occur only in the age to come, at Jesus' second coming. Then the prophecy Nathan made about David will be fully realized: "Your house and your kingdom shall be made sure forever before me; your throne shall be established forever" (2 Sam. 7:16). Many prophetic references to the "coming day" refer to Jesus' second coming (for example, see Jer. 23:5,7; 33:14; Joel 3:18-21; Mic. 4:1-13). It's wrong to apply them to literal, physical Israel today or to this age prior to the Messiah's restoration of all things.

From the vantage point of the OT prophets, only two ages existed. They expected the Messiah's coming to usher in the age to come — the age of plenty and prosperity, with Israel's fortunes reversed. Yet based on NT revelation, we understand that Jesus entered "this age" and brought into this age some of the blessings of the age to come. That reality explains Paul's statement that Christ's body, the church, is now seated in the heavenlies in Christ (see Eph. 1:3; 2:6; Col. 3:1).

This means that some of the prophecies about Israel or Zion are now in the process of fulfillment in the church, Christ's body. Other prophecies about Israel won't be fulfilled until the end of this age, at Jesus' second coming. Be alert to this "already — not yet" element of biblical prophecy.

Several other important cautions:

Some prophecies have more than one fulfillment. For example, Daniel's prediction of the "abomination that causes desolation" (Dan. 9:27; 11:31; 12:11) was fulfilled by Antiochus IV (also known as Epiphanes, who built an altar to Zeus in the second temple of Jerusalem). Then Jesus used the image to refer to the Roman general Titus, who destroyed Jerusalem in AD 70—a figure who might also stand for the Beast of Revelation, also called the Antichrist (see Dan. 9:27; 11:31; 12:11; Mt. 24:15; Mk. 13:14). Isaiah's prediction of a woman to give birth to a child who would be a sign of God's presence, Immanuel or "God with us" (Is. 7:14), was probably fulfilled in his own time, with the birth mentioned in 8:3-4 as well as in Jesus' birth (see Mt. 1:23).

Many prophecies are unconditional. God announces what he'll do, and he does it. But not all prophecies are like this. Sometimes a prophet's pronouncement of what God will do might have unstated conditions. For example, God asserted through Jonah that he planned to destroy Nineveh. But when the wicked city repented, God changed his mind about the intended judgment, much to Jonah's dismay (3:10–4:2). Jeremiah clarified the issue of conditional prophecies (18:7-10). God takes into account the purpose of his action when his message goes forth. At times, both blessings and cursings depend on people's obedience to God's will, and in his sovereignty God may reverse his formerly announced intentions.

Prophecies can be fulfilled in a variety of ways. What does it mean for a prophecy to be "fulfilled"? In the case of Micah 5:2, noted earlier, Bethlehem was quite literally the city where the Messiah was born. The prophecy seemed to point straightforwardly to historical fulfillment. Sometimes the details in the OT are less precise, but the prophecy still finds a clear historical fulfillment (for example, the mission of the Messiah foreseen by Isaiah 61:1-2; see Lk. 4:16-21). Isaiah's prophecy of a literal birth finds historical fulfillment (7:14). Clearly that's one type of fulfillment.

At times, however, a prophecy points to a historical fulfillment in the future but its realization is more figurative or spiritual than concrete. For example, in the following verses, we might expect that Amos predicts the return of Israel's people from exile into the land of Israel in a concrete, historical way:

"IN THAT DAY I WILL RESTORE

DAVID'S FALLEN TENT.

I WILL REPAIR ITS BROKEN PLACES,

RESTORE ITS RUINS,

AND BUILD IT AS IT USED TO BE,

SO THAT THEY MAY POSSESS THE REMNANT OF EDOM

AND ALL THE NATIONS THAT BEAR MY NAME,"

DECLARES THE LORD,

WHO WILL DO THESE THINGS. (9:11-12)

Yet in his comments at the Jerusalem Council, James cited this text as a prophecy that now the Gentiles should be granted entrance into the people of God solely by their faith in Jesus, without adherence to the Mosaic Law (see Acts 15:15-17). James gives this prophecy a spiritual fulfillment in the church: The Gentiles are streaming not into Israel but into the church.

In the OT, we rarely find specific predictions about the course of this present age prior to the second coming of Jesus and the end of this age. Despite the well-meaning attempts of some interpreters to pin current events on obscure verses in the OT prophets, which often they alone seem to be able to interpret accurately, the NT gives us little reason to engage in such speculation based on OT texts.

By the way, throughout church history, all such attempts have proved ungrounded. For example, despite many attempts in the last five hundred years to identify the Antichrist, all were misguided. Similarly, assertions that the rapture of the church would occur within a generation of Israel's refounding as a nation in 1948 have proven false. We should give up such unprofitable speculations; Jesus himself affirmed as much (see Mt. 24:36).

In contrast, NT writers understood most prophecy to show three things:

1. Jesus was the anticipated Messiah.
2. Israel's covenants and mission are being fulfilled in the church.
3. The final events culminate in the end of this age.

I'm not saying that the OT doesn't suggest any future role for the nation of Israel as God's plan culminates in the age to come. At the same time, the NT writers often equate Israel with the church or argue that the new chosen people of God consist of Jews and Gentiles in one body, the church (see Eph. 1:3-4; 2:11-22; Ro. 2:28-29; Gal. 6:16; 1 Pet. 2:9-10). These descriptions should alert us to spiritual fulfillments for most OT prophecies about God's people Israel.

WISDOM

This vital genre of literature in the Bible comprises several entire biblical books: Proverbs, Job, and Ecclesiastes. But "wisdom" as a category occurs more broadly, including some parts of the NT. To navigate life successfully, we need to be wise, and wisdom literature provides us with the insights we need.

The created world and daily life illustrate the wisdom these texts record. We can learn crucial lessons from ants (see Prov. 6:6-8) and from springs of water (see Jas. 3:11). It makes sense to work hard and plan well if we want to be successful in life. That's wisdom. If a spring doesn't pour forth both bitter and fresh water, both evil and good words can't come out of our mouths. In other words, wise people will use their tongues to bless, not curse.

Because the wisdom writers of the Bible find wisdom by observing how life works and life's inevitable consequences, they don't proclaim their messages in direct commands or instructions. We must reflect on what they say and then act.

Here's an example. Proverbs 12:11 says, "Those who till their land will have plenty of food, but those who follow worthless pursuits have no sense" (NRSV). So a wise farmer plans out a yearly schedule, gets up early each day, cultivates and fertilizes the soil, plants good seed, weeds the growing plants, keeps the fence around the field in good repair to keep out scavengers, and harvests the crop at the optimum time. Farmers who do all these things are wise and put themselves in the best position to harvest a good crop.

This is wisdom, but it's not a promise. Farmers are wise to engage in these tasks, but doing them doesn't guarantee a bumper crop—other factors may come into play. Hailstorms at the wrong time, lack of rain, or an invading army that destroys the crops might alter the outcome.

Here's another wise proverb: "Train children in the right way, and when old, they will not stray" (22:6, NRSV). This is the best course of action for parents, but the proverb doesn't promise that if parents train well, their children will never stray. Is it pointless, then, to act wisely? Of course not; wisdom puts us in the best position to succeed, but it makes no guarantees. Proverbs aren't promises.

Beyond proverbs, wisdom in the OT comes in the form of instructions—often also found in the book of Proverbs. In one such instruction, "Do not enter the path of the wicked, and do not walk in the way of evildoers" (Prov. 4:14, NRSV), we learn to avoid those who do evil things. But that bit of wisdom might also be conveyed through stories that serve as examples. In Proverbs 7:4-27, the writer tells the story of a man corrupted by a seductive woman—and the disastrous consequences. Engaging in immorality is not the way of wisdom.

The book of Ecclesiastes conveys wisdom through the author's reflections on what he's learned. When we're prone to conclude that life simply doesn't make sense, we'll find an ally in the musings of this "preacher." He gives us permission to be honest with our questions and doubts.

The body of wisdom literature also includes the book of Job. Job, a righteous man, suffers afflictions through no fault of his own — an insight that Job affirms and his friends dispute. Why, then, does Job suffer? Job maintains his innocence and asserts that he has a valid case against God (16:7-14). He finally despairs of finding justice or even hearing from God, hopelessly expecting his inevitable death. But then the Lord enters the narrative and reduces all human arrogance to humble acceptance of God's sovereignty (38–41). Of this book's many lessons, one stands out: The principal character, Job, and his friends don't have all the available information to understand Job's plight. What an important reminder for us! The wise realize that they don't understand all the issues or all the factors in any situation. More might be going on than we realize or are even able to know. As a result, we should remain humble.

Insights for interpretation. Wisdom literature contains a vast assortment of insights that can help readers avoid life's pitfalls and live successfully. We don't need to travel down every path of life to see the likely outcomes. Why not follow the wise routes and avoid the ones that lead to trouble. Wisdom is ours for the reading, but only if we'll be doers of the Word and not hearers only (Jas. 1:22). These are divine instructions and insights; we must hear them and put their truths into action.

At the same time, because we know that proverbs don't guarantee outcomes, we won't have unrealistic expectations. Job reminds us that we don't have all the information we might like to have about our situation. Although as readers we know more than Job does, the book doesn't promise that God will eventually explain to us the reasons behind our circumstances. We might never know the reason we experience an illness or tragedy.

Still, Ecclesiastes provides some comfort in dark or perplexing times. Even when the answers aren't apparent, we can learn lessons. In Ecclesiastes 4:7-12, we learn that it's better to find a companion to share life with than to navigate its pitfalls alone. In Ecclesiastes 5:18-19 we find the wisdom in savoring whatever opportunities for happiness we have—celebrate when we can.

CONCLUSION
The earliest Christians included the Hebrew and Aramaic Scriptures in the Bible because they grasped the crucial role of the OT for understanding God's plan of redemption. Any Christian who neglects the OT misses the majority of God's revelation and the wealth of benefits these books provide. This emphasizes the importance of being biblical Christians and not merely New Testament Christians. And it underscores the importance of carefully studying all of the OT genres, not just the Psalms or a few other favorite sections.

Genres of the New Testament
Following the same approach, let's look at the four genres we find in the NT. Again, our goal is to examine each genre's essential features to understand how it works so we can think literarily in our study of the Bible. And again, after the description of each genre, I'll supply insights to guide our interpretation.

GOSPEL
Our English word *gospel* comes from the Old English word *godspel*, which means "a good story." It translates the Greek word *euangelion*, which means "good news." The writer Mark used this word in the beginning of his account of Jesus: "The beginning of the gospel about Jesus Christ, the Son of God" (Mk. 1:1). The label stuck,

and thereafter the four accounts of Jesus' life in the NT (and some noncanonical documents) were given the title "gospel." But the title "good news" did not originally describe a literary genre, so we need to look more closely at these four documents to see exactly what their writers achieved.

As we look at the four gospels, we discover that they omit many of the features we'd expect in a modern biography. Equally, many scholars note that the Gospels don't correspond to typical biographies in other Greek literature. For example, the Gospels have gaps: things we'd like to know but the authors didn't include. Yet in the end, "biography" seems to capture the writers' essential objective to explain the significance of Jesus' life, ministry, teachings, death, and resurrection. Luke's explained this objective as follows:

> Many have undertaken to draw up an account of the things that have been fulfilled among us, just as they were handed down to us by those who from the first were eyewitnesses and servants of the word. Therefore, since I myself have carefully investigated everything from the beginning, it seemed good also to me to write an orderly account for you, most excellent Theophilus, so that you may know the certainty of the things you have been taught. (Lk. 1:1-4)

Luke's goal was to explain in an orderly fashion the truth or certainty of what occurred. After careful investigation of the facts from eyewitness and prior accounts, he compiled his own version. We might call the result a "theological biography" — the significance of Jesus for salvation history. Both words are essential to understanding the Gospels as intended.

First, they are *biographies*. The writers share the events of Jesus' life that were significant and convey the purposes of those events. As a result, we find the names of Jesus' parents, the unusual circumstances surrounding his birth, the names of some of the villages he visited, some of the truths he taught, some of his astonishing actions, how he related to various kinds of people, the events of his death, and the declaration that he rose from the dead.

Yet not all of the four Gospels contain some or all of these events; their accounts are selective and nuanced. At the same time, the first three gospels, called the Synoptic (meaning "viewed together") Gospels, more closely match each other than the fourth gospel, John.

Second, the Gospels are *theological* documents. The authors have little interest in simply recording events, actions, or teachings. Written thirty or more years after Jesus' departure, the Gospels exhibit several decades of theological reflection on the significance of—as Luke wrote—"the things that have been fulfilled among us" and "the things you have been taught" (Lk. 1:1,4). Each gospel writer (they are often called evangelists based on the Greek word for gospel, *euangelion*) reflected in his own way on the significance of Jesus. That partly accounts for the differences among the four books. In rare instances, all four record the same incident (such as the feeding of the five thousand); often an incident appears in only one, two, or three of the accounts.

Again, more similarity exists among the Synoptic Gospels. Yet even they sometimes place incidents in different places in their accounts. For example, Luke inserts Jesus' sermon in Nazareth early in his account of Jesus' Galilean ministry (see Lk. 4:16-30), while the other synoptic writers save it until later (see Mt. 13:53-58; Mk. 6:1-6). Matthew collects much of Jesus' ethical teachings into the so-called Sermon on the Mount (see Mt. 5–7), while Luke spreads much of that teaching throughout his account.

In some places where the accounts are parallel, we find that the authors go their own way in giving the order of events, details, or other features (compare the order of Jesus' three temptations in

Mt. 4:1-11 with Lk. 4:1-13). God's words at Jesus' baptism differ in the accounts (compare Mt. 3:17 with Mk. 1:11). In addition, each gospel has unique material not found in any of the others. The wise men show up only in Matthew; the shepherds at the manger only in Luke.

While the basic order of their accounts of Jesus' life agree, each gospel reflects its own individuality—in its wording and arrangement, what it includes or excludes, and how it portrays the details of the story. That's why we see them as theologically motivated. Under the guidance of the Holy Spirit, each writer constructed his own account in a unique way to compose his own portrait of Jesus. Each one adds his own brushstrokes, textures, and lighting. While they don't mirror every detail (and if they did, why would we need all four gospels?), together they provide the full picture.

Insights for interpretation. Much of what we said earlier about interpreting OT narratives applies when we read the Gospels (and, as we'll see, Acts). The gospel stories tell us what happened in Jesus' life, but because they were written by Christians—people under the New Covenant, as are we—they have more direct application to our own lives.

We should employ all the basic steps discussed for interpreting OT narratives (historical background, literary context, word studies, and grammar) to understand what the writers intended to say to their audiences. Then we can take the following steps to apply their messages.

Start by allowing each evangelist to tell his own story. Follow his account step-by-step. See how the narrative unfolds and how each section builds on the preceding one. At this point, avoid the temptation to compare a parallel account, if it exists. Appreciate the portrait that the writer composed. How does he tell his story? What roles do the important characters play? Who are the heroes and villains? Who are Jesus' followers? How does Jesus relate to the crowds and his opponents? What are the key themes that recur? What leads to Jesus' death, and how do the various characters in the story respond?

Compare one gospel with another to see each one's uniqueness and to fill in gaps. Again, take this step after you've studied one gospel account straight through. Here a resource called a gospel synopsis or harmony can be invaluable; it displays the four gospels in parallel columns. For example, you can ponder why the order of the temptations is different. Perhaps Luke wanted to save Jesus' temptation in Jerusalem as a foretaste of Jesus' final temptation culminating in Jerusalem.

For another example, consider the account of Jesus quieting the storm on the Sea of Galilee. Matthew quotes the disciples as saying, "Save us, Lord; we are perishing" (8:25, ESV). In Mark they say, "Teacher, do you not care that we are perishing?" (4:38, ESV), while in Luke they say, "Master, Master, we are perishing" (8:24, ESV). Remember, Jesus and his disciples most likely spoke Aramaic. The Gospels were written in Greek based on the accounts the writers received (recall Luke's prologue in 1:1-4 on page 213). What different impressions do you get from the various quotations? What might the differences suggest about the authors' intentions in this story?

Within larger narratives of Jesus' teaching in the Gospels, we sometimes find parables. Jesus often used this literary device to teach about the nature of the kingdom of God. The word *parable* (*parabolē* in Greek) refers to several devices within Jesus' teaching: riddles (see Mk. 3:23), proverbs (see Lk. 4:23), sayings (see Mt. 13:44-45), lessons (see Mt. 24:32), and—what we most often think of as parables—short stories.

The purpose of a parable is to illustrate and instill a spiritual truth. Parables use a down-to-earth, concrete image to teach or shed light on a spiritual reality. Essentially, when you "get" the point of the parable, you understand a spiritual issue more clearly. For example, it's somewhat of an abstract ideal to say that followers of Jesus should love their neighbors. However, the story of the Good Samaritan allows us to appreciate what loving our neighbors really means from Jesus' point of view. Like the Samaritan who "proved to be a neighbor to the man who fell among the robbers" (Lk. 10:36, ESV), Jesus' followers now see concretely what it means to love others.

Of course, getting Jesus' point in a parable doesn't mean we'll put it into practice or respond in the correct way any more than other teaching devices. Often, even Jesus' opponents understood his point: "When the chief priests and the Pharisees heard his parables, they realized that he was speaking about them. They wanted to arrest him" (Mt. 21:45-46, NRSV). As we interpret a parable, just as in all our study of the Bible, we must grasp Jesus' intention in it and then rigorously put that meaning into practice.

How can we make sure we understand the intention of Jesus' parables? Let's consider several points.

1. See if the writer of the gospel provides a clue to the point Jesus was making. In Luke 18:1, we read, "Jesus told his disciples a parable to show them that they should always pray and not give up." In this instance, we know the main point of the parable before we even read about the widow and the unjust judge. See Luke 18:9 and 19:11 for other places where Luke informs his readers of Jesus' point.

2. Study the context of the parable and seek to understand the cultural features of the parable itself to be sure you can grasp the meaning Jesus intended to teach, as well as its impact on the original hearers. How did farmers plant seeds in Palestine? How much flour did women use when making bread? Why would a shepherd leave ninety-nine sheep to search for one lost sheep? That Jesus makes a hated Samaritan the hero of his story about being a

neighbor would shock his Jewish hearers. Failure to show social concern for those in need makes one a goat heading for hell (see Mt. 25:31-46). Is that shocking?

3. Pay special attention to the main characters in a parable; often you'll find two or three primary characters. For example, read the story of the prodigal son (see Lk. 15:11-32) from the perspective of its three characters: the father, the prodigal, and the older brother. This parable shows God's compassion as a father anxiously waiting for his lost son to return and running to receive him when he does; the prodigal reminds us of our sin and our need for repentance as the way back to our loving God; and the older brother speaks loudly to those who are lost but don't feel lost — those who might be self-righteous and not admit that they also need to repent.

4. Take care not to allegorize Jesus' parables. In other words, not all the features in a parable convey spiritual meaning. Some of them merely make the story work or make it interesting. For example, the Good Samaritan put the wounded man on his "horse" and transported him to an "inn," but we shouldn't look for deep spiritual meaning or implications in the horse and inn. In the past, people interpreting these narratives fell prey to this tendency to allegorize. But apart from any evidence that Jesus intended to invest the parable's details with meaning, we should resist that impulse. Stick with the main characters. What role do they play? How do they advance the main thrust or point of the story?

5. Put into your own words the main lesson or point of the story. Sometimes this is simple and easily determined. For example, the parable of the pearl teaches that the kingdom of God is the most precious possession you can obtain, and

so you should enter it at all costs (see Mt. 13:45-46). But sometimes the point is more complex, although it usually revolves around the main characters. For example, in the parable of the prodigal son, the main point might be that God welcomes lost sinners who repent; those who insist on their own righteousness will miss God's approval.

Throughout the Gospels, we should keep in mind the distinction between what they *describe* and what they *prescribe*, just as we remarked earlier about OT narratives. For example, John 9 describes how Jesus cured a man of blindness. The account tells us what happened, and we must investigate how the writer of the gospel employed that account in his portrait of Jesus. Jesus healing a blind man is reason for worship; it doesn't imply that Jesus will heal every blind person who has faith.

The Gospels, then, accomplish many goals. They inform us of the demands of following Jesus. They instruct us about the dangers of religious formality and arrogance. They portray Jesus for who he is—the one to worship as Lord of all. And they introduce us to the kingdom of God—how to enter and what life in the kingdom entails.

ACTS

Rather than the "Acts of the Apostles," Luke's second volume actually depicts the Acts of the Holy Spirit. In Acts, he continues the narrative of his gospel, going beyond what "Jesus began to do and to teach" (Acts 1:1) to what the Spirit did through Jesus' earliest followers. A quotation of Jesus serves as the grand outline of Luke's story: "You will receive power when the Holy Spirit comes on you; and you will be my witnesses in Jerusalem, and in all Judea and Samaria, and to the ends of the earth" (Acts 1:8). While Jesus' life moved from Galilee to Jerusalem, the Acts narrative takes the reader in widening circles from Jerusalem to Rome.

Acts is a phenomenal story of church growth and evangelistic expansion. In a little more than thirty years, the message of Jesus spreads from an obscure outpost of the Roman Empire to the capital itself and in dozens of key cities in between.

But like the Gospels, Acts is a theological story—a nuanced portrait of that amazing expansion. Luke has his purposes and priorities, so his story is selective. Though the twelve apostles appear in the first two chapters, Luke focuses the rest of the story on Peter and John, to a lesser extent on Stephen and Philip, and then from chapter 13 to the end on his hero, Paul.

Yet even in telling Paul's story, Luke is selective and purposeful. He never mentions Paul's letter-writing ministry. We learn very little of Paul's two- to three-year stay in Ephesus beyond a couple key incidents. The story contains heroes and villains. Barnabas shows his character as a mentor and encourager. Ananias and Sapphira illustrate God's hatred of hypocrisy.

Insights for interpretation. Again, we need to emphasize the distinction between what's descriptive and what's normative in Acts. Luke's purposes must guide us. Barnabas shows up repeatedly as an encourager (see Acts 4:36; 9:27; 11:22-25; 13:43). We might even laud him for taking on Mark as his companion when Paul had disowned Mark (see Acts 15:39). It would seem that Luke wants his readers to admire and imitate Barnabas. On the other hand, while God judges the hypocrisy of Ananias and Sapphira with immediate death, clearly such an action isn't typical; God doesn't punish all sins so drastically. We must keep this distinction in mind whenever we encounter stories in Acts.

As we read Acts, we find that when some people come to faith, they receive the gift of tongues. Is that descriptive or normative? In other places, we find no mention of tongues at all. Is that descriptive or normative? In one instance, it appears that the reception of the

Spirit is delayed and comes by the laying on of apostles' hands (see 8:15-17). Is that descriptive or normative? Was it a special occasion or does the Spirit always await apostolic (or other) hands?

The eleven disciples in Jerusalem employed the Jewish practice of casting lots to select Judas's replacement (see 1:23-26). Did Luke include that incident merely because that's how the disciples did it (descriptive), or did he intend that churches always use that method to determine God's will in selecting leaders (prescriptive or normative)? These questions are crucial because we can't simply do things we want to and avoid those we don't.

Often the answer comes when we see that an incident is isolated or a unique occurrence, such as the casting of lots. When selecting "the Seven" in Acts 6:3-6, Luke gives no hint they used lots. Most likely, then, Luke did not consider casting lots as the prescribed way to select leaders.

The fact that tongues sometimes does and sometimes doesn't follow conversion suggests that neither is normative. The sole incident of the Spirit's delay also indicates that it simply describes what happened on that occasion rather than prescribing all future practices. The uniqueness of Ananias and Sapphira's death also shows that it describes a single incident but doesn't prescribe how God operates.

It seems to be a matter of common sense to consider many features of Luke's story as descriptive. Others are more debatable. Some readers think that Paul went only to the major cities when he evangelized in what we call Turkey and Greece. If this is true, should missionaries today follow suit and let the new converts move into and evangelize rural areas?

What about Paul's practice of first preaching in synagogues in the cities he visited? Is there a normative principle involved, even if we can't follow his practice literally? Should we begin our evangelistic efforts with people who share some common ground—those who have been "pre-evangelized"—before we move to people more distant from our own beliefs? At times, Paul abandoned his efforts to reach some of his hearers who rejected his words. When do we abandon efforts to reach people? Is such abandonment descriptive or normative? Such questions require careful thought.

On the other hand, Luke seems to intend some things as normative for his readers. God repeatedly fills his people with the Spirit so they have the capacity to accomplish his purposes (see Acts 2:4; 4:8,31; 9:17; 13:9). The apostles and early Christians agree on the central core of the gospel message that they proclaim throughout Acts (see 2:16,22-23,32-41; 3:13-14,18-26; 4:10-12,26-28; 13:13-43): Salvation is found only in Christ, and everyone needs to understand what's involved in becoming a follower of Jesus. Indeed, Luke emphasizes the mandate to proclaim this saving message to Jews and Gentiles.

Contextualizing the message so each audience can understand its significance for their own lives is normative as well. A comparison of Paul's approaches to Jews, with the superstitious at Lystra and with the philosophers in Athens, illustrates this point. While there is just one message, evangelists need to present it so that various hearers can grasp its meaning.

Epistles

You might be more familiar with the letters (or epistles) in the NT—at least many of them—than other sections of the Bible. Some are more obscure (for example, Jude), and we sometimes avoid others because they seem to be less useful (2 Corinthians) or too complicated (Hebrews). Paul's letters probably get the most attention.

Though most of us intuitively understand how letters work, let's cover several basic points.

First, by their nature, letters are the most instructive of the NT genres. Authors write letters to teach their readers and, usually, to exhort them to embrace their messages and live accordingly. So where psalms, proverbs, or narratives convey messages in roundabout ways, letters says things more directly.

Second, in letters, authors address specific occasions rather than write systematically to express or summarize their ideas. For example, Paul wrote 1 Corinthians because he learned of problems occurring in the house churches in Corinth (see 1 Cor. 1:11) and because he wanted to respond to questions posed to him (see 7:1). Similarly, because Paul wrote to address the problems in the Philippian church, we have a great hymn about the incarnation and glorification of our Lord Jesus Christ (see Phil. 2:5-11).

Because epistles are written for specific occasions, we can analyze the kinds of tactics an author employs to address the readers' needs. In fact, we can categorize these tactics and arrive at a list of subgenres of NT letters. These parallel the typical kinds of letters others composed in the Greco-Roman world of the first century AD. Think about some of the letters or e-mails you compose. Do they serve any of these kinds of purposes, which NT letters employed?

1. Exhortation letter (also called *parenesis*): An appeal to readers to act in certain ways. Ephesians is an example.
2. Diatribe: Conversational style that deals with hypothetical objections that were raised and answered, often using questions and answers. Romans is an example.
3. Letter of introduction or recommendation: This introduces the individual who brings the letter prior to making a request or asking for a favor. Philemon is a good example.
4. Apologetic letter of self-commendation: A carefully worded defense by the author or response to criticism. Paul's self-defense in 2 Corinthians fits this category.
5. Family letter: A personal letter that someone would send

to members of a close-knit group or family. Philippians is a good example.

In addition to assessing the kinds of letters we find in the NT, we should also be aware of some interesting features they might contain or employ. Often we might not immediately recognize these features of the ancient world. Just as the Gospels contain parables, letters might contain self-contained forms. As you study the NT letters, look for these four examples:

1. Creeds or hymns: Important summaries of doctrine in poetic style and parallelism (see Phil. 2:6-11; 1 Tim. 3:6; Col. 1:15-20).
2. Domestic code: Writing that provides instruction about household relationships (slave/master, parent/child, husband/wife—see Col. 3:18-41; Eph. 5:22–6:9; 1 Pet. 2:13–3:7).
3. Slogans: Common sayings quoted by letter writers. For example, in 1 Corinthians, Paul quotes views held by some at Corinth that he wants to challenge. In effect, he adopts a "yes/but" approach. "Everything is permissible" (1 Cor. 6:12), "yes, but . . ."
4. Vice and virtue lists: Inventory of behaviors to avoid or to adopt (see Ro. 1:29-31; 1 Cor. 6:9-10; Gal. 5:19-23; Jas. 3:17-18).

Insights for interpretation. When we study the Epistles, we need to interpret what each writer says in light of the historical and cultural setting of the specific letter. To do this, we need to use the basic tactics for understanding literature that we've outlined; that is, we should study a specific passage from a letter in light of the literary context where it occurs. We should consider any parts of the passage that might be obscure due to their distance from us in time or culture. We also need to take into account the meaning of the words the author uses and the grammatical structures the author employs to convey his or her meaning.

Beyond these basic tasks, we should also be aware of the nature of the letter we're studying: What's its purpose, and how does the author accomplish it? What arguments does the author use? How does he appeal to the readers? What rhetorical devices does the letter include?

For example, does the author try to convince the readers of a point of view or of the rightness or wrongness of a behavior? Does the author want to motivate the readers to take action? Does he praise or blame them? How does he get their attention? What values does the author appeal to?

All of these approaches help us understand both the content of the message as well as the strategies the author uses to convey his message and motivate the readers to accept it. These insights help us decipher what we need to know and how we should respond to the message of the letter.

REVELATION

Sadly, many Christians avoid reading the Bible's final book. Do you avoid it for any of the reasons people often give? It's too bizarre and complex. It doesn't have much use for practical Christian living. Preachers and writers present wildly competing and often contradictory interpretations of Revelation. Who knows what it means? You might think you can get along quite well as a Christian without paying much attention to Revelation.

That's a sad thought for several reasons.

First, Revelation is a book in the Bible, so it is inspired Scripture written for the benefit of God's people. We shouldn't ignore what God inspired and what the early church included in the Canon.

Second, Revelation is a glorious book that reveals God as sovereign and Jesus as Lord in spectacular terms. Don't miss these grand portrayals.

Third, Revelation is a clarion call to the people of God to follow Jesus' words closely despite all the pressure to follow other ways. We need that message.

Finally, Revelation promises God's people of his final victory over sin, death, and the Devil. It's an inspiration to God's people to persevere in his way, knowing they'll share in God's final triumph.

Revelation, or the Apocalypse (the transliteration into English of the Greek word that means "revelation" or "unveiling"), is its own genre in the NT, although it's one of many apocalypses written from about the second century BC to the first century AD. As a group, apocalypses claimed to unveil the ways God was at work in the world even though his followers might not readily see his presence or activity. They assured readers that God would break into history in his own time, destroy God's enemies, and vindicate his people. Until that climax, his people might suffer many hardships and temptations to abandon God. Apocalypses were calls to God's people to remain faithful to him with the assurance that they'll be rescued and vindicated at the end of history.

The NT book of Revelation shares this essential outlook but conveys its message in a form that is unique, as it also uses tactics of epistles and prophecies. To interpret Revelation, we need to understand how it functions.

First, the book is an epistle. It starts as many other NT epistles begin (see Rev. 1:4-5,11); it includes seven self-contained letters in chapters 2 and 3, and it ends like a letter (see Rev. 22:21). Because it's a letter, we understand that it was sent to specific people to address issues they faced.

Second, Revelation clearly claims to be a prophecy (see Rev. 1:3; 22:18-19). This means we should be alert to both its forthtelling and foretelling properties. It contains important messages for John's readers (John is the author, see Rev. 1:1). Prophetic books, like those in the OT, communicate God's messages for readers about their current behavior and how God is at work among them. Prophecy can also be predictive, and Revelation certainly claims to show what will happen in the future (see Rev. 1:19).

Third, Revelation uses apocalyptic tactics to convey its message. Jews and Christians wrote apocalypses to the faithful. As a genre, apocalyptic employs dreams and visions; it uses symbols and allusions readers would understand; angels convey God's messages to his spokespeople; beasts—both mythical and real—appear with frequency; and battles rage between the forces of good and evil.

Often it appears that evil will triumph, until God finally appears to defeat his enemies. The message to the readers stresses the need to remain faithful despite adversity or the lures of the dominant culture. The message is a blend of despair and confidence. Current times are tough, but God and his people will triumph in the end.

Insights for interpretation. Unfortunately, many prophecy "experts" have become so enamored with the element of prediction that they ignore John's message for his readers and for us as contemporary readers. These experts have been revealing the identity of the Antichrist for more than five hundred years and predicting the time of the Rapture for at least the last sixty—and all have been wrong so far! Their wildly contradictory interpretations should remind us to be wary of blindly following their interpretations and, more importantly, missing the lessons that Revelation can teach us.

In keeping with Revelation's character as an epistle, we should first try to discern its message to its original readers. Revelation was also written for a specific occasion. If we were studying Ephesians, for example, our first task would be to try to determine the message to the original readers: What did Paul seek to say to his readers, and how can we understand and apply that message to our churches and lives today? Similarly, John was writing a message that his readers needed to hear, and that message was largely instructive for them. We should be asking what he said to them and how that message can apply to us.

Our primary tactics for understanding Revelation are the ones outlined earlier for understanding the meaning of NT letters. The meaning of many images and symbols will come from John's world. We must research the historical and cultural background to understand John's allusions. We must do word studies and examine how John develops his arguments. We need to trace John's structure and how the message of the book develops from the heavenly scene in chapters 4 and 5 through the seals, trumpets, bowls, Babylon, Jesus' triumph, Satan's demise, and finally the new heaven and new earth.

So instead of spending our energy trying to predict who the great prostitute Babylon will be in the Tribulation period, we should aim to understand what Babylon represented for John's readers. Why did John use Babylon to convey this idea? How did this "prostitute" seduce the people of John's time? John refers to Babylon's materialism, for example (see Rev. 18:3,7). He calls his readers to abandon her ways (see v. 4). What are corresponding seductions of materialism for us today? Are we taken in? Because we know this prostitute will be destroyed (see v. 21), we need to be sure we're not seduced by her promises and allures.

This example of Babylon highlights the difficulties we have in deciphering apocalyptic literature. Symbols and allusions are the stock in trade of this genre, and we must become adept at deciphering them, at least as much as we can. In some places, the author tells us what the symbols stand for. For example, we learn that the seven lampstands (see Rev. 1:12) stand for seven churches (see v. 20) and that the golden bowls of incense are the prayers of the saints (see 5:8).

But John doesn't provide all the keys to understanding the symbols.

At times, we can find crucial clues from the OT, where John gets many of his allusions. From the OT, we know that olive trees are a standard symbol of people, especially God's people (see Jer. 11:16; Hos. 14:6; Zech. 4:3,11; see Ro. 11:17,24). That insight can help us make sense of Revelation 11:4. In fact, Zechariah 4 provides many allusions that inform Revelation 11. The book of Daniel is another common source for John's allusions. The scroll John must eat (see Rev. 10:9-10) refers back to Ezekiel 2:9–3:9.

At other times, we might be at a loss to explain some of John's symbols, the number 666 being a prime example. Other allusions from Jesus' teaching might have become part of subsequent Christian theological understanding. For example, in his Olivet discourse (see Matthew 24–25) Jesus used the picture of a "thief in the night" to alert his disciples about the sudden or unexpected nature of his coming (see Mt. 24:43-44). Paul (see 1 Thess. 5:4) and Peter (see 2 Pet. 3:10) repeated the image, and finally John employs it as well (see Rev. 16:15). In other words, Jesus' return is imminent. The clear message is "Be ready."

The prophetic element of Revelation will continue to challenge readers. We must avoid several extremes. We can't brush off the entire book as just a collection of symbols. Although Revelation uses many symbols, the book is more than an extended allegory. Similarly, another extreme to avoid is to deny any predictive element to the book, as if it should be read just as an epistle. It's an epistle, but it's also a prophecy. It does speak to John's readers, but it also foretells.

Here we need to use utmost caution and humility. Revelation does predict God's final victory accomplished by Christ's glorious and triumphal return, but many of the details of that grand and victorious narrative don't correspond literally to the events they portray.

I suggest that when we study Revelation, we remember that it doesn't give specific details about how the events of the end will unfold. Most likely we should view such words as "the stars of the sky fell to the earth" and "every mountain and island was removed from its place" (Rev. 6:13-14) as symbolic. Likewise, when we realize that locusts are stock symbols of marauding hordes of enemies (see 9:3-11), we understand their significance for John's vision. Locusts symbolize untold devastation.

As we study the Bible, we must be aware that though Revelation may tell us about end events, it doesn't portray them precisely as they'll happen. Just as John portrays the church as a lampstand to shine the light of the gospel, he describes Jesus as a triumphant warrior. Jesus will return, but he probably won't be riding on a horse (see Rev. 19:11). There will be a final battle, but it might not occur on the Plain of Sharon in Israel (near Mount Megiddo, Armageddon in Hebrew).

CONCLUSION

As we strive to interpret the variety of genres in the OT and NT, we can circle back to our goal of studying the Bible: to understand it the way the authors intended their readers to understand it. So as we close, let's review the questions that can help us interpret the Bible:

1. What were the biblical authors seeking to do when they wrote? What were their motives and purposes in writing?
2. What meaning did they want to convey through their writings?
3. What can we do to understand what the writings mean?

I hope this chapter has helped prepare you to answer these questions in your own study of God's Word. Certainly, your own understanding and application of the Bible will be enriched as you faithfully undertake these tasks.

FOR FURTHER STUDY

Alter, R. *The Art of Biblical Narrative*. New York: Basic Books, 1981.

Bray, G. *Biblical Interpretation: Past and Present*. Downers Grove, IL: InterVarsity, 1996.

Dockery, D. S., K. A. Matthews, and R. B. Sloan, eds. *Foundations for Biblical Interpretation*. Nashville: Broadman, Holman, 1994.

Fee, G. D., and D. Stuart. *How to Read the Bible for All Its Worth*. 3rd ed. Grand Rapids, MI: Zondervan, 2003.

Fokkelman, J. P. *Reading Biblical Poetry. An Introductory Guide*. Westminster John Knox, 2001.

Goldingay, J. *Models for Interpretation of Scripture*. Grand Rapids, MI: Eerdmans, 1995.

Green, J. B., ed. *Hearing the New Testament: Strategies for Interpretation*. Grand Rapids, MI: Eerdmans, 1995.

Klein, W. W., C. L. Blomberg, and R. L. Hubbard Jr. *Introduction to Biblical Interpretation*. 2nd ed. Nashville: Nelson, 2004.

Osborne, G. R. *The Hermeneutical Spiral*. Rev. ed. Downers Grove, IL: InterVarsity, 2006.

Ryken, L., and T. Longman III. *A Complete Literary Guide to the Bible*. Grand Rapids, MI: Zondervan, 1993.

Schneiders, S. M. *The Revelatory Text: Interpreting the New Testament as Sacred Scripture*. 2nd ed. Collegeville, MN: Michael Glazier Books, 1999.

CHAPTER 6

BIBLE STUDY METHODS

A re you a gardener? Maybe you spend hours and hours each year growing enough vegetables to feed your family and even more to preserve or give away. Or maybe your green thumb is limited to caring for a few houseplants.

Many gardeners, at all levels, have discovered the pleasure that comes from taking a bare patch of dirt, adding amendments to improve the soil, tilling the land, planting seeds, cultivating and weeding, and finally enjoying the bounty of harvest.

In a similar way, many Christians have discovered the joy of digging into the contents of the Bible. Although the process of studying God's Word takes extended effort, those who spend time in Bible study find themselves enjoying the bounty of harvest. Because the Bible conveys God's Word, we can enjoy digging into its contents to learn more about him.

The Bible, written over many years in different cultures and at different times, provides a rich resource that deserves careful study. This diversity means we can take a variety of approaches to studying it. The different genres invite us to use multiple ways to grow and learn from its pages. Its narratives tell the life stories of people — some we might want to imitate, and others who teach us through their mistakes. Its epistles pass on instruction to followers of Jesus. Each genre holds something for us to learn. The Bible's origin is divine; that means we can learn *theology* from its pages—what God wants his people to know and believe and how he desires them to live.

You can use different study methods depending on your specific goal. For example, you might want to understand what Paul means by *justification* and how it compares with how James uses the term. Or you may be interested in Jesus' mother, Mary—what kind of person was she that God selected her to be the mother of our Lord? Maybe you're interested in the theological question of whether true Christians can lose their salvation, so you decide to study the book of Hebrews in depth to see what it says about this.

BASIC BIBLE STUDY METHODS

In this chapter, we'll look at a variety of methods we can use to benefit from our study of the Bible. Dividing methods into "basic" and "in-depth" isn't a precise division because we can lengthen or shorten most methods depending on how much time we'd like to spend on a topic. However, first we'll look at study methods that take smaller amounts of time. The later in-depth list includes methods you can use when you have more time or when you'd like to do a study over a period of days or weeks. Trial and error will determine what works best for you. Let's look at fifteen methods: using ABCDE, seeking the purposes of Scripture, looking for the meaning of a word or phrase, learning from the kings of Israel, systematically studying the book of Proverbs, exploring God's Creation, meeting Jesus, answering questions Jesus asked, understanding the commands of Christ, exploring what prompted Jesus to say "amen," studying spiritual fruit, personalizing Scripture, comparing stories to your own experiences, journaling reflectively, and using *lectio divina* (sacred reading).

Method One: As Easy as ABCDE

To begin an ABCDE Bible study, select a passage of Scripture you want to study. This method works best on a self-contained passage of the Bible, no more than a short chapter. It works well if you're reading a book and want to study one section at a time. Here's what to do:

1. Read the passage at least three times.
2. Read it again and jot down your reactions and questions.
3. Organize your study under the following five sections, each identified by a letter of the alphabet.

A. Create A Summary Title

You might want to wait to finalize your title until you've finished the rest of your study. To choose a title, jot down two or three titles that come to mind as you study; then either select the best one from this list or develop a new one from a combination of your suggestions. The title should express what the passage is about and be as complete as possible. Don't worry about being clever or catchy. Aim for a title between five and ten words.

B. Identify the Basic Verse or Text Cluster

Decide whether you're choosing a basic verse or a text cluster. A basic verse is a single reference that stands out as you read the passage or chapter; it doesn't have to include the central theme. You might want to write out the basic verse and memorize it. A text cluster is a small group of verses (two or three) that highlight the central message or are crucial to the message of the passage. Write the references of the verses under the section title.

C. Look for a Personal Challenge

As you study the passage, ask God to challenge you in a personal way through what you're studying. Your job is to accept this challenge and apply its truth to your life. It might be something that God wants you to do or stop doing, or it could be an attitude to develop or stop.

Using the heading "Challenge," list the verse or verses where you found your challenge. First, state in your own words the truth of the verse. Then write how the challenge applies to you: what needs it reveals in your life; what shortcomings, sins, or faults it indicates; and what new appreciation or understanding it opens up to you. Because the challenge is personal, use the pronouns *I*, *me*, *my*, and *mine*.

Next, write a specific action you'll take to correct the weakness, to build the needed quality into your life, or to increase your understanding of that particular truth. Choose something practical you can do during the following week. Pray for the help of the Holy Spirit, who helps you grow in Christ.

D. Pinpoint the Difficulties

Consider each verse in your study passage. Did you find anything you couldn't explain to someone else? If so, under the heading "Difficulties," write down the number of the verse and the question or problem it raises in your mind. As you have time, use the principles and procedures of biblical research from chapter 5 to answer the question or solve the problem.

E. Describe the Passage's Essence

In the last section of your study, summarize in your own words or outline the passage under the heading "Essence." Write only what the passage says, not what it means. Rather than applying it to your life at this point, simply put in your own words what the Scripture says.

This summary is a condensed version of the passage. Summarize all parts equally. A way to do this is to write one sentence for each thought in the passage. Then condense your summary into fewer words, combining your sentences and making them shorter. You should aim for an average of two to eight words per verse.

An outline divides the passage into its natural paragraphs and gives a brief title or heading to each section. Write down the verses included in each section. List as many subpoints under the main headings as you need to define its content. Just like with the summary, include all parts of the passage in equal proportions.

Method Two: Seeking the Purposes of Scripture

This method starts with a simple question: What is the Bible for? The answer comes from a text we have mentioned several times, Paul's words in 2 Timothy 3:16: "All Scripture is God-breathed and is useful for teaching, rebuking, correcting and training in righteousness." Asking key questions about these four purposes of Scripture—teaching the truth, rebuking our sin, correcting spiritual weaknesses, and training in righteousness—can guide us as we evaluate and apply Scripture.

Teaching the Truth

After you've selected a passage or chapter, begin with the first purpose of Scripture listed in 2 Timothy 3:16: teaching. Ask yourself, *What does this passage teach?* Boil it down to a simple statement. To help clarify what the passage teaches, ask these questions:

1. What does this passage say about God?
2. What does it say about people?
3. What does it say about my relationship with God and others?

You'll soon realize how much of what you discover in God's Word relates to these simple questions. Jesus said that the entire Bible hangs on the two commands to love God and love others (see Mt. 22:34-40; compare with Ro. 13:8-10). How can your study of the Bible help you increase your love for God and others? Scripture becomes incredibly practical when we look at it in light of these questions. To help cement the truths you find, write down the lessons you discover. Writing out your thoughts will help solidify your understanding of God's Word.

REBUKING OUR SIN

The second purpose of God's Word is to rebuke our sin. Scripture rebukes us by showing our sins and the ways we fall short of God's standards. Once you see what a passage teaches, prayerfully ask if there's any way that you're not obeying this truth. For example, *Am I falling short in this area?* If you sense conviction, ask, *Where and why is this sin happening?*

It's important to identify as specifically as possible how you fall short. For example, it's not enough to know that you have an anger problem. Responding properly to rebuke means specifically confessing where this sin is rearing its head. Don't just say, *I have a problem with anger.* Instead, identify the triggers: *I get angry when . . .* or *I respond to* [fill in the blank] *by getting mad.* Also identify how you express that anger in harmful ways: *When I'm angry, I'm critical of my spouse.* Next, ask, *Is this angry response the problem or just a symptom of a deeper issue?*

Many times sin manifests itself in our lives as a response to other underlying problems. Criticizing a spouse might be the result of frustration at work. Unless we deal with the root, weeds will grow again. Real change demands that we go below the surface.

CORRECTING SPIRITUAL DEFICIENCIES

The third purpose of the Bible is correction. The Word of God not only rebukes us when we get off track but it guides us back to the right road. Correction begins by asking, *What's the opposite of my sin?* For example, if one has a problem with uncontrolled anger, God desires patience and self-control.

Next, ask, *What action will get me back on track?* Write down specific ways to correct your behavior. For example, *I'll listen to my wife's point of view before I respond. I'll try to hear what she needs and not take her words as attacks. When I respond, I'll respond with a calm voice.* Ask God to help you make the changes you need.

TRAINING IN RIGHTEOUSNESS

God's Word trains us in righteousness. The goal of the Christian life is finishing well — getting back on the right track and staying there. Hebrews 12:1 instructs us to "throw off everything that hinders and the sin that so easily entangles, and . . . run with perseverance the race marked out for us." When we're gaining too much weight and losing strength in our bodies, we adopt a training regimen to get back in shape. But what about our spiritual fitness? The Word of God trains us to run with perseverance.

Ask yourself, *What spiritual training regimen do I need?* The answer might surface in the passage you're studying. However, you might also need to look for other Scriptures to answer this question. Perhaps you need to pray about the issue or memorize verses on the subject. Long-term change demands that we transform our minds and hearts.

Method Three: What's in a Word?

Words, even in the Bible, can be either "sweeter than honey to my mouth" (Ps. 119:103) or "things that are hard to understand, which ignorant and unstable people distort" (2 Pet. 3:16).

While words are the building blocks for language and communication, they can also cause confusion with their many meanings and uses. For example, the *Oxford English Dictionary* lists more than seventy different meanings for the word "round." Our study of the Bible needs to include the careful study of its words so we understand their authors' intentions.

Word studies uncover the most appropriate meaning of a particular word within the context and reveal how that meaning affects the whole passage. Word studies can be as simple as following some easy steps with only a Bible in hand, or they can be as complicated as an in-depth study based on the original languages and Greek or Hebrew references. Decide how deeply you need to dig based on the resources and time you have and the nature of the word.

The following three steps form a basic word study. Your study will get more complex as you dig deeper into these steps.

Step One: Determine Meanings and Uses

Decide what word to study by looking for keywords within the passage or for words you don't know. Let's say you're studying Ephesians 1:7: "In him we have redemption through his blood, the forgiveness of sins, in accordance with the riches of God's grace." You could do word studies on *redemption, forgiveness, sin,* or *grace.* First, try to find possible meanings of the word. It might be used differently in other parts of the Bible or even within the passage itself. Use what you've found to try to determine how Paul uses it in Ephesians 1:7.

Use Bible dictionaries, concordances, and other resources to find different meanings of the word. A Bible dictionary (which contains articles on most biblical names, places, images, themes, and important words in alphabetical order) or lexicon (which provides a complete listing of a language's vocabulary) would tell you that the word *forgiveness* in Ephesians 1:7 means "to dismiss or release."

Only God can release us from sin, a theological truth emphasized in both the OT and the Gospels (see Mk. 2:7). This is where we get the term *scapegoat* from; in ancient Israel, the sins of the people were confessed over the head of a goat, which was then sent into the wilderness, never to be seen again (see Lev. 16:6-28).

STEP TWO: CHOOSE THE BEST DEFINITION

As you study words, you'll find some that have only one meaning. That makes your job easy. But many words have multiple meanings, and you need to decide which meaning fits the passage and context best. Try substituting each definition for the word in the passage. Ask which meaning fits best and is consistent with the context. Determine which meaning makes sense with other passages of Scripture that teach similar truths.

In Ephesians 1:7, "redemption" can either mean "a deliverance," such as freeing a prisoner, or "a release achieved by the payment of a ransom." Here, the second sense fits Paul's context better because Christ's blood paid for our release from sin.

STEP THREE: STATE THE PASSAGE'S MEANING

Word studies are useful only when the word is studied in context and we're able to see how its meaning explains the passage we're studying. When we see how the word's definition sheds light on the passage's meaning, we're able to apply the passage to our lives.

For example, I mentioned that the word *round* has many meanings. But when it's used in a discussion about guns, such as when someone says, "I took the round out of the chamber for safety," we can narrow down the definitions to what the author meant. The best definition of a word helps us interpret the meaning of the entire passage.

TYPES OF WORD STUDIES

Here are six types of word studies that use the same basic steps we just went over but that rely on different resources.

English-definition study. An English dictionary shows various meanings of a word as well as word origins and foreign-language uses. But English dictionaries aren't always helpful for Bible study because the meaning of a word in English might be completely different from how it's used in the Bible.

Basic-meaning study. You'll need a good Bible dictionary, such as *Mounce's Complete Expository Dictionary of Old and New Testament Words.*[1] This book will help you discover the background and range of meanings for the words you discover. If you know Greek or Hebrew, dictionaries in those languages can help. See additional resources at the end of this chapter as well as the more complete list in chapter 7.

Usage study. A good concordance is all you need to see how the word is used in other passages. Study every place the word is used, looking for other meanings and patterns. A concordance that traces words in the original language texts is best. If you looked up the word *trial* in some concordances, you might not find that the same Greek word for *trial* or *test* (*peirasmos*) is also translated *temptation* in James 1. A concordance will show what words are unique to specific authors or specific books.

Historical study. A good Bible dictionary or encyclopedia will trace how a word's meaning changed over time. You'll find information about the word's origin, history, meanings, and theology. You'll also see which Hebrew words were translated into Greek words in the Greek OT (LXX) translation of the Bible. Look up the word, write its basic idea and meanings, and then try to pick the best meaning for the passage before looking at what the book recommends. For the OT, see Willem A. Van Gemeren, ed., *New*

International Dictionary of Old Testament Theology and Exegesis. For NT studies, see C. Brown, ed., *New International Dictionary of New Testament Theology.*

Synonym study. Most words have synonyms; their meanings overlap in some of their uses. The dictionaries edited by C. Brown and W. A. Van Gemeren listed in the previous paragraph are also useful here. List each synonym of the word you are studying and its meaning, and then take what you learned from knowing that the author chose that specific word instead of one of its synonyms. A look at the words for *sin* in the NT will turn up many entries, such as *offense, trespass,* and *lawlessness.* Discerning the subtle differences of each one will give you information about the passages where the author uses one or the other.

Translation study. Various translations of the Bible can help you understand word meanings. Look up your word in several different translations and paraphrases to find possible word meanings or wording that's easier to understand. This will often show that you need to do more research to understand the differences and see which translation is on target. Use many types of translations: formally equivalent translations such as the King James Version and the New American Standard Bible; dynamically equivalent translations such as the [Today's] New International Version, [New] Revised Standard Version, and New Century Version; and paraphrases such as *The Message* and The New Living Translation.

Method Four: Learning from the Kings of Israel

Have you read about the kings of ancient Israel? If you study the career of King Amaziah, you'll find he began well but then turned from the Lord (see 2 Chron. 25). Uzziah's story in chapter 26 isn't much better: He, too, started strong and then stopped pleasing God. But that's not the whole story. "Jotham grew powerful because he walked steadfastly before the LORD his God" (27:6). What can we learn from these ancient kings?

If we let go of any preconceived ideas, the kings' stories have a lot to offer us. Within them are rich lessons about walking with God for a lifetime. Remember from chapter 5 how narratives work? Grab your Bible and a notebook and pen (or laptop) and get ready to dig up buried treasure from these historical books of Scripture. Here's what to do.

STEP ONE: RECORD OBSERVATIONS

First, choose a king's story and read the whole account, writing down biographical information you find in the text. Then consider these questions:

- What were this king's strengths and weaknesses?
- How did these traits affect his relationship with God over the long haul?
- How did he finish his reign as king?
- Why did he finish the way he did?

Asa, for example, was committed to God although his father, Abijah, had been evil. Asa expelled the temple prostitutes, got rid of the idols his father made, and dethroned his grandmother, the queen mother, because she made an Asherah pole (monument to a pagan deity). However, Asa didn't remove the high places dedicated to pagan gods.

Remember that many stories in 1 and 2 Kings repeat in 1 and 2 Chronicles. For example, you'll find Asa's story in both 1 Kings 15 and 2 Chronicles 14–16.

STEP TWO: COMPARE HIM TO YOU

How are you like the king you're studying? List the character traits—good and bad—that you share with him. For example, many Christians share Asa's passion to do mighty things for God. But we may also share a significant weakness with him. At a critical moment, Asa relied on the king of Aram instead of the Lord (see 2 Chron. 16:9), just as we sometimes look to people for help before we look to God. When an emergency arises, God can seem less powerful and real than flesh-and-blood friends or family.

Identifying similarities between the lives of the kings and our own makes us less likely to see them as failures. We'll see that our struggles and decisions are very similar to theirs.

STEP THREE: WRITE AN APPLICATION

Next, write down the king's attitudes and behaviors you want to imitate and those you want to avoid. You might write, "I want to have godly attitudes and actions, just like Asa in the early years of his reign. I plan to do what's right in the eyes of the Lord by putting God first. Specifically, I need to give more intentionally to God's work in my church—both money and time. I also need to deal with areas of idolatry (putting other things before God) in my life. Materialism has become an idol for me."

STEP FOUR: ETCH THE TRUTH

Now think about ways to etch God's truth into your heart and your actions. Did a particular verse grab your attention? Memorize it or write it on a piece of paper and stick it on your mirror. Or look for a song about what you want to do. Be creative as you consider how to drive home what you've learned.

STEP FIVE: RESPOND IN PRAYER

Respond to what God has taught you. Look back at step 3 and ask God to help you do what's right and avoid wicked actions. You might want to write your prayer in a journal or notebook.

STEP SIX: TELL SOMEONE

Finally, share your discoveries with someone else. Maybe you can ask your prayer group to pray with you for the character traits you want to develop. Ask a friend or mentor to question you gently when he or she sees you stumbling into habits you're trying to break.

Method Five: Growing Through Proverbs

The book of Proverbs is a thirty-one-chapter catalog of short, concise statements about God's perspective on daily life. You'll find truths on everything from keeping a lid on your temper to the effects of drinking too much.

Proverbs also comments on relationships, mentioning more than 180 different kinds of people. So how about studying it chapter by chapter? Using this method, you'll study each chapter on the day of the month it matches. This will help you look for different kinds of content and spur you to think deeper about how to apply each proverb's wisdom to your daily life.

This study approach uses nine keywords to help you see the text from different points of view and locate treasure buried just beneath the surface. The first letters of each keyword forms an acronym: CHARACTER. Applying truth from Proverbs to your daily life will grow your character and your walk with God. Let's look at the process using Proverbs 15.

KEYWORD ONE: COMMUNICATION

Start your study with prayer. Ask God to increase your powers of observation and show you how the verses relate to your life. Make the psalmist's prayer your own: "Open my eyes that I may see wonderful things in your law" (Ps. 119:18). When you finish praying, read the Proverbs chapter that corresponds to the day of the month.

KEYWORD TWO: HOME

Home is one of the main places we apply Bible truth to our lives. As you read the day's chapter, try to connect what it says to your life. Does a verse make you think of your relationship with your spouse, roommate, children, or neighbor? If possible, find a verse that gives insight for your life now.

Look at Proverbs 15 and think about this question: "Which verse speaks loudest about the things I'm experiencing at home?" Maybe the Holy Spirit will direct your attention to verse 1: "A gentle answer turns away wrath, but a harsh word stirs up anger." The verse might make you remember an incident when you used harsh or inappropriate words. Through this memory, the Holy Spirit answered your initial prayer and was faithful to point out a connection between this verse and your experience. An appropriate response is to confess your sin to the Lord and apologize to the person you spoke harshly to.

KEYWORD THREE: ATTITUDES

An attitude is a feeling or internal reaction we have toward a person or circumstance. Words such as *humble, joyous, teachable, pessimistic, resentful,* and *thankful* describe some attitudes. As you read each chapter of Proverbs, consider these questions: What attitudes does the text praise? What attitudes does it say are sinful?

These questions help us when we read Proverbs 15:32: "Those who ignore instruction despise themselves, but those who heed admonition gain understanding" (NRSV). What attitude does this commend?

This verse glorifies a teachable spirit—a willingness to learn from others. When we take this verse seriously, we'll seek feedback from others, even if it's painful at times. To avoid instruction that others give us is the same as hating ourselves. God doesn't ask us to agree with everyone, but he does instruct us to listen to and consider what others say.

KEYWORD FOUR: RELATIONSHIPS

Relationships are one of the most common topics in Proverbs. What connections do you see between the chapter and relationships outside your home? Each chapter might speak to the way you relate to friends, neighbors, coworkers, and even your enemies. Does one verse prick your conscience and make you want to change in the way you're relating to someone?

For example, review Proverbs 15 with relationships in mind. Note verse 22: "Plans fail for lack of counsel, but with many advisers they succeed." If you'd been wrestling with a decision for days but couldn't sort through the issues to reach a conclusion, this verse might challenge you to meet with a close friend or counselor to talk about it. More input might clarify your alternatives and help you think clearly.

KEYWORD FIVE: ACTIONS

Some proverbs refer to behavior patterns that God either approves of or hates. As you read each chapter, try to pinpoint one behavior that God wants you to start or stop. However, don't compile a long list of action plans from each chapter. When we try to make too many changes at once, we get overloaded and are not able to make any meaningful changes, resulting in frustration instead of increased obedience.

Sometimes the action we need to take will relate to another observation in the study. For example, perhaps the "Home" phase of the study (see page 247) already convicted you about speaking harshly. A few minutes later, meditating on the chapter in light of those actions, God might remind you again to apologize to the person you offended. Two steps in this study work together to move you toward one specific action.

KEYWORD SIX: CONSEQUENCES

Other passages in Proverbs describe the positive or negative consequences of our actions, motivating us to get rid of bad behavior. What consequences do you desire and which do you want to duck?

Proverbs 15:25 warns about the damaging consequences of pride: "The LORD tears down the house of the proud" (NRSV). This verse might remind you of another proverb: "Pride goes before destruction, a haughty spirit before a fall" (16:18). To avoid God's judgment and inevitable destruction, remain humble.

After reflecting on these verses, thank the Lord for helping you achieve success. These proverbs remind us of the danger of accepting credit the Lord deserves.

KEYWORD SEVEN: TONGUE

More than a hundred verses in Proverbs talk about the tongue. Finding these verses will help you understand God's wisdom for our speech. These verses describe both sinning and serving others with our words.

Proverbs 15:23 grabs our attention: "To make an apt answer is a joy to anyone, and a word in season, how good it is!" (NRSV). Providing an appropriate answer or the right word requires listening. Reflecting on this wisdom might move you to ask God to help you stop interrupting others.

KEYWORD EIGHT: EXPRESSION

The word *expression* refers to something we say or convey to others. We express our faith when we witness to an unbeliever, lead a Bible study, or share an idea that changed our lives. As you probe the proverbs, pick a principle to express to someone else.

- Did a verse encourage you?
- Did the Holy Spirit expose a problem you need to discuss with a friend?

- Did something remind you of a wayward friend who needs your encouragement or loving criticism?

Ask the Lord for the right opportunity to express something you learned in the chapter, and share the wisdom of God's Word with someone else.

KEYWORD NINE: REMEMBRANCE

Which principle from the chapter challenged you the most or left the biggest impression? Meditate on that verse; then memorize it. Memorization gives the Holy Spirit fuel to work with throughout the day and increases the chance of applying Bible truth to your life. The verses you've already identified in your study are good ones to memorize. Review the sections on "Bible Intake" from chapter 4.

Say you decide to memorize Proverbs 15:1 to remind you to refrain from harsh speech. Then when you're tempted to overreact to a coworker, you might remember that verse's words: "A gentle answer turns away wrath, but a harsh word stirs up anger." These memorized words can inspire an emergency prayer and keep you from a major blowup.

Method Six: Learning from God's Creation

It's hard to imagine a book that relates more to life than the Bible; however, sometimes we need to hear its words in fresh ways. And if we've been walking in faith for a while, a different angle can enhance our Bible reading.

Anyone who's visited Colorado has seen the majesty of the mountains. Fifty-four peaks reach up more than fourteen thousand feet above sea level. Can nature's splendor be a springboard to Bible study? Yes!

Think about the mountains in the Bible. You might remember several prominent "mounts" in God's Word: Mount Sinai, Mount

Zion, the Mount of Transfiguration, and the Mount of Olives. With the help of a concordance, you'll find more than a dozen mountains in the Bible.

Obviously, your goal isn't to learn about mountains; it's to read and contemplate the Bible events involving them. Use your interest in a natural feature to guide you into how God has worked in our world. What happened on those mountain peaks? Beyond them, what can we learn by studying passages that included a feature of the natural world that God created?

Mountains might not captivate you. Maybe you love the ocean instead. As a change from your usual mode of study, choose an aspect of the natural world that interests you and examine it in the Bible:

- Are you a beach person? Look at stories that involve water, including the Nile, the Red Sea, the Jordan, the Sea of Galilee, and Paul's Mediterranean journeys.
- Maybe the sky interests you. You might want to study the heavens, the sun, the moon, the stars, Creation, the day the sun stood still over Joshua and his army, the Day of the Lord in Joel, the wise men's star, or the black sky at Jesus' death.
- Are you an animal lover? God's Word is full of animals. Begin with the Creation story, but don't overlook Noah's passengers, Balaam's donkey, Elijah's ravens, David's sheep, Daniel's lions, Jonah's worm, and Jesus' Triumphal Entry donkey.
- If plants fascinate you, consider the Garden of Eden, Moses' burning bush, Jonah's vine, the parable of the sower, and Jesus' vine and branches illustration.

To do this study well, you'll need some basic Bible reference tools to look up verses and understand them in context: a good concordance, a Bible dictionary, and a commentary to do more in-depth study of the passages.

Let me show you how this method works with a short study about mountains.

FIND THE NATURE VERSES

First, identify verses about the element of nature you're studying. You can work from memory or use a concordance. For example, here are some verses about mountains in Scripture:

- The mountains of Ararat: Gen. 8
- Abraham's mountain: Gen. 22:1-19
- Mount Sinai: Ex. 19:1-25; 24:12-18; 32:7-16
- Mount Carmel: 1 K. 18:16-46
- Mount Moriah: 2 Chron. 3–7
- The mountains in Psalms: Ps. 46; 121; 125
- Mount Zion: Ps. 28; 74; 78; 125; 133; Is. 4; 8; 10; 18; 24; 29; Lam. 5; Joel 2; Ob. 1; Mic. 4; Heb. 12; Rev. 14
- The mount of temptation: Matt. 4:1-11
- The mount of Jesus' famous sermon: Matt. 5–7
- The Mount of Transfiguration: Matt. 17:1-9; Mk. 9:2-8; Lk. 9:28-36
- The Mount of Olives: Mt. 24:3–25:46; 26:30-56; Lk. 19:28-40
- The mount of ascension: Mt. 28:16-20; Acts 1:1-12

DEVELOP YOUR QUESTIONS

Next, form questions to guide you through each passage of Scripture. Some questions should help you make basic observations from the passages you've chosen. Others might be application questions to help you relate what you find to your life. You might use the following questions to look closer at the mountains in the Bible:

- What do I see about God?
- What do I see about people?
- What happened when people spent time on this mountain?
- Would I have liked being on this mountain then? Why or why not?
- What can I learn about myself from the experience on this mountain?
- What new name could I give this mountain in light of my study?

LET QUESTIONS AND ANSWERS SURFACE

Depending on the number of passages you select, you might finish your study in one sitting or you might stretch it out over several days. Each time you sit down to study the Bible, ask the God of nature to reveal truth you can apply to your life. Visualize the images in the stories, and answer each of the questions you brainstormed in the previous section. Allow other questions to come up, and be prepared to think about familiar passages from a fresh perspective.

THE EXPLORATION'S END

You don't have to come up with a single application or idea that summarizes everything you discover. The purpose of this study isn't to find answers as much as it is to see God's Word with new eyes. You might look at old familiar passages differently and study some obscure ones for the first time. Use it as an opportunity for the Holy Spirit to speak to you while exploring your personal interests.

To conclude the study, you might consider summary questions such as these:

- Has my view of mountains changed?
- Has my view of God changed?
- Has my view of myself changed? While we tend to think

of "mountaintop experiences" as high points of life, events that happened on biblical mountains were often difficult. Mountains are beautiful monuments to our Creator. They're also places where God has met people. Now when you experience "mountain peaks," do so more expectantly, seeking God and anticipating significant change in the process.

• What lessons have these passages shown me? After studying different mountains in the Bible, you'll realize that the God of those mountains is also the God of the individual.

Method Seven: Meeting Jesus

Most Christians want to be close with Jesus, so why can such a worthy goal cause so much frustration? It's hard to become personal with someone whose face we haven't seen, whose voice we haven't heard, and whose hand we haven't touched.

Encountering Jesus through Bible study can help us know him more intimately. All we really need is the Gospels; however, a Bible atlas and a gospel synopsis or harmony (a book that presents the texts of Matthew, Mark, and Luke in parallel columns) might add meaning.

Jump into Jesus' Ministry

Select a passage from one of the Gospels—one of the self-contained sections typically separated by headings. The book of Mark is a good place to start because it leaps right into Jesus' ministry. Then follow these steps:

Read the passage through once. This will help you become familiar with the background and setting. As you read, jot down some basic information: Where is Jesus? Record the town, if it's mentioned, as well as the specific location, such as the synagogue, a mountaintop, on the lake, or in someone's home. If you have time, and if the event you choose occurs in more than one gospel, use the synopsis or your Bible's cross-references to read all versions of the incident.

Determine the background of this event. This will help you put Jesus' words and actions into context.

- Where had Jesus been just before this event? Where did he go after this? Using a Bible atlas, locate the places Jesus visited. You won't always be able to discover this information, but when you can, it will help you see the extent of his travels.
- Now imagine his physical and emotional circumstances. Would he be tired, hungry, sweaty, refreshed, encouraged, discouraged, or excited?
- Consider the people who were with Jesus. Is he in a crowd or with an intimate circle of friends? Are the people Gentiles or Jews, common people or leaders? If they're Jews, are they followers of Jesus, friends, or antagonists? To what sect do they belong?

Summarize or quote what Jesus says. Also consider what Jesus doesn't say, but be careful not to put your own ideas into his silence. For example, in all three gospel accounts of Jesus casting demons out of a man (or men, as recorded in Matthew) and into a herd of pigs, the people plead with Jesus to leave them (see Mt. 8:28-34; Mk. 5:1-17; Lk. 8:26-37). No one mentions if Jesus answers them — he simply gets into his boat and leaves. What might he have said?

Note his feelings, tone, and attitude. These help us relate to Jesus on a human level. For example, look at the times Jesus is amazed, angry, distressed, or compassionate. See how he rebukes (see Mk. 3:12), orders (see 5:43), strongly warns (see 1:43), and exhorts (see 5:36).

Observe how he responds to people. Does he grant their requests? Does he answer their questions? Does he act or react to people?

Consider people's impressions of Jesus. Don't limit this to human dialogue. God, Satan, and the demons also talk to or about Jesus, and what they say helps us understand him better. How do they feel about Jesus? Does he surprise, entertain, or anger them? Who do they think he is? What do they call him? Where do they think he gets his power? Often these impressions are stated directly, but sometimes you may have to read between the lines.

Look for how people respond. After their encounter with Jesus, what do people do? Do they follow him? Laugh at him? Ask him to leave? Plot to kill him? Everyone who meets Jesus responds to him in some way. Evaluate whether the people you're observing respond appropriately or surprisingly. What can you conclude? How else could they have responded?

Your Impressions of Jesus

The final questions guiding this study focus on application. After working through the eight steps, you might find that your impressions of Jesus have changed. Sometimes you might feel confused by Jesus. Other times you could be drawn to him. You might even find yourself frustrated by some of his actions. Does he ever make you want to leave him? In response, ask the following questions.

How has your impression changed? Is your impression of Jesus different from how you used to think about him? Share your feelings about Jesus with him.

How will you respond to Jesus? No one meets Jesus and remains the same. By this point in your study, a personal application might already be obvious. If not, review your notes, praying for insight as you do. What characteristic of Jesus' life would you like to see more of in your own life? Did the people's responses to Jesus convict or inspire you? How can you worship, witness, or minister more effectively because of your encounter with Jesus? Ask yourself, *What is Jesus saying in this passage that could change my life, and how can I work with him to make it happen?*

For example, after reading in Mark about Jesus putting aside his plans to listen to and care for the people who constantly interrupted him, we might realize how our own frustrations with interruptions prevent God from using us to serve other people. We need to repent of this selfish attitude and allow the Lord to make us more open to the interruptions some call "divine appointments."

Once you're committed to applying what in the passage the Holy Spirit has taught you, end your study time by thanking Jesus for what you've learned from him and what you appreciate about him. Or tell him what questions you still have or what about him confuses or disturbs you.

Method Eight: Answering Questions Jesus Asked

Jesus often asked questions as he taught. When you study the Gospels, you might discover that these questions make great material for group or individual Bible study. Most of Jesus' questions fall into one of three categories:

1. **Questions that validate his teaching.** Jesus asked questions to prove that what he said actually made sense. In Matthew 6:25, Jesus made the statement, "Do not worry about your life." To validate this teaching, he followed it with a series of questions: "Isn't life more important than food and clothes?" "Aren't you more valuable than the birds?" "Can worry add a single hour to your life?" When we honestly answer these questions, we'll find we agree with Jesus' original statement. Other examples of validating questions appear in Luke 6:27-32 and 9:23-25.

2. Questions that challenge false ideas. Just as we do, Jesus lived in a religious culture where false ideas flourished. He challenged these ideas by asking questions. In Luke 13:1-2, Jesus challenged a common understanding of suffering. Many people thought that suffering was a result of sin (see Jn. 9:2). Following a tragedy involving some Galileans, Jesus challenged that assumption by asking, "Do you think that these Galileans were worse sinners than all the other Galileans because they suffered this way?" (Lk. 13:2). His question forced listeners to reconsider their views. You'll find other examples of challenging questions in Matthew 15:1-3 and 16:13-15. These questions confront our traditional, and sometimes wrong, views of God.

3. Questions that deepen faith. Jesus often set up a miracle with a question, such as, "Do you want to get well?" (Jn. 5:6). It seems like a crazy thing to ask. Yet in this situation, maybe Jesus wanted to force the man to think about what was truly important. Or maybe it was to help the disabled man deepen his faith in Jesus.

Jesus also asked faith-building questions after episodes that showed a lack of faith. In Matthew 14:31, for example, Jesus rescued Peter from his water walk and then asked, "Why did you doubt?" That question had to ring in Peter's ears for the rest of his life and probably helped him through difficult situations.

WORKING QUESTIONS INTO BIBLE STUDY

How can we work Jesus' questions into a Bible study? For both individual and group studies, you can use this tactic:

Find a question of Jesus. In the Sermon on the Mount alone, Jesus asked at least a dozen. At the end of this section, you'll find twenty questions to get you started.

Identify the question. After selecting a question, determine whether it's a validating question, challenging question, or faith-deepening question. Sometimes a question will fall into more than one category.

Analyze the context of the question. Zero in on Jesus' purpose by addressing the following issues:

- For *validating* questions, find the statement being validated. List possible objections to the statement, and then describe how the objections are resolved.
- For *challenging* questions, identify the false ideas being challenged. Discuss the reasons for these false ideas. Then you'll see the clearer understanding Jesus gave.
- For *faith-deepening* questions, determine the context of the question and the question's significance. Finally, ask how the question elicits or deepens faith.

In a group study, you can choose one of two routes. For a structured study, the leader can select a question for study, ask group members to answer the questions in advance, and write discussion topics to bring to the study. In a more relaxed group, you might want to let members choose a question on the spot and then answer the questions together.

Concluding with Prayer

After you've worked through the steps, close your study with prayers that relate to the issues you have discussed.

- For *validating* questions, pray that God will help you clearly see the spiritual reasons behind Jesus' teachings.
- For *challenging* questions, ask God to help you understand him based on truth, not false assumptions.
- For *faith-deepening* questions, ask God to help your faith

grow. Ask him to help you recognize that you can experience abundant life only through him.

Twenty Questions from Jesus

Here are some questions to get you started. Classify each as a validating, challenging, or faith-deepening question. Some fall into more than one category.

1. "Why do you look at the speck of sawdust in someone else's eye and pay no attention to the plank in your own eye?" (Mt. 7:3, TNIV)
2. "Which of you, if your son asks for bread, will give him a stone?" (Mt. 7:9, TNIV)
3. "Who is my mother, and who are my brothers?" (Mt. 12:48)
4. "How long shall I put up with you?" (Mt. 17:17)
5. "Which is greater: the gold, or the temple that makes the gold sacred?" (Mt. 23:17)
6. "How many loaves do you have?" (Mk. 8:5)
7. "Who do you say I am?" (Mk. 8:29)
8. "Why do you call me good?" (Mk. 10:18)
9. "Why are you bothering her?" (Mk. 14:6)
10. "Why have you forsaken me?" (Mk. 15:34)
11. "If you love those who love you, what credit is that to you?" (Lk. 6:32)
12. "Why do you call me, 'Lord, Lord,' and do not do what I say?" (Lk. 6:46)
13. "Were not all ten cleansed?" (Lk. 17:17)
14. "What do you want me to do for you?" (Lk. 18:41)
15. "Did not the Christ have to suffer these things and then enter his glory?" (Lk. 24:26)
16. "Will you give me a drink?" (Jn. 4:7)

17. "You do not want to leave too, do you?" (Jn. 6:67)
18. "Woman, where are they?" (Jn. 8:10)
19. "Are there not twelve hours of daylight?" (Jn. 11:9)
20. "Shall I not drink the cup the Father has given me?" (Jn. 18:11)

Method Nine: The Commands of Christ

Sometimes we wish the Bible told us exactly what we should do. Actually, sometimes it does! We can discover commands that come directly from Jesus' lips.

A careful reading of the Gospels will unearth a wealth of clear commands that bring stability, direction, and fulfillment to our lives. In fact, the NT is emphatic about knowing and following Christ's commands. Keeping his commands is the strongest evidence of knowing (see 1 Jn. 2:3-6), following (see Jn. 8:31), and loving (see Jn. 14:15,21-24) Christ. Even more, rejecting Jesus' commands brings judgment (see Mt. 7:21-23; Jn. 12:48). The Master said, "Therefore everyone who hears these words of mine and puts them into practice is like a wise man who built his house on the rock" (Mt. 7:24).

When we study and obey Jesus' commands, our intimacy with him grows stronger as we hear him speaking again and again to the issues of life. Knowing and obeying the will of our Lord will invigorate our spiritual lives.

RECORDING THE COMMANDS

How can we study the commands of Jesus? First, make a reasonable plan for reviewing each gospel. Consider the amount of time you can devote to the study and divide each gospel into manageable segments. If you're studying Jesus' commands in a small group, you might want to assign different portions of a gospel to each person.

We can find Jesus' commands in any verse that says what should or shouldn't be done, thought, said, or allowed. As you read the words of Christ, list each command and its reference on a page. Some people also like to highlight Jesus' commands in the text of their Bibles or on a printout from their Bible software.

STUDYING THE COMMANDS

After you've recorded the commands from a chapter or section, reread the verses around each one to be sure you're interpreting Jesus' command in context. Keep in mind the principles and tools for correct Bible study that we covered in chapters 3, 4, and 5, and then consider these questions:

- What topics does the command address?
- How does the context shed light on the command?
- How did the command challenge the original audience?
- What timeless principles does this command incorporate?
- What is the command telling me, and how should I apply it?
- Are there related passages?

You might want to create a chart that lists some or all of these questions to help focus your study. You can jot down short phrases or longer notes for each command using these questions as headings.

CATEGORIZING THE COMMANDS

After you've listed the commands and studied them, group them into categories, such as warnings, beliefs, discipleship, humility, forgiveness, the Holy Spirit, and endurance.

You might also want to break some categories into subcategories. For example, subcategories under the topic of love might include love of God, people, self, enemies, and fellow believers. These subcategories can serve as a reference tool for further study themes.

APPLYING THE COMMANDS TO LIFE

Before finishing the study, decide on a personal response to what Jesus has commanded. Consider what changes in your life are necessary to obey each command. Here are several ways to match your life with the will of God as you apply his commands.

Pray for the Holy Spirit to counsel, teach, and remind you to obey Christ's commands. Jesus said this was one of the primary roles of the Holy Spirit. "The Counselor, the Holy Spirit, whom the Father will send in my name, will teach you all things and will remind you of everything I have said to you" (Jn. 14:26).

Memorize commands that correct or encourage you. Post them in visible places in your home or car so you can reflect on them often.

Review your life by comparing it to each category. Are you truly pleasing God, or are you deceiving yourself (see Mt. 7:21-24; see Jas. 1:22-25)? Would your spouse, children, friends, neighbors, or coworkers agree or disagree? Do you dare ask them?

Choose a command you struggle with. Develop an action plan to obey it. Write down your plan and share it with a friend who can help keep you accountable.

Confess sin as necessary (see 1 Jn. 1:9). This study on Jesus' commands will probably uncover some shortcomings. Your repentance and confession will bring spiritual healing and increase your intimacy with the Lord.

Evaluate your life regularly in light of your findings (see Ps. 26:2; 139:23-24). If you keep the results of your study in a notebook, your summary will help you keep an ongoing spiritual inventory.

Christians should be captivated by the promises, deeds, and love of Christ. However, we can't neglect his commands, which are also expressions of his love for us. While some ask, "What would Jesus do?" it's more crucial to ask what *we* should do. No substitute exists for finding the answers in the directions that he's given us in his Word. As we obey them, we will find stability, fulfillment, and joy.

Method Ten: What Does Jesus Say "Amen" About?

Remember the childhood rhyme "Cross my heart, hope to die, stick a needle in my eye"? With these words, kids promised to tell the truth. Making an *X* over their heart after uttering the words emphasized the commitment. Adults have other phrases, such as "Swear on a stack of Bibles," "Swear on my mother's grave," and "Scout's honor" to confirm the truthfulness of our words.

The OT used the word *amen* often (for example, Dt. 27 uses it repeatedly), and Jesus used it to underscore some of his statements. The double use of the word—"amen, amen"—occurs twenty-five times in the gospel of John (though not in the other gospels). Taken from the Hebrew language, the phrase has been translated a variety of ways. The KJV translates it "verily, verily." Both the RSV and the NASB translate the double amen as "truly, truly," while the NIV renders it, "I tell you the truth." Other variations include "most assuredly," "very truly," or "I tell you for certain." *The Message*, though it doesn't translate the phrase consistently, uses many interesting options: "Take it from me," "It's urgent that you get this right," "I say this with absolute confidence," "Believe me," and, "The truth is . . ."

When Jesus said, "Amen, amen" (however we translate it), he emphasized the authority of his teaching by reminding listeners that his words were true and reliable. He proclaimed the truth and he was the embodiment of that truth. Truth matters because each of us lives according to what we believe to be true. If we make decisions based on something untrue, we'll reap the consequences of that error.

The idea of absolute truth isn't a popular concept today. In a postmodern era, subjectivism, pluralism, and relativism often push any notion of truth aside. Because much of the world operates without any regard for truth, we must examine what Jesus said was true.

By studying his "amen, amen" sayings, Jesus will remind us of some unchanging realities of our world. We can study and reflect on these teachings with a three-step process. Here's how to conduct an "amen, amen" study from the book of John:

1. **Identify the truth statement.** Choose one of the twenty-five passages that Jesus begins with the words "amen, amen" (see Jn. 1:51; 3:3,5,11; 5:19,24-25; 6:26,32,47,53; 8:34,51,58; 10:1,7; 12:24; 13:16,20-21,38; 14:12; 16:20,23; 21:18). After reflecting on the passage, identify the truth of Jesus' words. What does he say is true? Pay careful attention to the context of Jesus' statement.

2. **Determine how this truth affects your life.** Knowing a truth isn't enough; we must change our lives through practical and concrete steps. How would your life be different if this "truth" was "true for you"? Write down what you discover. While many of these passages are well-known, don't ignore their truths simply because they're familiar.

3. **Identify the world's lie.** Jesus' words reveal the lies of the Devil and the world. Almost all of the "amen, amen" statements have a corresponding lie that the world seeks to defend. Just as Jesus reveals the truth, Satan does his best to make us believe a lie. When you reflect on truth, these lies will become clear. Write down the lie that the truth in each passage uncovers so you can remember it when Satan tempts you.

Here is how this might look for one of the "amen, amen" sayings.

"Amen, Amen" Saying: "Very truly, I tell you, servants are not greater than their master, nor are messengers greater than the one who sent them." (Jn. 13:16, NRSV)

Truth Statement: Because Jesus served, and he is greater than we are, we should imitate his example by serving others.

Lifestyle Decision: I need to look for avenues to serve. Spiritual leadership includes a willingness to meet others' needs in submissive, humble ways.

World's Lie: Leadership isn't about serving others; it's about being served. As a leader, I shouldn't have to perform acts of service that are below me.

The truth frees and empowers us to live the kind of life that pleases God. Jesus said, "Then you will know the truth, and the truth will set you free" (Jn. 8:32).

Method Eleven: Studying Spiritual Fruit

You're probably familiar with Galatians 5:22-23. In it, Paul describes what a fruitful life looks like: "The fruit of the Spirit is love, joy, peace, patience, kindness, goodness, faithfulness, gentleness, and self-control."

As followers of Jesus, we want to see these qualities in our lives more and more, but it's easy to sprint through the passage, barely noticing what they mean. We pray, "I'm not doing too badly on self-control this week, but I am kind of low on patience and gentleness. I guess I need to get more of them. Lord, please make me more patient and gentle today. Amen." Then we leave our Bibles beside our empty coffee mugs and set off on our busy days, no more patient or gentle than we were before our time in the Word.

It's possible, though, to approach the fruit of the Spirit in a way that brings these traits to our lives. We can let our thoughts linger on each character attribute Paul mentions. We can delight in the fruit of the Spirit. This could be a nine-day project if we pick a fruit a day.

FRUITFUL CHARACTER BUILDERS

Savor the Spirit's fruit by following these steps:

1. **Pick a fruit of the Spirit.** Prayerfully select the spiritual quality that's most lacking in your life or that you want to focus on, or just work through the list in order.

2. **Define its meaning.** Using an ordinary English dictionary, look up the "fruit" you're studying and record its definition and characteristics. A Bible dictionary might give additional insight.

3. **Identify synonyms and antonyms.** Using a thesaurus, look up the word you're studying (say it's *joy*) and write down other words that mean the same thing. Now identify the antonyms to the fruit you're studying. Antonyms can give you better understanding of a word because sometimes we understand a concept most clearly by identifying what it isn't. For example, the antonym of *joy* is *sorrow*.

4. **Identify related words.** These will come from the dictionary, a thesaurus, and resources such as Willem A. Van Gemeren, ed., *New International Dictionary of Old Testament Theology and Exegesis* and C. Brown, ed., *New International Dictionary of New Testament Theology*. For example, *rejoice, rejoices, rejoicing, rejoiced, joyous,* and *joyful* are all related to *joy*. A study of *joy* wouldn't be complete without examining related words.

5. **Look up Scripture passages that include the word.** You'll need a concordance for this. You might also want to look up all (or a representative sample of) the verses that include the synonyms, antonyms, and other words related to that fruit. Write down the verses that are significant to you. This should give a broad perspective of what the Bible teaches about the character trait. Take your time with this step. Remember, you want to savor the fruit. Be sure you understand each verse in light of its context so you're not mixing apples and oranges (pun intended).

6. Write down your observations. Consider the following questions:

- How do I see this quality in God?
- Why is this quality important to God, others, and me?
- How can I cultivate this quality in myself?
- What would hinder the growth of this quality?
- What biblical character shows me what this quality looks like in real life?
- What is a key verse about this quality?

After you think about these questions, you might find that you want to rewrite your definition of the fruit based on what you've learned.

7. Write a summary with a personal application plan. What are the core elements that grow out of your study? How can you make this attribute more central in your life? Summarize what you've discovered into a few sentences that can motivate you to put the truths you've learned into practice.

8. Memorize a key verse. Memorization will allow the Holy Spirit to bring this quality to mind at appropriate times in the future. Eventually, you'll see God working more and more of this fruit into your life.

9. Choose another fruit. Now that you've finished studying one fruit, it's time to study another. Repeat the process until you've studied all nine.

When you come to Galatians 5:22-23 in the future you'll linger there, recalling the sweet flavors of the attributes of God, amazed that the Holy Spirit is cultivating these choice fruits in you.

Method Twelve: Paraphrase Makes Personal

"Practice makes perfect," the saying goes. How about another: "Paraphrase makes personal"? One way to give new life to your time with the Bible is to paraphrase verses to make them more personal to you. Paraphrasing allows you to see the Scriptures from a new perspective.

Here's a step-by-step method for personalizing Scripture through paraphrase.

WRITING YOUR PARAPHRASE

To select a section to paraphrase, consider the following:

- Has a particular verse (or sentence, if it includes more than a single verse) been appearing often in your life? Perhaps it addresses an issue God wants you to consider.
- Has a theme emerged in your life recently? Is there a text that captures that theme well?
- Choose a verse or passage that's been comforting or meaningful to you.
- Select a text related to a personal struggle, such as anger, worry, pride, or temptation.
- Look through the list of words in an abridged concordance, perhaps the one in the back of your Bible. When a particular subject grabs your attention, choose a verse related to it.

Once you've chosen a verse, here's what to do:

1. **Proceed with caution.** As you paraphrase a particular passage of the Bible, be sure to employ what you've learned about studying God's Word so you restate it accurately. Also, pray that you'll know and experience the truth of his Word more intimately. The purpose of paraphrasing God's Word is to apply what God has said to your

situation, not to change the meaning of Scripture so that you like it better!

2. **Read the verse slowly several times.** Pay attention to the way it naturally breaks into words and phrases. Write one word or phrase per line in a notebook and then skip two or three lines to allow room for your paraphrase.

3. **Begin paraphrasing by rewriting each phrase using your own words.** As you do this, personalize the verse to fit your situation. For example, when you see the words *you* or *we* in reference to an individual Christian or God's people, substitute your name or the name of your church. When you come across general words such as *trial* or *sin* that relate to your circumstances, use specific terms to describe what you're facing.

As you personalize your verse, use appropriate synonyms where you want to replace a word. If you're not sure how to restate something, check a thesaurus. Make sure the words flow from one line to the next. You want your final paraphrase to read as a complete thought, not a group of unconnected words and phrases.

4. **Meditate on the facets of truth you've discovered.** Ask God to show you what he wants you to learn and how to apply it to your life.

Method Thirteen: Comparing Stories

Are you looking for meaningful ways to understand and deal with situations in your life? Maybe you're in a rut and your life feels colorless and barren. Maybe you've experienced a lot of change and you feel overwhelmed or lost. Maybe you want to start a new ministry or a new business and you need courage and insight.

We all like stories, and the Bible contains many good ones. Comparing the Bible's stories to our own stories can spice up our study. Connecting your personal story to a Bible story can empower you to continue in a God-honoring way.

STUDYING YOUR STORY

We always carry our own stories with us in all we do, but we're not always intentional about using our current situation to structure our study of the Bible. Bringing your own feelings and situation to the Bible can be like looking in a mirror: You see yourself and your situation more clearly and get a better idea of what direction to take.

Use the following steps to study your own story:

1. **Reflect on your situation and seek a corresponding biblical story.** Ask yourself:

- What am I feeling?
- What are the questions my situation brings to mind?
- What biblical story or character involved a similar situation?
- What about my story parallels issues or concerns in a biblical story?

For example, maybe you're leading a group or ministry and you feel lost and confused. You could study Moses leading God's people through the wilderness in Exodus. If you're in a stormy situation, choose Jesus calming the storm in one of the Gospels. Many stories in the Bible can help us see God's touch on our lives.

To select an appropriate story, use one from the list on page 273 or think of another one that might have some connections to your situation.

2. **Read your chosen story slowly, reflecting on it.** Then ask more questions:

- What's the problem in the story?
- How is it similar to my situation? How is it different?
- How do the characters react to the problem?

- Is their reaction similar to mine, or am I reacting differently? If so, why?
- Do the outcomes in the story reflect good or bad choices by the characters?
- Is God present in the story? If so, what's he doing? Is he providing something? Is he fulfilling a promise? Is he guiding the characters in a new direction? Is he at work behind the scenes?
- How does God's action in the story relate to what he might do in my life? Has he made promises I can rely on? Is he leading me in a new direction?

3. **Let the story simmer slowly in the back of your mind between readings.** You might need to come back to it after several days of reflection. Let your story and the Bible story intermingle. You might take an hour on consecutive Sunday afternoons for the same story.

4. **Ask God to speak to you from the Bible story as it simmers in your mind.** Write down how the story applies to your life and how God might be directing you in this situation.

Sarah's Example of Barrenness

Consider this example of comparing stories. Imagine that life seems monotonous to you. Because everything looks gray and barren, you choose the story of Abraham and Sarah (see Gen. 11:30; 15:4-6; Gen. 16). Their story is symbolic of your problem. They were past the years of bearing children, so they thought they would never have a child to fulfill the promise God made to them.

Their situation looked hopeless. In fact, they concocted a solution themselves: Abraham would sleep with Sarah's servant Hagar to produce the child of the promise. It wasn't a smart plan. Ask, *What's hopeless about my situation? Have I tried to devise my own solutions? Have I tried some, only to see them fail?*

Next, think about Sarah. She actually laughed to herself when she heard the Lord say she would bear a child. Sarah was a skeptic. But God accepted her feelings, even though she lied and said she didn't laugh. How do you feel about God delivering you from your situation? Do you doubt that he cares? You can share your feelings honestly with the Lord.

God made Abraham and Sarah a promise. The promise came true. God makes promises that you can rely on. In Psalm 91, for example, God promises to protect and deliver his people. In Lamentations 3:22, we find the promises that the Lord's love never ceases and his mercies never end. God will never abandon his people (see Heb. 13:5).

No one expected Sarah to have a child at her age, yet God brought new life into a situation that was hopeless. Can you name expectations in your situation? Do your expectations come from your own resources? Can you hold your barrenness up to God and let him bring you surprising new life, whatever that might look like?

This particular story can be helpful in times of emptiness, separation from family and friends, and illness or when deciding on a new course of action. God can use it to give new perspective, hope, and direction for dealing with challenging situations, even when the way forward doesn't involve a miracle as it did with Sarah. Other Bible stories can help in different ways. Let them speak into your life. Here are several other stories you could consider, depending on your life's storyline at the moment.

1. Jacob's Dream at Bethel (Gen. 28:10-22)
   - When you wonder where God is
   - In times of exile
2. Joseph Interprets Dreams in Prison (Gen. 39:20–41:40)
   - When you feel trapped

- During hard times
- When you wonder if it's worth being faithful to God
3. Elijah and the Famine (1 K. 17:1-16)
   - When you hunger for something
   - When in need
4. Nehemiah Rebuilds the Wall (Neh. 2:1-20)
   - When you face a difficult challenge
   - When you're trying to rebuild amidst opposition
5. Esther Intercedes (Est. 4:4–5:2)
   - When you need courage and strength
6. Jesus Tempted in the Desert (Mt. 4:1-11)
   - When tempted
   - When you question your motivation
7. The Gerasene Demoniac (Mk. 5:1-20)
   - When you feel fragmented or pulled in many directions
8. A Storm at Sea (Lk. 8:22-25)
   - During a turbulent period
   - When you need a fresh glimpse of who Jesus is
9. Jesus Heals a Blind Man (Lk. 18:35-43)
   - When you can't see clearly
   - When you need mercy
10. Elijah's Victory over the Priests of Baal (1 K. 18:20-40)
    - During spiritual dryness
    - When God seems powerless in your life

Method Fourteen: Reflective Journaling in Bible Study

We all have different learning styles, so different approaches to Bible study can help us. We also need variety to stay fresh and to open ourselves up to new insights. One way to do this is through reflective writing. Written meditation in God's presence is a way to keep track of what you discover as God reveals himself and his truth. Putting your thoughts into writing makes you think more reflectively and concretely. Sometimes you find out what you think only when you put general impressions into words.

You might decide to keep your meditations in bound journals, which can be an excellent way to track your spiritual journey. Other systems might work better for you, such as using a spiral notebook or entering text in a word-processing document on your computer. No matter how much time you devote to reflective writing, each meditation is worth keeping. Over the years, you'll be amazed how clearly God communicates when you make yourself available to him, taking time to focus on Scripture and being receptive to his truth.

LEARNING TO WRITE REFLECTIVELY

During a quiet time for your reflective study, imagine sitting at Jesus' feet as Mary did (see Lk. 10:39) while he talks to you. Of course, this can work for any portion of the Bible, not only where Jesus actually speaks. Here's how it can work.

1. **Prepare a spiritual journal to hold your meditations and other entries.** Choose one of the following suggestions or another system that works for you:

- Blank journals. Use a journal you can set up chronologically; it will help you track your spiritual journey.
- Three-ring notebooks. These can be divided according to the book or topic of study. Supplemental materials can easily be inserted anywhere.
- File folders, or folders on your computer. Like ringed notebooks, these give you the flexibility of arranging your meditations in ways that work best for you. You can print out typed meditations and file them for future use.

2. **Set aside at least thirty minutes of uninterrupted time.** If you can devote more time, whether every day or periodically, that will be even more productive.

3. **Select a passage (perhaps a chapter or more) for your reflection.**

4. **Read the passage and mark it.** Highlight words or phrases that stand out. It's also good to make notes in your journal to remind you of your first impressions of the text.

5. **Handwrite or print out the part of the passage you want to focus on.** A particular portion of a chapter or book may stand out for some reason. Allow plenty of space in the margins and between lines so you can respond in writing. If you have a computerized Bible program, you might want to print out the text you're studying with generous margins rather than marking up your Bible.

6. **For ten minutes, respond on paper to what's in the passage.** Simply write your thoughts. This isn't structured writing. Don't edit or delete insights, questions, problems, or tangents that seem to be off track. Write down everything; even draw diagrams or pictures if that helps.

7. **Write a summary of what you learned.** This is the place to organize your thoughts. Don't be overly concerned about the structure. Write down what you're thinking as you reflect on the overall effect of the passage.

8. **Include creative writing ideas or topics for later use.** After completing the previous steps, you might want to write a poem, song, or creative essay in response to what God shows you. Or maybe your meditation caused something to surface and you need to research answers. It might lead to a more in-depth type of Bible study. Include in your notebook either your piece of writing or what you plan to research.

9. **Be receptive to God's truth.** In the days following your meditation on a passage, be open to what God will show you that

emphasizes his truth and its meaning for your life. As this happens, add it to your journal. You might collect news articles, magazine pictures, sermon notes, quotes, and even cartoons to add to your notebook or file folder. These are important connections to what God is teaching you. Poetry, essays, and other projects might emerge from your meditations. They become living documents and commentaries on your life. As you continue to build your journal, God can take you even deeper into the meaning of the passages to bless you repeatedly.

Method Fifteen: *Lectio Divina*

An ancient use of the Bible, *lectio divina* (sacred reading), puts readers into a different position than many other types of Bible study. With *lectio divina*, you make a conscious effort to allow the text itself to guide your study so that your main concern is no longer the human author or what the author intended the text to mean. Under the prayerful guidance of the Holy Spirit, you adopt a meditative stance and allow the text to shape and move you. You might find this a useful complement to other kinds of study.

Imagine sitting under a gentle waterfall on a hot afternoon as the cooling waters wash over you. Now imagine the Holy Spirit pouring the Word of God over you—cooling and refreshing but also urging and inviting. With *lectio divina*, you put yourself into the text while the Spirit uses it to speak to you beyond or in addition to how God speaks when you study the Bible in more cognitive ways.

The church historically used four steps or stages of the *lectio divina* process: *lectio, meditatio, oratio,* and *contemplatio.* Translated from Latin, they mean reading, meditation, a response in prayer, and contemplation—rest in God's presence. You might want to return to our discussion of meditation and contemplation in chapter 4 for further insight on these steps.

Set aside a half an hour in a quiet place where you won't be interrupted. Bring your Bible and sit in a comfortable position. Pick a text—a gospel section is a good place to start—that will serve as the basis for your "divine reading." You might try the story of Jesus visiting Martha and Mary in Luke 10:38-42, or Psalm 131, but any Bible passage can work for *lectio divina*.

1. **Reading.** Read slowly, reflectively, and attentively. Listen to what the text says about your life. Pay attention to words that stick out, any ideas the text triggers, and thoughts and feelings that emerge. Try imagining yourself as one or more of the participants.

While this reading acknowledges the value of more critical kinds of study, for this exercise don't expend energy figuring out what the text means. The goal of *lectio divina* is to guide you to a prayerful approach to Scripture. Your main goal isn't critical study but the text's significance for your life.

2. **Meditation.** Slowly read through the text again. Then meditate on what you observed in the first reading and what was confirmed or added in your second reading. How does the passage address your motivations, feelings, thoughts, and heart? Spend five to ten minutes prayerfully reflecting on what the Holy Spirit says to you through the text as you spend time with him. Ponder the words. Go back and memorize one of the verses if you feel led to do that. This is the stage where you consider the significance of the text for your own life.

3. **Prayer.** If you'd like, read the text a third time in a more prayerful mode. The progression from meditation to prayer isn't clear-cut, and you don't want to think of the process of *lectio divina* as a rigid progression of steps. The goal is to connect with God through his Word, not to follow the "steps" in the correct way. Moving from meditation to prayer comes naturally. In meditation, you deeply engage a passage of Scripture, and this personal engagement leads to prayer. Speak the Word to God as he has spoken words

to you. How is God calling you to respond to the passage? Speak to him about it.

4. **Contemplation.** Here you can reread the passage or simply enter a time of rest after your prayer. Allow God's Spirit freedom to connect you to the Lord without words. It's God's work to make his Word live in you. Remain open to God's communication. Rest without effort in God's presence, trusting that all God wants is your willingness to receive him and his purposes for you.

At the same time, God might impress you with insights or actions that stand out — that pull your heart in certain directions. Perhaps these insights or sensations arose during your time of meditation. Perhaps God's Spirit channeled your prayers in certain directions. Now as you contemplate your experience of *lectio divina* (this sacred reading of his Word) and prepare to return to life's daily activities, God might well communicate words of encouragement and even direction. Take in those divine words with gratitude for God's active presence in your life.

IN-DEPTH BIBLE STUDY METHODS

The following in-depth list includes methods you can use when you have more time or when you want to continue a study over days or weeks. Some of them work well during a time of personal retreat, whether for a full day or over several days or more. We'll look at seven methods: conducting a manuscript study, doing topical studies, finding truths from the OT, making the stories live, reading the Bible as literature, learning to avoid characters' mistakes, and completing a comprehensive book analysis.

Method One: Making Your Mark — Manuscript Study

In a manuscript study, you begin by turning the Bible passage you want to study into a manuscript you can mark up. You should consider a manuscript study if:

- You're looking for a fresh way to interact with a book of the Bible
- You're interested in finding patterns in Scripture
- You like using colors and other creative methods for your study

You'll need to decide in the beginning how much time to give to this study. You can use it individually or in a small group.

To begin, type (or import from your Bible software program) the passage you want to study. Format the pages using double- or triple-spacing and huge margins. Delete verse numbers, chapter numbers, paragraphing, and notes.

WALK THROUGH THE MANUSCRIPT

We'll use 2 Timothy as an example to illustrate a manuscript study for individual study. With a small group, you could take two weeks to complete a study of one section or a small book. Focus the first week on observations and questions the text raises. During the second meeting, discuss your answers and share significant lessons and personal applications. With your text printed out before you, follow these steps:

1. Read the entire text through three or four times over several days. On the second reading, start marking repeated words and phrases or other elements that stand out. Use colors, boxes, arrows, and other creative tactics to make connections and note patterns, repeated words, or themes.

2. By the third reading, your manuscript should be alive with color as you note themes, commands, key phrases, and more. You'd

hesitate to mark your Bible with total abandon, but when doing a manuscript study, you can be creative. For example, imagine using the following for 2 Timothy:

- Green circles for repeated words, such as *grace, ashamed, sound,* and *endure*
- Blue double-underscores to note one of the underlying themes (things we have in Christ, such as faith and love, grace, and salvation)
- Purple boxes to note another theme (our partnership with God in ministry)
- Yellow circles to note Paul's warnings (against fear, false teaching, the flesh, and fatigue)
- Red circles to mark references to the power and usefulness of God's Word
- Black circles for commands, such as "Fan into flame the gift of God" or "Do not be ashamed to testify" or "Present yourself to God as one approved"
- Orange boxes for descriptions of Paul's character and lifestyle (for example, he was a finisher, he wasn't ashamed of the gospel, he endured suffering, and he lived with purpose)
- Orange double-underscores to note words Paul used to describe himself (*apostle, servant, herald,* and *teacher*)
- A highlighter to mark key verses, or verses you want to memorize later

These techniques are only examples. Use any system that works for you. Different books will yield different treasures. Other features to note are comparisons and contrasts, cause-and-effect statements (look for "if . . . then" or "therefore"), key people, and statements of purpose ("in order that" or "so that").

3. Now read through the text again and make notes. For example:

- Jot down references to other parts of the Bible that come to mind.
- Write in the margin any observations or points of application. For example, where Paul writes, "I am not ashamed, because I know whom I have believed," you might note in the margin, "Paul's fearlessness isn't the result of confidence in himself but confidence in Christ. The cure for Timothy's shyness—and mine—is to focus on my all-powerful Savior."
- Look up in a Bible dictionary the meanings of any words that are new or unclear.
- Draw arrows or dotted lines to connect related ideas.
- Write in the margin any questions you have. For example, you might want to know who Jannes and Jambres were, as Paul spoke of them as opposing Moses. You might also ask, *What does this mean?* You'll try to answer those questions in step 4.

4. At this stage, you might want to read a commentary or check a few reference books for background information on the book, such as the cultural and historical setting. Try not to check the commentaries and references too early in your study. You don't want them to replace your personal study and discovery, but they'll give insight and information you can't discover in any other way. Write in the margins any insights you gain from this research. Also look for and record any answers to your "What does this mean?" questions.

5. It's often helpful to decide where you'd put the paragraph breaks. Sometimes we're so locked into existing chapter and verse divisions that we miss the crucial flow of thought from the end of

one chapter to the beginning of another. This process can reveal a flow and relationship of ideas and principles that you wouldn't otherwise notice.

6. In the end, personal change is the purpose of all this coloring, circling, and underlining. Your final question should be, *Lord, how do you want me to respond to this passage?* You might already know the answer, having spent days, weeks, or months on the study. Or you might need to let the study roll around in your head and heart for a few more days to discern what God is saying to you. Write down what you decide.

Consider telling a friend what you've learned, for accountability. Your application might require a change in behavior. It might require taking a step of faith, such as initiating a spiritual conversation with a friend or coworker. Perhaps God will tell you, "Write a letter to _____ and encourage her, as Paul did Timothy."

BOTH VERSATILE AND VALUABLE

You can use manuscript studies for personal insights and in small groups. Group members love seeing the creative ways others have marked their manuscripts. You'll find that the hands-on involvement with the text deeply impresses it on your brain and in your heart. No two studies are alike.

One helpful hint for using this method in small groups: Have one person produce and duplicate the master copy of the manuscript for others to use. Number the lines on each page. Because you're working without chapter and verse numbers, you'll need some way to direct each other within the text. Numbering each line accomplishes this.

Method Two: Doing Topical Studies

A topical study will help you study something that interests you. You'll make your own set of conclusions — even convictions — on the subject, complete with application to your own circumstances.

The first step in a topical study is choosing a good, manageable topic. Your topic might be one you've wanted to research for a long time. It might have come up as a side issue during another type of study, or maybe you heard a sermon that started you thinking on the subject. You might be mentoring someone who's asked you searching questions on a matter of importance and you want further insight.

Be careful of topics that are too broad, such as "love." If you're interested in something like that, you'll need to divide it into several studies, such as "The Nature of God's Love," "Human Love of God," or "Love of Neighbor" (or enemies).

SELECT THE SCRIPTURE PASSAGES

Once you've selected your topic, pick ten to twelve passages that address the topic most directly. Some passages include only a single verse, others a paragraph or maybe a whole chapter. A topical Bible or concordance—print or computer-based—will help you find the passages relating to your topic. Try to discover the key or central passages that address the topic. At some point, your study may become too broad or you might have too many passages to consider, so you'll need to set limits.

If your Bible has a subject index, you might find references on your topic listed there. The process of selecting the best passages will take some time as you look up and compare various Scriptures. Be patient; by choosing your best passages you'll have limits for your study and won't wander through the Bible searching for one more truth. Once you've listed your passages in your notebook or computer, jot down a key thought beside each one for quick identification.

SUMMARIZE OR OUTLINE THE PASSAGE

The Scriptures you've chosen and listed form the basis for the rest of your topical study. Using your skills of Bible analysis, summarize each passage separately. Then read your summaries several times, noting the main points the passages teach, how they fit together, and where they have different emphases.

On another page, summarize your summaries—condensing, rearranging, and combining where possible. This should be a compilation statement of what Scripture teaches on the topic. However, avoid making the main point of any of the passages less clear as you form a synthesis. Remember that each passage was written to make its own point under the Spirit's guidance.

You might prefer to put your findings in outline form once you've written your summaries. When you've rewritten the summary or outline to your satisfaction, copy it in final form in your study notebook.

Find a Key or Favorite Verse

As you read each passage for study, find one that seems to have the key point of what that passage teaches on this topic. Or simply choose the verse you like best. Record it under the heading "Key Verse" or "Favorite Verse." You might want to memorize this verse as a reminder of the topic.

Think of Topic Illustrations

The passages you select, as well as your summary or outline, might have some illustrations of the topic. If so, list them by Bible reference under the heading "Illustrations." For example, in a study on faith, you might use Abraham as an illustration, listing Hebrews 11:8-10 (actually, the point of Hebrews 11 is to provide multiple illustrations of faith).

You might also think of other illustrations from the Bible, your own life, nature, or the experiences of others.

WRITE AN ACTION APPLICATION

Review each of the passages you've studied, asking God to show you what you should apply to your life. First, write a brief statement of the truth you select for your application. Then add a brief statement about the need or condition in your life (your relationship to the Lord, or your relationship to others) that you want to change or improve because of what you discovered in this study.

Finally, record a simple plan of action you'll follow to help make the change in your life. This might include spending time in prayer about the need, memorizing a verse, making good on something, serving someone in need, or scheduling a special project. Although it's not always easy, this part causes excitement because you'll see the payoff of your study, and you see God use his Word to make changes in your life.

Method Three: Finding New Truths from Old Testament Books

An OT book study teaches important lessons from the Israelites as they encountered God many thousands of years ago. In the study, you'll focus on two qualities: God's character, and principles to live by. If your time is limited, however, you can study one of these aspects and leave the other for another time. However you approach the OT, you can find things you already knew as well as fresh insights in its pages. Here are the steps to follow.

STEP ONE: PICK A BOOK

Pick an OT book to study. One of the more action-packed books filled with events is a good place to start. Plan to read the book in segments, taking one to three chapters at a time.

STEP TWO: MAKE A CHART

Make a chart with the following headings across the top: Biblical Reference, Events, God's Character, Principles to Live By, and Application.

STEP THREE: LIST THE EVENTS

Make a list of the events in the book, being sure to write their references as you read about them. You might not want to write down minor events, just the detailed ones. For example, from Joshua 1:1-9, you might include the following:

- God commissioned Joshua to go in place of Moses to take possession of the Promised Land.
- The commission promised God's presence and that he would give them the Land.
- God told Joshua to keep the Law and meditate on it to bring success.

STEP FOUR: IDENTIFY GOD'S CHARACTER TRAITS

List God's character traits in the account as he interacts with people. What can you see about the nature of God—his heart, mind, and will? For example, again from Joshua 1:1-9, God makes promises, gives instructions, expects obedience, and understands his people's fears and addresses them.

STEP FIVE: TRACE THE PRINCIPLES

Trace the principles you discover when you read about the transactions between God and his people. What is a principle you could look for? Think of principles using these definitions: a rule of conduct, a primary law or truth, and the requirements and obligations of right actions. What can you learn from the book that provides guidance for how God's people should live? What actions please God? What conduct does God require or expect? What fundamental laws make life go well?

Try to discover principles that God wants you to pattern your life after. For example, when God speaks, we should listen and act on what he says. The Bible was written for our instruction; we're to follow it and cling to it for success in life.

STEP SIX: WRITE APPLICATIONS

Work to relate what you're reading to your personal life. In what specific ways can you incorporate the principles you discovered? When it's your conscious motivation, the Holy Spirit might speak to you about a specific circumstance in your life in which a principle from Scripture applies.

Write out your application and commit to doing something in response to God's leading. When the Bible events are so far away from your life, you might see only general ways of relating the passage to your life. List these, too. The purpose of this step is to note what God is trying to tell you.

STEP SEVEN: SUMMARIZE THE COMMENTS

When you've finished going through the entire book, review your notes. Reread your comments on the character of God and summarize them in a paragraph. Compile a list of the attributes of God that you found, and then review the principles you discovered. Which ones were found most often throughout the book? Which seem most important?

Finally, look for patterns in your applications. One point might stand out above all the others, or they might be leading to one specific need in your life.

If you tend to avoid studying the OT, this method might help, both in your daily study or during more extended times. It can help you get a better handle on the OT's content. In this way, its message can become relevant to your life as you see God's character throughout its pages and principles that relate to everyday life.

Method Four: Making the Stories Live

Rewriting a Bible story from a new viewpoint can bring fresh insight and make the story personal. Instead of just knowing facts about the story, you can feel it more intimately. Filtering it through your own mind, experiences, and imagination helps the narrative to emerge as a part of you.

You might find that this method boosts your devotional life. It puts the story into your mind in ways that other kinds of Bible study might not. Try the following steps.

Write Your Essay

Obviously, the first step is to write the story yourself. Follow these guidelines to bring out the writer in you:

1. **Choose your story.** Pick a Bible story you want to write about. You might want to start with a familiar story. Later you might choose a lesser-known story as a way to help you grasp its meaning.

2. **Read through the passage.** Do this enough times to familiarize yourself with the details. If possible, read it in several different translations to get a feel for the story behind the words.

3. **Investigate the background.** You might start with a study Bible and read over the notes carefully. Or use tools such as a Bible commentary or a Bible dictionary to dig deeper into the background of the story. Learn as many new things as you can about the characters, their situation, and the relevant customs of the time. Try to get a feel for life at the time of the narrative.

4. **Pick your viewpoint character.** Decide who will narrate the story. Choose a person who was there, but not the main

character. For example, in retelling the story of Jesus' crucifixion, you might make Pilate the narrator. In the Bible account, the narrator focuses mostly on Jesus and the Jews wanting to execute him. What was Pilate thinking beyond the few words recorded in the Gospels? What if *he* told the story?

5. **Write your story.** Begin to write from the viewpoint of the character you've chosen. Incorporate biblical facts and new things you've learned from your background study. You can write your essay as if it were a journal entry, a newspaper article, a letter, a play, an obituary (if applicable), or any other form of writing. Be creative and enjoy writing it.

ADDITIONAL GUIDELINES

As you write, keep these guidelines in mind:

1. **Take the pressure off yourself.** You don't have to be a professional writer to do this exercise. Everyone has an imagination. Use yours! No one has to see what you write.

2. **Stick to the facts.** The point of this method is to understand a familiar Bible story in a new, more intimate way, not to rearrange the facts to say something other than what God intended. Base your essay on the truth of God's Word. You can embellish the biblical account, but don't throw it out!

3. **Keep a flexible time limit.** You can finish your essay in thirty minutes or take thirty days. You can scribble something down and come back to it in a few days to refine your work, or you can think about the story for a week before you write anything. There's no right or wrong way; do what works for you.

When the essay's finished, you'll find you know your chosen story well because you've used your intellect, emotions, and imagination to compose it. Take some time to record insights you gain from this experience. Thank God for the new things you've learned and how his Word has influenced you on new levels. If you're feeling brave, share your story with others.

Rewriting a Bible story requires a level of study, thought, and creativity that could be draining if used all the time. But it's a great way to take a break, step back, and refresh your devotional life when you're in a slump. Try using this method as a good break or whenever you find yourself intrigued by a particular person or story in the Bible.

Can't decide on a story? Try one of these:

- The story of the Flood from the perspective of Noah's wife or one of his sons (see Gen. 6–8)
- The crossing of the Red Sea from the perspective of an Israelite child (see Ex. 14)
- The destruction of Jericho from the perspective of Rahab (see Josh. 2; 6)
- The story of David from the perspective of a Philistine soldier (see 1 Sam. 17)
- The story of David, Bathsheba, and Uriah from the perspective of Bathsheba (see 2 Sam. 11–12)
- The resurrection of Lazarus from the perspective of Lazarus or one of his sisters (see Jn. 11)
- The story of the Last Supper from the perspective of Judas (see Lk. 22)
- The story of Paul's conversion on the road to Damascus from the perspective of one of Paul's fellow travelers or Ananias (see Acts 9:1-18)

Method Five: Reading the Bible as Literature

Many Christians believe that the Bible is God's revelation to his people. It tells God's people what they need to know and how they should live. But people who pick it up for the first time find it very different from the guidebooks and manuals they usually use. The Bible doesn't give an indexed list of instructions dealing step-by-step with the issues of life, such as "This is what you should do if . . ." or "Here are eight criteria for finding a good church . . ." or "If you've come to Christ from a totally secular or unchurched background, your worldview now needs to change in these ways: . . ."

Instead, when we thumb through the Bible, we find different kinds of writings. What kind of a guidebook is this then? We soon discover it's a brilliant one! Through the various literary genres in the Bible, God has given us instruction, the story of his grand plan, inspirational examples of the faith and failure of his people, songs that help us express our deepest hurts and longings to God, and practical insight about living day to day with our lives centered around God and his purposes. Because the Bible uses various literary styles, we need to know how to read each type so we can better understand God's Word for our own situation.

In this section, we'll review several of the Bible's genres that we explored in chapter 5, and then see helpful ways Bible study can make the most of that genre's features. The following sections will help you study these genres:

- Narrative
- Poetry
- Wisdom Literature
- Parables
- Prophecy

Reading Biblical Narratives

The most common literary type in the Bible is the narrative. A narrative is a story—an account of something that happened in the past. Most of the OT consists of narratives, such as Genesis, Joshua, and

1 Samuel. In the NT, the Gospels and Acts are narrative texts.

In contrast to childhood stories such as *The Wizard of Oz* or novels such as *Moby-Dick*, Bible narratives are based in history and convey vital truth about God and his purposes. They are not merely fairy tales with a moral twist.

However, we can't reduce Bible narratives to mere history. They reveal God to us. The individual narratives combine to tell the story of God at work among his people: creating them, delivering them, teaching them, warning them, fighting for them, and showering them with his love and mercy. Ultimately, we could say that the Bible narratives tell us the story of redemption. They tell how a loving God saved his people from their awful plight. Jesus Christ is the centerpiece of this plan.

Each of the individual Bible stories communicates certain features of the grand narrative. They teach us lessons about God and life. But when looking for these lessons, we need to be careful not to read into them things that weren't intended. The following guidelines should help us discover truths in narrative texts.

1. **Read the whole story at least three times.** A basic familiarity with the story and its details is crucial to interpreting correctly. In the first reading, aim for a general appreciation for the story. In later readings, focus on finding some of the crucial elements of the story that are mentioned in the following paragraphs. Some Bible books, such as Genesis, hold many individual narratives. Be sure to read each passage in light of the entire book's story; however, the entire book of Ruth is one story.

2. **Identify the plot and the principal characters.** In reading any story, we naturally identify the characters and try to understand the plot. In many stories, after the characters are introduced, conflict emerges and a resolution follows. The story of Joseph (see Gen. 37–50) gives a good example of this pattern.

3. Learn about the historical setting. Because each biblical narrative took place in history, knowing the setting and circumstances of the narrative helps us better understand the story. Let's say you're reading Luke's account of Paul's ministry in Ephesus (see Acts 19). To gain a greater appreciation for the story, you'll want to learn something about the city of Ephesus, the worship of the goddess Artemis, and the nature of occult practices in that part of the ancient world. Bible encyclopedias and good commentaries are necessary for this part of the task.

4. Find the moral or other lessons the story teaches. Each biblical writer intentionally picked certain stories to narrate. That purpose often relates to telling truth about God, his plan of redemption, and how we're to live in relationship with God. As readers of the inspired text, we want to learn the author's purpose for writing it. What's the lesson to learn? Again, be sure you're discovering the author's purpose, not inserting your own.

For example, in John's account of the feeding of the five thousand (see Jn. 6:1-15), he ends the narrative by referring to this spectacular event as a "miraculous sign that Jesus did." This story shows that Jesus is indeed the Messiah, the Son of God (see 20:31). John points out that the crowds drew their own conclusion about Jesus as the Messiah that was different from what Jesus himself taught (see v. 15).

The narrative can also give additional truth about God and his purposes. However, we need to be careful not to overinterpret the passage. For example, the fact that Jesus used fish and bread when he fed the five thousand, or the number of fish and loaves (two and five), or even the fact that it was a small boy who originally provided the food that Jesus multiplied probably means very little. These details are simply parts of the story.

We can conclude, however, that Jesus cares about our physical well-being and can miraculously provide for us. Even more significant is Jesus' declaration of himself as "the bread of life" (Jn. 6:35) who "comes down from heaven and gives life to the world" (v. 33). Because of this, we need to put a much higher priority on obtaining "food that endures to eternal life" (v. 27). The bigger idea can provide important clues for interpreting the meaning and relevance. But we can't conclude that God will miraculously respond to our needs. Remember our distinction between what is descriptive and what is normative.

5. **Research what the rest of Scripture teaches about the lessons.** To check your interpretation, look for support elsewhere in Scripture. Commentaries might provide some aid in this; your own knowledge of Scripture will also help.

6. **Think about how the story contributes to the book's overall theme.** As we interpret each of the biblical narratives, we should always ask ourselves how they contribute to the overall purpose of the book. The book itself might give clues to help us interpret the significance of narrative sections.

EXPERIENCING THE BIBLE'S POETRY

The book of Psalms is the well-loved collection of poetry in the Bible. Some poems also occur in narrative portions of the Bible, such as the "Song of Moses" (see Ex 15:1-18) and the "Song of Deborah" (see Jdg. 5). Even in the NT we can find poetic pieces within narratives and the letters of Paul, such as Mary's song to the Lord (see Lk. 1:46-55) and the poem of praise to the Lord Jesus Christ (see Col.1:15-20).

To interpret poetry, we must first understand the role emotions play in poems. The book of Psalms reveals how God's people responded to him as they faced both dangerous and happy situations. The book holds cries to God for help or deliverance, joyous prayers of thanksgiving to God, expressions of grief over great loss, and compositions to lead the people of God in worship.

All these words spoken to God by his people are Spirit-inspired compositions preserved to help us express ourselves to God through the variety of life experiences. As we interpret individual passages of poetry, the following rules will aid our understanding:

1. **Determine what type of poem it is.** The 150 psalms—like other biblical poetry—represent a wide variety of poetic styles. While we normally interpret an individual passage in light of the thought flow in a book, we interpret the psalms separately from their context. More important, we need to understand why each psalm was written. The reason will be similar to the type of poem it represents. Here are a few examples. Consult a good commentary or Bible encyclopedia for additional help and a complete listing of the types of psalms.

- **Prayers for deliverance.** This is the most common kind of prayer in Psalms. See Psalm 22, which includes the cry, "O my Strength, come quickly to help me" (v. 19).
- **Songs of thanksgiving.** These songs express gratefulness to God for his help and deliverance. David begins his song of praise to God with the words, "I will exalt you, O LORD, for you lifted me out of the depths" (Ps. 30:1).
- **Hymns of praise.** These are songs of praise to our awesome God for who he is and what he's done (for example, Ps. 8,19,66).
- **Poems of grief.** Many psalms share a deep sense of pain and suffering at times of death, loss, or serious struggle (see Ps. 39,42,44).
- **Calls for action.** Portions of some psalms (usually the prayers for deliverance and the poems expressing grief) record extreme emotions against people who do evil. The language of these psalms is often exaggerated. It's vital to

realize that these words are expressed to God with the clear conviction that he's the one who avenges evil.

2. **Interpret the imagery.** In contrast to the language of prose, poetry uses many more metaphors (for example, "the Lord is a rock"), similes (comparisons using *like* or *as*), and other figures of speech. For example, the word *like* occurs 188 times in the Psalms (NRSV) and only 26 times in Genesis. Security and productivity in life are compared to "a tree planted by streams of water, which yields its fruit in season" (Ps. 1:3). The Twenty-Third Psalm elaborates on the metaphor of the Lord as a shepherd. In it, the rod and staff (see v. 4), tools of the shepherd, represent God's ministering and comforting presence with us.

3. **Observe the literary style.** Learning about common features of Hebrew poetry will help us interpret the book of Psalms and other poetic texts in the Bible. You might want to review some of these from our discussion of Hebrew poetry in chapter 5.

- **Repetition.** Repetition is a common feature of Hebrew poetry. Sometimes a keyword occurs repeatedly in a psalm, such as the word *righteous* in Psalm 11. This gives us insight into the theme or key thought.
- **Parallelism.** Hebrew poetry also frequently uses various types of parallelism, with one line helping interpret another. "Echo" parallelism occurs when the second line echoes or contrasts the first in different words: "Israel came out of Egypt, the house of Jacob from a people of foreign tongue" (Ps. 114:1) or "Happy are those who do not follow the advice of the wicked. . . . *But* their delight is in the law of the LORD" (1:1-2, NRSV, emphasis added). Parallelism might make the second or subsequent lines less important than the first, it might continue the first line, it might compare

the second with the first, or it might give more details about what the first line states.

THE WISDOM WORDS IN THE BIBLE

A truly wise person knows firsthand, often by years of observation, the consequences of decisions. But biblical wisdom travels beyond this. It establishes God as the source of wisdom. Proverbs 1:7 says, "The fear of the LORD is the beginning of knowledge, but fools despise wisdom and discipline." According to biblical wisdom, the starting point for gaining wisdom is centering our lives around God and working to please and learn from him.

The books of Proverbs and Ecclesiastes are the largest collections of wise sayings designed to help people make responsible decisions. The original writers worded most of the sayings in short and catchy ways to help the Hebrew people memorize them. Some of this word-play is lost in the translation from Hebrew into English. Like poetry, proverbs use parallelism and metaphors.

In applying proverbs to our lives, we need to avoid taking them too literally for two reasons:

1. **Proverbs point to the truth.** The Proverbs should be seen as general principles for guiding our behavior and choices. When we read in Proverbs 12:5 that "the plans of the righteous are just, but the advice of the wicked is deceitful," it doesn't mean we should take advice only from Christians. Not all unbelievers are wicked or give wicked advice.

A non-Christian financial planner might have some sound ideas for helping a Christian avoid unnecessary debt and put together a good budget. The proverb suggests that God's people need to be discerning in taking advice from unbelievers who might have different values, especially in ethical and spiritual matters.

2. **Proverbs aren't formulas or guarantees.** Proverbs give us principles, not promises. They point to particular outcomes that

are likely when we choose a certain course of action. We can think of many exceptions to the saying "If a king judges the poor with fairness, his throne will always be secure" (Prov. 29:14). This verse certainly can't guarantee that leaders will remain in political office as long as they act righteously and fairly (or that scoundrels won't survive as rulers). In essence, the proverb teaches that people will typically respect and favor a civic or political leader who acts out of principle and fairly resolves disputes and allocates resources.

GRASPING THE POINT OF JESUS' PARABLES

Jesus was a storyteller, often relating a story to make a point. The gospel writers refer to his stories as parables.

Over the course of the centuries, some biblical scholars have misunderstood Christ's parables as elaborate allegorical mysteries in which every detail had a hidden meaning. This was especially true of some of the early and medieval church theologians.

Some more recent scholars argued that a parable could have only one point and that the details of the story only add to the color and drama of the parable. For example, they might say that in the parable of the prodigal son, the point is the generous forgiveness of the father. But this might simply have swung the pendulum to the other extreme. In the parable of the prodigal, even if the father's readiness to forgive is the focal point, we also learn valuable lessons from the prodigal and the older brother.

Most modern scholars maintain that a limited amount of allegorical interpretation is appropriate when interpreting the parables—when it's clear that Jesus meant for the parable to carry additional meaning. Use the following guidelines when you study parables:

1. **Remember that context rules.** The writer's introduction to the parable, the context of the parable within a gospel, and the

historical circumstances when Jesus spoke the parable will help in grasping what the parable teaches.

Jesus told a parable about a king going on a trip and leaving money for his servants to invest (see Lk. 19:11-27). As it turns out, some invest well, but one doesn't; the good investors are rewarded and the poor one is punished. Luke introduces the parable, however, with the comment that Jesus told the parable "because he was near Jerusalem and the people thought that the kingdom of God was going to appear at once" (Lk. 19:11). So the main point of the parable is the fact that the King (Jesus) would delay establishing his kingdom. It also teaches that until he returns, his followers must invest their lives wisely.

2. **Investigate the historical details.** As in all Bible study, we can't fully understand the meaning of the parables until we understand the relevant cultural, social, political, and historical features. For example, without sensing the racial tension between the Samaritans and Jews, the parable of the Good Samaritan loses its punch.

3. **Consider the viewpoint of each main character.** The characters in the parable provide different points of view about the action described in the parable. The central points of the parable often revolve around these characters and their relation to the main story line.

For example, in the parable of the prodigal son (see Lk. 15:11-32), we can take away three lessons from the three characters: (1) the prodigal son teaches us the importance of repentance; (2) the father's response to his repentant son helps us appreciate God's incredible love and forgiveness; and (3) the older brother warns us against self-righteous pride.

4. **Apply the lessons to your context.** The final step is to identify the lessons that come from the main points of the parable. Ask how they relate to the key characters. Look for ways to apply those

lessons to your life. How are you like a prodigal in need of repentance? In what ways are you like the older brother looking down on the "less religious"?

DECODING PROPHECY

One of the hotly debated areas of Bible interpretation centers on prophecy. Much of the debate focuses on the books of Daniel and Revelation and other passages throughout the Bible that speak about what will happen in the future. Some Christians avoid studying prophetic texts. They might not want to debate, or they might think that if experts disagree, what chance do they have of figuring it out? However, the main function of prophecy wasn't to predict the future; it was to announce God's message to his people. It alerted them to what he thought about their behavior and to what he was doing, as well as what he would do in the future.

Almost one-fifth of the Bible consists of prophecy, so it's important to spend time thinking about how to interpret those particular passages properly. Keep these points in mind as you interpret biblical prophecy:

1. **Read the whole prophecy.** You can't isolate one verse or passage from the context of the complete prophecy; you can't do this with prophecy any more than you can with other parts of the Bible. Carefully read the whole section in light of the entire book. What is the writer's message to his readers? How can you apply that message to your circumstances?

2. **Learn the historical context.** All of the prophecies came to God's people for specific times and situations. Most of the OT prophecies relate to Israel's exile and return from exile. Once again, a good Bible encyclopedia or commentaries will help you understand the historical setting.

3. **See if the passage is messianic.** This means, does the

prophecy point to the coming and work of the Messiah, Jesus (for example, see Isaiah 9; 11; 52–53)? Determine this by looking in the NT at what prophecies are quoted or alluded to that Jesus Christ fulfilled. Be more doubtful about seeing OT texts as messianic if the writers of the NT did not.

4. **Ask if the passage has already been fulfilled.** Most of the predictive OT prophecies have already been fulfilled. For example, God has already judged Babylon, Assyria, the Philistines, Moab, Damascus, Cush, and Egypt in fulfillment of Isaiah 13–21. Aside from further clarification in the NT, how would you know that some still await fulfillment? Be cautious of "experts" who claim to know.

5. **Consider multiple fulfillments.** One unique characteristic of biblical prophecy is the possibility of double or even triple fulfillments. Daniel prophesied about an "abomination" that would desolate the temple (see Daniel 9:27; 11:31; 12:11). This was fulfilled in 167 BC when the Syrian ruler Antiochus Epiphanes entered the holiest place of the temple and forced the Jews to sacrifice pigs on the altar. But this prophecy was fulfilled *again* in events surrounding the destruction of Jerusalem in AD 70, and it will be finally fulfilled during the events at the end of time (see Mk. 13:14). The NT explains this; it's *not* merely the speculation of prophecy "experts."

6. **Discern the literal from the symbolic.** This is the hardest part of interpreting the book of Revelation. The genre of "apocalyptic" uses symbols to convey messages, so we should avoid viewing those literally. The author of Revelation obviously doesn't mean that a literal eagle rescues a pregnant woman from a dragon (serpent) and flies her to the desert (see 12:13-17).

The symbols represent realities either in the past (from our perspective) or yet to occur in the future. The eagle probably doesn't represent the United States, as someone once suggested, in spite of the fact that the eagle is our national symbol. We need to interpret the symbols in terms of their significance to the original readers.

Because the interpretation of prophetic symbolism can be difficult, it's best not to hold on to any interpretation too tightly. Read commentaries from a variety of perspectives to avoid this error.

7. **Ask what you can learn.** Because the primary purpose of prophecy wasn't to give a timetable for future events, we can't limit our expectations to what we might learn from its texts about the future. For example, try reading the book of Revelation to answer these questions: Who is Jesus? What did he come to do? What other themes emerge as you read?

Method Six: Studying and Avoiding the Mistakes Characters Made

David's affair. Noah's drunkenness. Jacob's conniving. Abraham's lying. Peter's denial. Ananias and Sapphira's hypocrisy. The Bible candidly reveals people's shortcomings, even of God's faithful followers. Apparently, the biblical authors and the Holy Spirit had good reasons for recording the failures as well as the successes of God's people. Paul explains, "Everything that was written in the past was written to teach us, so that through endurance and the encouragement of the Scriptures we might have hope" (Ro. 15:4). He added, "These things occurred as examples, to keep us from setting our hearts on evil things as they did. . . . These things happened to them as examples and were written down as warnings for us" (1 Cor. 10:6,11). The Scriptures can warn us against making the mistakes that believers before us made.

A Mile in Their Sandals

How can we benefit from these failures? One good way is to study the biblical accounts of people who made mistakes.

1. **Choose a biblical character to study.** Perhaps you already have someone in mind, somebody who's always intrigued you or

made you ask, "Why is that person's story in the Bible?" Does it matter that Abraham lied? That Jonah was a coward? That Sarah suggested that her husband Abraham sleep with her servant girl? That David covered up his adultery by having a loyal soldier killed? If you need help selecting a candidate for study, flip through Paul D. Gardner's *New International Encyclopedia of Bible Characters.*[2]

2. **Use a concordance to locate every reference to that person.** Be sure to include NT references to OT characters because these can provide valuable insight. For example, the account of Lot in Genesis mentions few positive things about him, but Peter describes his inner turmoil and calls him righteous three times: "If [God] rescued Lot, a righteous man greatly distressed by the licentiousness of the lawless (for that righteous man, living among them day after day, was tormented in his righteous soul by their lawless deeds that he saw and heard)" (2 Pet. 2:7-8, NRSV).

3. **Prayerfully read your character's story several times.** Look for character traits—what made this person "tick."

4. **Put yourself in that person's shoes and consider these questions:**

- What did the character do right? Wrong?
- What motivated this person? What was he or she after?
- What were the character's strengths and weaknesses?
- Was there a clear point when a decline began, or was it gradual?
- What opportunities did this person have to repent? How did he or she respond to these?
- What could the character have done differently to avoid failing God?
- In what ways am I like this person?
- What do I need to do to avoid making the same mistakes?

In a spirit of humility, record your observations.

5. **Write a summary that includes a personal application plan.** Often this will become obvious as you answer the questions from step 4.

6. **Finish your study with a prayer of thanksgiving and praise.** Thank God for using "jars of clay" to reveal his all-surpassing power (see 2 Cor. 4:7).

SAMPLE STUDY: SAMSON

Here's an example based on a study of Samson in Judges 13–16, using the questions listed in step 4.

What did Samson do right? Wrong?

Samson had godly parents who feared, trusted, and obeyed the Lord. They believed the angel of God, who told them their unborn son would deliver Israel from the Philistines. They obeyed all of God's commands about how to raise Samson as a Nazirite. The Lord blessed Samson and began to move within him while he was still living at home with his parents.

But Samson made his first wrong move when he visited the Philistine town of Timnah. In that city, he met and soon married a Philistine woman, even though God had prohibited marriage between his children and the Canaanites (see Ex. 34:16; Dt. 7:3). Later, Samson visited a Philistine prostitute. Ultimately, he allowed Delilah, his Philistine mistress, to rob him of the source of his strength.

Despite these failures, however, the author of Hebrews still included Samson in his list of the OT heroes of the faith (see Hebrews 11:32). Flaws don't exclude people from faith.

What motivated Samson?

Although God's extraordinary call on Samson's life should have motivated him to greatness, he had weaknesses for sensual pleasure and revenge. Even in the final victory, where he slaughtered more than three thousand Philistines, he didn't destroy the pagan temple because of the idol worship that was taking place. Instead, he asked God to give him the strength to topple the massive structure to "get revenge on the Philistines for my two eyes" (Jdg. 16:28).

What were Samson's strengths and weaknesses?

Samson had amazing physical strength, and he acknowledged God as the source of that strength. However, Samson was self-willed, impulsive, and proud. He ordered his parents around: "I have seen a Philistine woman in Timnah; now get her for me as my wife" (Jdg. 14:2). By insisting on marrying a Philistine, he failed to honor them and the Lord.

Samson had other character flaws as well. He had a blazing temper and could sometimes be cruel. He once tied three hundred foxes' tails together with lit torches between them. And strong as he was physically, he couldn't resist Delilah's manipulation.

Was there a clear point at which Samson's decline began, or was it gradual?

Samson's defeat first became apparent outwardly when he visited Philistia and came back demanding a Philistine wife. But it must have begun earlier than the text records, when he first began putting pleasure before God. Why wasn't Samson's first priority to seek God for wisdom about how to defeat the Philistines, since that was God's purpose for his life? Why didn't Samson respect the desires of his godly parents? Did he think he was above moral failure and compromise?

What opportunities did Samson have to repent, and how did he respond to these?

To accomplish his purposes, God was able to use Samson's poor choice to join with the Philistine woman: "This was from the LORD, who was seeking an occasion to confront the Philistines" (Jdg. 14:4). But Samson never realized that God had used the unholy union to establish him as Israel's mighty leader.

In Samson's life, we repeatedly see this pattern of blindness to God's work: when his wife died, when God's Spirit strengthened Samson for mighty acts, when God miraculously supplied a spring of water, when God helped him escape entrapment in Gaza, and when God allowed Samson three opportunities to recognize Delilah's treachery before his ultimate downfall. All of these were times of God's mercy and opportunities for Samson to repent. But he didn't. The book of Judges never indicates that Samson asked for forgiveness for his sins against the Lord.

How could Samson have acted differently to avoid failing God?

Samson could have avoided failing God in these ways: obeying his parents and honoring their wishes that he marry an Israelite; obeying God concerning intermarriage and not considering himself above God's Law; making God's call on his life his first priority; examining his heart and his ways; asking God for wisdom, purity, and an undivided heart to lead Israel; asking the Lord to avenge him rather than taking matters into his own hands; avoiding sexual immorality; and running from Delilah when he saw that she couldn't be trusted.

In what ways am I like Samson?

Samson's most basic flaw seems to be his failure to put God's will above his own. God worked in spite of Samson rather than with his willing cooperation. What might God have done through this strong man if Samson had been motivated to honor God instead of being consumed by his own interests and pleasures?

In response, we might ask these questions: How often am I driven by my own desires? Am I using my God-given gifts and abilities for my own agenda rather than God's? Do I limit what God would do through me because I want to serve him on my terms rather than his? Does God have to work in spite of me?

What action should I take to avoid repeating Samson's mistakes?
We should make the prayer of Jesus in the Garden of Gethsemane a regular part of our prayers: "Not my will, but yours be done" (Lk. 22:42).

Let's work to use our spiritual gifts for God's purposes and not our own, ask the Lord to search our hearts, and repent of any sins he reveals. We should also pray for those closest to us — that they would completely fulfill God's plan for their lives, avoiding the traps of immorality, unholy partnerships, and revenge. Finally, let's praise God that he can use even our foolishness and sin to accomplish his purposes.

Method Seven: Completing a Comprehensive Book Analysis

Building on many of the Bible study methods described in previous chapters, a comprehensive book analysis engages in a more thorough examination of the various aspects of the book you're studying. The book survey and book summary will help you see an entire Bible book as a whole.

The books of the Bible were originally written as single units. If you want to master the Bible, grasping the message of an entire book leads to a better understanding of its details. Understanding the meaning of the details will give you greater mastery of the book and Scripture as a whole.

Three steps to studying any whole book of the Bible include the book survey (the whole), chapter analysis (the particulars), and the book summary (conclusions).

In the study of each chapter, there are also three steps following this procedure: the passage description (the whole), the verse-by-verse meditation (the particulars), and the theme and conclusion (conclusions).

Because application can come from any step of the Bible study, I won't list it separately. The order represents the steps used to discern truth from God's Word. Application involves putting this truth into practice in daily life.

GETTING STARTED

Begin your study by selecting a book. You might start with an epistle from the NT. Or you might want to try an OT book such as Jonah, Nehemiah, or Ruth.

A good pace is a chapter a week. If a chapter is especially long, you might split it into two studies. In addition, you should spend a week on the book survey as your first session and another week on the book summary as your last session. That means that a six-chapter book like Ephesians would take eight weeks for your study.

THE BOOK SURVEY

A book survey gives you an overview of the entire book. This overview will help you understand and relate the details you discover later. The book survey contains five main sections: principal personalities, historical setting, purpose, themes, and overview. You might also want to expand this list by adding sections for literary style, keywords, additional personalities, and the geography of the book. You will have the skills and know about the tools for engaging in these various tasks from many of the prior studies in this *Handbook*.

Principal Personalities. Who's the author of the book? To whom was he writing? What other people does the author mention in the book? Why are they included? Do the characters relate to one another, and if so, how? How well do they know and understand one another?

Historical Setting. When was the book written? What's the historical setting in which it was written? What were the circumstances of the author? What's the situation of the recipients? What was happening in that part of the world at that time? Are other circumstances mentioned that you need to understand to grasp the message?

Purpose. Why was this book written? Sometimes the author gives a purpose statement (for example, see 1 Jn. 5:13), but that's rare. If there was a problem to correct, what was it? What was the writer trying to accomplish?

Themes. What's the main emphasis of the book? What are some of the recurring ideas? What topics does the author address?

Overview. Summarize the book in an outline, chart, or diagram. Be as creative as you like. You might want to use the theme and outline given in a reference book or study Bible for a starting point, but you'll find it more useful to produce your own. As you complete your study, you'll revise your theme and outline.

Other Observations. Other questions that might be important include:

- What's the style of writing? How does the author use elements such as illustrations, logical arguments, and emotional appeals?
- What are the keywords in the book?
- What else do you need to discover about the culture and background of the author and recipients as well as others mentioned in the book? What were their lives like? What are

some of their customs and habits? What culture dominated the world?

- How does the geography and topography of the places mentioned help you understand the book?

Some of these questions become more important for some books than for others. The more you study, the more you'll know which questions are important to ask.

You'll find most of this information by researching a variety of sources. In addition to the information contained in chapters of this *Handbook*, you can find background material for a book survey in the following reference books:

- Bible dictionary or encyclopedia
- Contemporary Bible handbook
- Recent Bible atlas
- Survey of the Old Testament or New Testament
- Commentary
- Concordance and lexicon

THE CHAPTER ANALYSIS

When working on your chapter analysis, begin with a passage description, then do a verse-by-verse meditation, and finish with your theme and conclusions.

The chapter analysis Bible study incorporates the Bible study essentials of observation, interpretation, and application. In the passage description, you'll make observations on the passage as a whole; in the verse-by-verse meditation, you'll make observations on each verse, ask questions to help you interpret the verse, and use cross-references to relate the verse to the rest of the Bible. You'll draw these thoughts together and record them in the theme and conclusion section. Finally, you'll complete the application section.

Passage Description. Read the passage several times and briefly describe the contents in your own words. Use a standard version (for example, [t]niv; nrsv; nasb) for your basic study, though you may supplement your reading from other Bible translations or paraphrases.

Don't try to analyze or interpret when writing your passage description. Carefully observe what the author is saying without explaining why or what it means. After reading your passage description, another person familiar with the passage should be able to identify it.

While you can describe a passage in many ways, the basic content of it should be uniform. Carefully use your skills of observation, and don't overlook crucial details in your description. Reread the passage to see if you've left out any details. You could try rewriting it without the modifying phrases and clauses, leaving only the subjects, verbs, and objects. This method is especially effective when the passage contains many modifiers. You'll quickly see the movement of the passage by seeing it so bare.

Another method of describing a passage is to make a summary outline. Divide the passage into paragraphs. Most recent versions of the Bible already have suggested paragraph breaks. The original text wasn't divided into paragraphs, so you might divide your passage as you think appropriate. Noticing changes of subject, natural divisions, and the use of conjunctions (such as *therefore* or *for this reason*) will help you determine the possible paragraph divisions.

After determining your paragraph divisions, write a sentence or two summarizing each paragraph's contents. Don't be concerned if you leave out some detail, but give a general framework that you can fit the details into later.

Verse-by-Verse Meditation. Verse-by-verse meditation gives you an opportunity to make more observations so you can interpret and reflect on the passage. Here you take a long look at the details as you proceed carefully from one verse to the next throughout the passage.

Take a concentrated look at each verse, recording your findings under these headings: "observations," "questions and answers," "cross-references," and "notes and comments." Place the verse numbers on the left of your findings under each heading. The first three categories are important aspects of your verse-by-verse reflection. Record additional information and possible applications under the "notes and comments" section.

- **Observations**—Proper observation is the foundation for building good interpretation and application. Because it's impossible to record every observation, record the observations that make you think more. Also record your observations about the relationship of each verse to other verses in the same passage.

- **Questions**—This section takes considerable time and effort, but it often leads to rewarding reflections. As you grow in your knowledge of the Bible, you'll have more questions, and they'll become more penetrating and significant. At the same time, your own knowledge and understanding will increase. There's no limit to the number or variety of questions for any particular passage. Who? What? When? Where? Why? and How? questions are obvious ones to start with.

- **Answers**—When you see that a question has several possible answers, you might record the possible options. Not every question or issue has a clear-cut answer, so be careful not to insist on always finding one. Focus on the answers that seem more certain. It's best to avoid answering questions prematurely. Give yourself time to think about them. Waiting may keep you from pursuing unnecessary tangents or jumping to wrong conclusions. In some cases, a succeeding verse will answer your question. In many cases, a question will stimulate further study in other sources. See whether you can discover answers from the Bible itself. A cross-reference might help. You might also need to consult a commentary or other resources.

• **Cross-References** — The Bible is its own best commentary. Scripture interprets Scripture. The content of one passage often clarifies the content of another. To help you apply this principle, use both internal and external cross-references. An internal cross-reference occurs in the same book; an external cross-reference comes from another portion of Scripture.

Be careful in applying this method, however, because you need to study each potential cross-reference in its own context. Just because a particular version or other resource lists another verse as a cross-reference, that's no guarantee it will shed light on the verse you're studying. A cross-reference might have only an incidental connection. Limit your study to those that have real connections to your passage.

Internal cross-references show the relationship of a verse to the paragraph, the chapter, and the book where it's found. This helps place the verse in context and typically gives the most insight. You encounter an internal reference when a verse uses a connective word, such as *wherefore, and, therefore,* or *hence.* What follows sheds crucial light. You'll pursue other internal references when crucial words or themes recur. For example, when studying Ephesians 1, you'll find Paul's reference to "heavenly places" (Eph. 1:3). Clearly the letter itself gives insight to this phrase through internal cross-references (see Eph. 1:20; 2:6; 3:10; 6:12).

External cross-references have the potential to give further insight on the verse under study. These might be helpful or not. When other writers of Scripture speak about the same topic, you can learn from their perspective. Important external cross-references are those that are parallel (saying the same thing), corresponding (dealing with similar matter), contrasting (taking an opposing stance), and illustrative (giving examples of the subject).

One superb source of cross-references is your own memory and knowledge of the Bible, but because no one's memory is exhaustive, we need to use other resources. If you're looking for a verse that contains a keyword, don't hesitate to use a concordance; it's your friend. In the space next to the cross-reference, add your linking thought— the thought that relates this cross-reference to the verse you're studying. Use a short phrase or keywords from the reference to help you remember its content.

- **Notes and Comments** — Use the space under this heading for your own reactions and remarks. You might want to use titles to identify specific topics or list things such as implications, possible applications, illustrations, definitions, and additional observations.

Theme and Conclusions. When you come to the "Theme and Conclusions" section of your chapter analysis, you're ready to report on the fruits of your study. Your analysis has led you to describe the passage, meditate on each verse, make observations, ask questions, answer many of them, and discover and assess various cross-references.

The theme is the central issue presented by the author in the chapter you're studying. It might be a topic, a proposition, a problem, or an argument. You could find several themes in a particular passage.

The best way to arrive at the theme is to ask, "What is the author talking about?" or "What is the basic subject of this paragraph?" for each paragraph. Combining and summarizing the paragraph themes will help you determine the major theme of the passage.

After arriving at the theme or themes of the chapter, record your conclusions. A paragraph could have more than one conclusion because the author might be saying more than one thing about the subject. The most accurate way to arrive at conclusions is to ask, "What's the author saying about the theme?" or "What's being said about the topic or subject of each paragraph?" It's not as important to have many conclusions as it is to have conclusions that follow logically from the main themes running through the passage.

Finally, you can give the chapter a title. Your title will reflect the theme and conclusions you've discovered.

Application. Your Bible study must always lead to application to life or it remains dry and pointless. Recording your application will help you clarify what you plan to do. It also encourages you to be specific. It's easy to say, "I am going to pray more," but we rarely follow through on that type of application. It's far more meaningful to write, "I'm going to spend the first five minutes of my lunch break each day in prayer." In addition to what we've seen in prior sections of this *Handbook*, the following four questions will help you write meaningful applications:

1. What truth do I want to apply?
2. What's my need?
3. What's my plan of action?
4. How can I check my progress?

Pray for the Holy Spirit's help in selecting and carrying out your application.

THE BOOK SUMMARY

To complete your study of a book of the Bible, you'll need to tie together what you've learned into a book summary. Your book summary will help you unify knowledge, consolidate facts, and grasp the whole book.

The first step in the summary is to reread the book several times. Do each reading in one sitting if possible. Because the material is now familiar, you should be able to read it quickly. Get a good grasp on the general thread that runs through the book.

Review your chapter titles to help you determine the overall flow, and then write an outline for the whole book. You'll find it interesting to compare your final outline with the overview in your book survey.

Next, review your passage themes and main conclusions. Decide which themes are most important and list them. Now do the same thing with your conclusions, choosing the most crucial ones.

Consider the book as a whole and give it a title. Keep your title short and use words that are descriptive or that illustrate the book's contents.

Finally, review your applications for each passage. Are there any projects you haven't started or ones you haven't finished? Using this review, chart out your next steps and make plans to complete them.

CONCLUSION

God's Word contains the riches of his revelation to his creatures. While a simple reading of a single verse can be meaningful, the Bible reveals its riches more and more to those willing to devote their energy to serious study. In this chapter, we've looked at twenty-two different approaches—some that might take only a few minutes in a day, and others that could extend to days, weeks, or a lifetime of study. We don't need to become bored with Bible study; there's always another way to approach it. And some of the tactics included in this chapter might suggest still other ways. This list of methods isn't complete. But you will find among them many means to the worthy end of getting to know our Lord and follow in his life-giving ways.

FOR FURTHER STUDY

Brown, C., ed. *New International Dictionary of New Testament Theology*, 4 vol. Grand Rapids, MI: Zondervan, 1986.

Duvall, J. S., and J. D. Hays. *Grasping God's Word: A Hands-On Approach to Reading, Interpreting, and Applying the Bible*. 2nd ed. Grand Rapids, MI: Zondervan, 2005.

Fee, G. D., and D. K. Stuart. *How to Read the Bible for All Its Worth: A Guide to Understanding the Bible*. 3rd ed. Grand Rapids, MI: Zondervan, 2003.

Fleming, Jean. *Feeding Your Soul*. Colorado Springs, CO: NavPress, 1999.

Goodrick, E., and J. R. Kohlenberger III, eds. *The NIV Exhaustive Concordance*. Grand Rapids, MI: Zondervan, 1990.

Klein, W. W., C. L. Blomberg, and R. L. Hubbard Jr. *Introduction to Biblical Interpretation*. Rev. ed. Nashville: Nelson, 2004.

Kohlenberger III, J. R., ed. *The NRSV Concordance Unabridged*. Grand Rapids, MI: Zondervan, 1991.

Mounce, W. *Mounce's Complete Expository Dictionary of Old and New Testament Words*. Grand Rapids, MI: Zondervan, 2006.

Van Gemeren, W.A., ed. *New International Dictionary of Old Testament Theology and Exegesis*, 5 vol. Grand Rapids, MI: Zondervan, 1997.

Warren, R. *Twelve Dynamic Bible Study Methods*. Wheaton, IL: Victor, 1981.

CHAPTER 7

RESOURCES AND HELPS FOR STUDYING THE BIBLE

Imagine trying to navigate your way around a strange country where you don't speak the language. In addition, you have limited knowledge and insights about the culture. At the very least, you'd need a good map and phrase book. Better yet, you'd have a guide and a translator.

We face similar difficulties when we study the Bible. For one thing, we don't fully understand the culture of the ancient world, and we don't speak ancient Hebrew or Hellenistic Greek. As we've already noted, to get the most accurate results as we study the Bible, we want to get our hands on the best tools and resources possible.

I emphasize the word *best* because not all the tools we can find easily are good or reliable, much less the best. Discount publishers and online sites offer all kinds of resources, often at little or no expense. But sometimes the old adage is true: "You get what you pay for."

Some books go out of print because they deserve to go out of print! Other books go out of print when better and more up-to-date sources replace them. Even though publishers reprint or make out-of-print materials available online doesn't mean we should rely on them for studying the Word of God. Would you go to a physician who relies on a medical textbook written in the 1950s? What if he said, "Well, it was the standard when it was written, and I was able to buy it for almost nothing"?

On the other hand, old isn't *always* bad. Some classic works deserve to be reprinted and made available. Often the best current sources use the finest scholarship from previous generations of authors. Here's my point: It makes little sense for students to use inferior sources simply because they're easy to find on the Internet, bundled "free" with some software package, or available from a used-book seller for minimal cost. Cheap inferior is still inferior, and easily searchable inferior is still inferior.

Because our goal of understanding the Word of God is so important, it makes sense to use the best tools and resources possible to tackle that task. In this chapter, I'll list what I believe are the best tools in major categories for Bible study. By the way, whenever these major reference works use common abbreviations, I list those after the titles; you might hear a pastor or Bible teacher use the abbreviations and know what sources he or she is referring to.

I need to insert some comments about some of the labels I'll use in this chapter. Bear with me, because they can be confusing. In the brief descriptions after the sources I list, I sometimes identify some as more or less *conservative* or *liberal*. I intend these rather imprecise adjectives to refer to points on a theological spectrum: Some writers hold more conservative theological convictions (sometimes called *tradition* viewpoints), while others tend to be more theologically liberal. In many cases, these convictions don't affect the quality of an author's work, but they might affect an author's conclusions.

I'll use another term occasionally: *ecumenical*. With this term, I mean to describe a broad range of writers from across the denominational and religious spectrum. That might well include Roman

Catholic, Eastern Orthodox, Protestant Christian, and Jewish scholars. In other places, I use the term *evangelical* to refer, broadly, to those Protestants who adhere to the National Association of Evangelicals' statement of faith[1], although the label is a slippery one. Alternatively, *mainline* imprecisely refers to denominational groups not considered evangelical (for example, Presbyterian Church USA, United Methodists, United Church of Christ, Evangelical Lutheran Church in America, and Church of the Brethren). Mainline churches tend to be more ecumenical or inclusive in outlook than many evangelical groups. Frequently they belong to interdenominational organizations, such as the National Council of Churches and World Council of Churches, while evangelical groups typically do not.

I'm not striving for precision in these terms, but I want you to have some idea of what I'm doing. I also use these categories to remind you that you may not always agree with various writers' conclusions about certain issues; I certainly don't. At the same time, I think these particular resources are among the most useful.

BIBLE INTRODUCTIONS AND SURVEYS

Need "the big picture"? Want to get an overview of the basic issues for a book in the Bible? In one volume and in relatively brief scope, Bible introductions and surveys supply the background information needed to put biblical books in context, covering areas such as authorship, recipients, locations, and dates. Here are some of the best:

Old Testament
Arnold, B. T., and B. E. Beyer. *Encountering the Old Testament: A Christian Survey.* Encountering Biblical Studies. Grand Rapids, MI: Baker, 1999. This book includes a CD-ROM with helpful

graphic illustrations and photographs that supplement the text.

Dillard, R., and T. Longman III. *An Introduction to the Old Testament.* Grand Rapids, MI: Zondervan, 1994. This resource features highlights of research rather than a complete treatment of past scholarship and deals with the meaning of each book of the OT in its context in the Canon. An electronic version is available on Pradis (see software section on page 350).

Hill, A. E., and J. H. Walton. *A Survey of the Old Testament.* 2nd ed. Grand Rapids, MI: Zondervan, 2001. This book emphasizes the content, background, and literary nature of the OT.

LaSor, W., F. Bush, and D. A. Hubbard. *Old Testament Survey.* 2nd ed. Grand Rapids, MI: Eerdmans, 1996. This text explores issues of OT authority, revelation and inspiration, Canon, and the formation of the OT. It also provides specific introductions and surveys of all the OT books as well as concluding background articles.

New Testament

Achtemeier, P. J., J. B. Green, and M. M. Thompson. *Introducing the New Testament: Its Literature and Theology.* Grand Rapids, MI: Eerdmans, 2001. This study adopts less conservative positions on some points than the others in this section do but provides excellent notes on the contents and narrative flow of each book.

Blomberg, C. L. *Jesus and the Gospels: An Introduction and Survey.* Nashville: Broadman, Holman, 1997; and *From Pentecost to Patmos.* Nashville: Broadman, Holman, 2006. Together, these two volumes span the entire NT and introduce the background issues for each book as well as a survey of their contents. Both books include helpful charts and maps.

Carson, D. A., and D. J. Moo. *An Introduction to the New*

Testament. 2nd ed. Grand Rapids, MI: Zondervan, 2005. This resource covers background issues, outlines of each book, and the theological significance of each NT document.

DeSilva, D. A. *An Introduction to the New Testament: Context, Methods, and Ministry Formation.* Downers Grove, IL: InterVarsity, 2004. Introduces the reader to the backgrounds and contents of the NT books, and surveys the various methods used in the careful study of the NT. A unique feature is the section at the end of each NT book that suggests practical implications for ministry.

Gundry, R. *A Survey of the New Testament.* 4th ed. Grand Rapids, MI: Zondervan, 2003. This volume provides the best basic-level survey of the essential content of the NT books.

HISTORICAL AND CULTURAL BACKGROUND SOURCES

Do you want to understand as much as possible about the historical and cultural background behind books of the Bible? As we've already discussed, you'll want to take this essential step for good interpretation and understanding during your study. You'll find many resources to choose from, but this list represents the best sources for background studies that will help shed light on the history, culture, and customs of biblical times.

Old Testament

King, P. J., and L. E. Stager. *Life in Biblical Israel: Library of Ancient Israel.* Louisville, KY: Westminster John Knox, 2002. With color photos and drawings, this book provides the best discussion about how people lived during biblical times.

Matthews, V. H. *Manners and Customs in the Bible.* 3rd ed.

Peabody, MA: Hendrickson, 2006. With vivid photos and images, this excellent resource supplies valuable cultural background on the biblical world, including what people wore, what they ate, what they built, how they exercised justice, how they mourned, and how they viewed family and legal customs.

Provan, Iain, V. P. Long, and T. Longman III. *A Biblical History of Israel*. Westminster John Knox, 2003. Taking a more scholarly approach, the authors provide thorough discussion of the history of ancient Israel in a very systematic fashion. They include a useful discussion of the method of writing ancient history.

Shanks, Hershel, ed. *Ancient Israel: From Abraham to the Roman Destruction of the Temple*. Rev. ed. Biblical Archaeology Society, 1999. Using a popular writing style, this easy-to-read resource features chapters written by one or two experts in the field of OT culture and history.

Walton, J. H., V. H. Matthews, and M. W. Chavalas. *The IVP Bible Background Commentary: Old Testament*. Downers Grove: InterVarsity, 2000. This commentary takes a verse-by-verse approach to provide insight into the historical and cultural background of the OT.

New Testament

Arnold, C. E., ed. *Zondervan Illustrated Bible Backgrounds Commentary*. 4 vols. Grand Rapids, MI: Zondervan, 2002. Many authors contributed to these volumes, which can help readers understand the historical and cultural background of the books of the NT. Includes full color photos and graphics.

DeSilva, D. A. *Honor, Patronage, Kinship, and Purity*. Downers Grove, IL: InterVarsity, 2001. This resource introduces readers to the cultural values reflected in the NT and provides applications to show how understanding the culture makes a difference.

Ferguson, E. *Backgrounds of Early Christianity.* 2nd ed. Grand Rapids, MI: Eerdmans, 1993. The book examines the Roman, Greek, and Jewish political, social, religious, and philosophical backgrounds of the NT and the early church. It includes fresh discussions of first-century social life, gnosticism, and the Dead Sea Scrolls as well as other Jewish literature.

Jeffers, J. S. *The Greco-Roman World of the New Testament Era.* Downers Grove, IL: InterVarsity, 1999. This work provides a scenic tour of daily life during the time of Jesus and the apostles, including legal codes, dinner foods, social hierarchies, apartment living, education, and family dynamics.

Keener, C. S. *The IVP Biblical Background Commentary: New Testament.* Downers Grove: InterVarsity, 1994. Like its OT counterpart, this commentary takes a verse-by-verse approach to provide insight into the historical and cultural background of the NT.

Witherington III, B. *New Testament History: A Narrative Account.* Grand Rapids, MI: Baker, 2001. As the title suggests, the author tells the story of the development of the Christian message as captured by the NT authors.

CONCORDANCES AND LEXICONS

Words serve as the building blocks of languages. Different kinds of resources can help us determine what words mean in the passages we study. A concordance lists all the places where a word occurs either in the original Hebrew or Greek languages or in a specific translation of the Bible. Some concordances bridge the biblical languages by identifying both the original language words and their English translations.

Lexicon is another word for dictionary. A lexicon contains the inventory of words in a given language. It supplies the range of meanings of the words in the vocabulary of a language.

Concordances

An early exhaustive concordance for the KJV of the Bible was produced under the direction of Dr. James Strong (1822–1894) and first published in 1890. He assigned each Hebrew or Greek word an entry number in the dictionary of those original-language words listed in the back of the concordance. These are now called "Strong's numbers." Many other reference works cross-reference words using Strong's numbers. The main concordance lists each word that appears in the KJV in alphabetical order, followed by each verse where that word appears listed in canonical order.

Not all concordances list every word that occurs in a given translation; the ones that do are called "exhaustive." Obviously, you need a concordance that parallels the version of the Bible you use for study because the list of words in each version will be unique.

Say you want to study the word *neighbor*, because "love your neighbor as yourself" is such a common command. In a concordance based on the NIV, you'll find 81 uses. In an NRSV concordance, *neighbor* occurs 102 times. Clearly, the translators of these versions used different criteria for which Hebrew and Greek words they would translate as *neighbor*.

Before I list recommended concordances, let's look at one of the instances of *neighbor* in the NIV to illustrate a key point. In Hebrews 8:11, the author uses the Greek word *politēs*, which the NIV, ESV, and KJV translate as *neighbor*, the NASB as *citizen*, and the NRSV *each other*.

The noun *politēs* occurs only four times in the NT. Let's look at another one of them. In Luke 19:14, the translations are: *citizens*

(NRSV; ESV; NASB), *subjects* (NIV), and *his people* (NLT).

That's part of the complexity in using various translations of the Bible. English versions use the same English word to translate different Hebrew or Greek words, and English versions translate the same Hebrew or Greek word with different English words.

Many Bible software programs allow you to produce concordances on the fly, using either root forms (such as all occurrences of *love*) or specific forms of a word (such as *loved, loving, was being loved*) in both modern and original languages.

Here are the most useful concordances in print:

Goodrick, E., and J. R. Kohlenberger III, eds. *The Strongest NIV Exhaustive Concordance*. Grand Rapids, MI: Zondervan, 2004. As the title suggests, this volume lists the occurrence of every word in the NIV. Its indexes define every Hebrew, Aramaic, and Greek word in the Bible, including the possible meaning of every proper name. More than two thousand keywords from the KJV are cross-referenced to their NIV equivalents.

Kohlenberger III, J. R., ed. *The NRSV Concordance Unabridged.* Grand Rapids, MI: Zondervan, 1991. This text includes all occurrences of all words in the NRSV, including the apocryphal books and alternate and literal translations of words found in footnotes.

The Strongest NASB Exhaustive Concordance. Grand Rapids, MI: Zondervan, 2004; *The New Strong's Expanded Exhaustive Concordance of the Bible*. Nashville: Nelson, 2001 (based on the KJV). For readers who use the NASB or KJV as their version of choice, these two concordances list the occurrence of all words. Both include many other sections or features and supply a wealth of information for readers.

Whitaker, R. E., and J. R. Kohlenberger III. *The Analytical Concordance to the New Revised Standard Version of the New*

Testament. Grand Rapids, MI: Eerdmans; New York and Oxford: Oxford University Press, 2000. Based only on the NT, this analytical concordance cites the various Greek words that were translated with each English term listed.

Kohlenberger III, J. R., and J. A. Swanson. *The Hebrew-English Concordance to the OT*. Grand Rapids, MI: Zondervan, 1998; *The Greek-English Concordance to the NT*. Grand Rapids, MI: Zondervan, 1997. These two works bridge the biblical languages and English language concordances. They list Hebrew or Greek words alphabetically and indicate the references where they occur, along with brief excerpts from the KJV. The words are keyed to Strong's numbering system and other reference works.

Lexicons/Dictionaries

As noted on pages 325-326, a lexicon or dictionary provides the meanings for the words in a language. Because most words have a range of meanings, we need to observe the options so we can select the one that best fits the context of the passage we're studying. Theological dictionaries start by tracing the history of a word's uses and meanings.

Mounce, W. D., ed. *Mounce's Complete Expository Dictionary of Old and New Testament Words*. Grand Rapids, MI: Zondervan, 2006. Although most dictionaries cover either the OT or NT, this one spans the entire Bible. So I suggest it if you can have only one in your library of Bible study tools. Because it covers both the OT and NT in one volume, the entries are briefer than a dictionary for each testament, yet it's exceptional for what it does.

OLD TESTAMENT

Harris, R. L. et al., eds. *Theological Wordbook of the Old Testament* [*TWOT*]. 2 vols. Chicago: Moody, 1980. This book contains a compact discussion of key Hebrew words and is readily accessible to most readers, even those without knowledge of Hebrew. It investigates each Hebrew word and its cognates (cognates are words that have common origins) and synthesizes the meaning of words in context in a concise format. Each entry is keyed to Strong's system. This makes *TWOT* an easy source to consult for the basic meanings of OT words. An electronic version is available.

Van Gemeren, W. et al., eds. *New International Dictionary of Old Testament Theology and Exegesis* [*NIDOTTE*]. 5 vols. Grand Rapids, MI: Zondervan, 1997. Volumes 1–4 are organized alphabetically by Hebrew words. The index, volume 5, lists topics according to English words or biblical book titles. Many topical entries discuss relevant Hebrew words. English readers can access Hebrew words by cross-reference numbers in Goodrick-Kohlenberger, *The NIV Exhaustive Concordance* (see page 327), which also has a *NIDOTTE*-Strong's numbers conversion chart. An electronic version is available on Pradis.

NEW TESTAMENT

Brown, C., ed. *New International Dictionary of New Testament Theology* [*NIDNTT*]. 4 vols. Grand Rapids, MI: Zondervan, 1986. This work discusses the theological significance of words over time. It's organized by groups of words connected in meaning, called semantic fields. The various terms used relating to power (for example, might, power, authority, throne, and so on) form a semantic field, so *NIDNTT* treats them together. This allows you to see words that might have similar meanings or can be used as synonyms. This valuable resource is very easy to use, even if you know only English or a bit of Greek. Most articles discuss the Hebrew background of NT words. The final volume consists of indexes that simplify searches. An electronic version is available on Pradis.

Verbrugge, V. *NIV Theological Dictionary of New Testament Words.* Grand Rapids, MI: Zondervan, 2001. This one-volume abridgment of *NIDNTT* works well for people who need only the "bottom line" rather than all the details. It's also less intimidating if you don't know Greek.

Bromiley, G. W., ed. *Theological Dictionary of the New Testament.* Exeter, UK: Paternoster; Grand Rapids, MI: Eerdmans, 1993. This one-volume book, known as "little Kittel," abridges a ten-volume work (useful mostly to scholars) of the same name. Even users who know little or no Greek find it accessible.

THEOLOGICAL DICTIONARIES AND ENCYCLOPEDIAS

As you study the Bible, you might want to investigate larger issues or specific topics that go beyond just understanding the meanings of words. Sometimes the boundaries between lexicons, Bible dictionaries, and encyclopedias aren't distinct, but in this category I've listed resources that treat biblical topics and subjects rather than single words. They discuss issues that might range over the entire Bible or those addressed within either the OT or NT.

Entire Bible
These four study tools engage the entire Bible:

Bromiley, G. W., ed. *The International Standard Bible Encyclopedia [ISBE],* revised. 4 vols. Grand Rapids, MI: Eerdmans, 1995 (an electronic version is available); Freedman, D. N., ed. *The Anchor Bible Dictionary* [*ABD*], 6 vols. New York: Doubleday, 1992 (an electronic version is available). These two multivolume encyclopedias reliably cover nearly all biblical topics in depth. Overall, the theological perspective of *ISBE*'s writers is more theologically conservative than you'll find in the *ABD*.

Freedman, D. N., ed. *Eerdmans Dictionary of the Bible*. Grand Rapids, MI: Eerdmans, 2000; Youngblood, R. F., and F. F. Bruce, eds. *Nelson's New Illustrated Bible Dictionary: An Authoritative One-Volume Reference Work on the Bible, with Full-Color Illustrations*. Rev. and updated. Nashville: Nelson, 1995. These two one-volume entries are hefty texts that include many illustrations, more than five thousand articles, and many color maps. The authors in the Freedman volume represent a broad base of scholars across the theological spectrum. The authors in the Youngblood volume are all evangelicals, so its entries are more uniformly conservative in theological perspective.

Old Testament

Alexander, T. D., and D. W. Baker, eds. *Dictionary of the Old Testament: Pentateuch*. Downers Grove, IL; Leicester, UK: InterVarsity, 2003; Arnold, B. T., and H. G. M. Williamson, eds. *Dictionary of the Old Testament: Historical Books*. Downers Grove, IL; Leicester, UK: InterVarsity, 2005. Exploring the major themes and issues of the Pentateuch (the first five books of the OT) and the OT historical books, these encyclopedic works offer authoritative overviews, detailed examinations, and very useful insights from the world of the ancient Near East. InterVarsity projects a total of four volumes in this series of OT dictionaries. These first two set a high standard.

New Testament

Green, J. B., S. McKnight, and I. H. Marshall, eds. *Dictionary of Jesus and the Gospels.* Downers Grove, IL: InterVarsity, 1992; Hawthorne, G. F., R. P., Martin, and D. G. Reid, eds. *Dictionary of Paul and His Letters.* Downers Grove, IL: InterVarsity, 1993; Martin, R. P. and P. H. Davids, eds. *Dictionary of the Later New Testament and Its Developments.* Downers Grove, IL: InterVarsity, 1998. These three resources provide focused study on all matters pertaining to the Gospels, Pauline studies, Acts, Hebrews, the general epistles, and Revelation. The final volume moves beyond the NT to trace the trajectory of the topics into the era of the apostolic fathers and early Christianity up through the middle of the second century. All of these IVP dictionaries are available in an electronic version.

GRAMMAR HELPS

Knowing the biblical languages provides the best access into how the biblical texts function and how to explore their grammar. Lacking that, students will find most help by using commentaries that use the original languages to arrive at their comments. Two additional sources for the NT are worth a mention.

Rogers, C. L. Jr., and C. L. Rogers III. *The New Linguistic and Exegetical Key to the Greek New Testament.* Grand Rapids, MI: Zondervan, 1998; Zerwick, M., and M. Grosvenor. *A Grammatical Analysis of the Greek New Testament.* Chicago: Loyola University Press, 1996. Both of these tools are useful for understanding the grammar of the NT. Both proceed verse-by-verse, alerting readers to significant grammatical (as well as other kinds of) features.

COMMENTARIES

Commentaries provide expert analysis of biblical texts. Good commentaries offer a deeper analysis of the background of biblical books than you'll find in study Bibles, Bible introductions, or dictionaries and encyclopedias such as those I've already listed. Because commentaries typically devote more pages to each book of the Bible, they also go into more depth commenting on individual verses (or sections) and, depending on the nature of the commentary, on theology and application.

While publishers sometimes offer individual commentaries, they often issue volumes in sets, usually for the OT or NT. Some words of caution: Not all entries in a set are of equal quality, and not all commentaries accomplish the same tasks. As you study the Bible and rely on these resources to help your study, you need to be aware of the nature of commentaries and the purposes they serve.

Obviously, a whole book that comments on a single book of the Bible (or several short ones) will provide the deepest level of help. However, you might not need that much help, or perhaps you don't want to purchase a commentary on each Bible book. In that case, a one-volume commentary on the entire Bible might be most useful.

With these thoughts in mind, here are two excellent commentaries.

Dunn, J. D. G., and J. W. Rogerson, eds. *Eerdmans Commentary on the Bible*. Grand Rapids, MI: Eerdmans, 2003. This volume includes commentaries on all the books in the Bible plus the OT Apocrypha. The authors, recognized scholars, represent a broad ecumenical constituency. Their comments reflect a more theologically liberal stance than the next volume.

Elwell, W. A., ed. *Baker Commentary on the Bible*. Grand Rapids, MI: Baker, 2001. Based on the NIV, this commentary is written specifically for laypersons, collegians, Bible teachers, and pastors. It offers comments, outlines, and introductions for each of the sixty-six biblical books, and, often, extended comments on specific biblical texts.

Before we proceed, I'll list the best commentary series currently available, along with their common abbreviations. Some series comment on both the OT and NT, while others focus on just one. My goal is primarily to alert you to these many options. Because the commentaries strive to do different things, it is very difficult to "rate" them adequately. I will use the following scale to identify broad, overall tendencies. But be aware that to assess a series is difficult because individual entries may not be alike in all respects. With some trepidation, here's how I will identify them:

T = technical: written for scholars and specialists in biblical studies, often for each other
S = scholarly in approach, though not written for other scholars; not as technical as the prior group
N = non-specialist: written for pastors or laypeople
E = ecumenical: written by authors across the denomination and, perhaps, religious, spectrum
C = conservative: authors fall generally toward the conservative side of the theological spectrum
L = liberal: authors fall generally toward the liberal side of the theological spectrum
C/L = volumes fall all along this spectrum

Major OT Commentary Series
AB   Anchor Bible—T, E, L
AOTC   Apollos Old Testament Commentary—S, N, C
BST   The Bible Speaks Today—N, C

CBC   Cambridge Bible Commentary—S, N, E

ConC   Continental Commentary—T, E, L

DSB   Daily Study Bible—N, L

FOTL   Forms of Old Testament Literature—T, E, L

HCOT Historical Critical Commentary of the Old
Testament—T, E, L

Herm Hermeneia—T, E, L

ICC   The International Critical Commentary—T, E, C/L

Int   Interpretation—S, E, L

JPS   Jewish Publication Society Torah Commentary; and
Jewish Publication

Society Commentary—S, L

NAC   New American Commentary—S, N, C

NCB   New Century Bible—S, E, C/L

NIBC   New International Biblical Commentary—S, N, E, C/L

NICOT New International Commentary on the Old
Testament—S, N, C

NIVAC The NIV Application Commentary—S, N, C

OBT   Overtures to Biblical Theology—S, E, L

OTL   The Old Testament Library—T, E, L

SBTS   Sources for Biblical and Theological Study—S, E, L

TOTC Tyndale Old Testament Commentaries—S, N, C

WBC   Word Biblical Commentary—T, E, C/L

WeBC Westminster Bible Companion—S, N, E, L

WEC   Wycliffe Exegetical Commentary—S, C

Major NT Commentary Series

AB   Anchor Bible—T, E, L

BECNT Baker Exegetical Commentary on the New
Testament—S, C

BNTC Black's New Testament Commentary—S, N, C/L

BST	Bible Speaks Today—N, C
EBC	Expositor's Bible Commentary—S, C
ECC	Eerdmans Critical Commentary—T, E, L
ICC	International Critical Commentary—T, E, C/L
Int	Interpretation—S, E, L
NAC	New American Commentary—S, N, C
NCB	New Century Bible—S, E, C/L
NCBC	New Cambridge Bible Commentary—S, N, C/L
NIBC	New International Biblical Commentary—S, N, E, C/L
NICNT	New International Commentary on the New Testament—S, N, C
NIGTC	New International Greek Testament Commentary—T, C
NIVAC	NIV Application Commentary—S, N, C
NTC	New Testament Commentary—S, N, C
NTL	New Testament Library—S, E, L
PNTC	Pillar New Testament Commentary—S, N, C
SP	Sacra Pagina—S, N, E
THNTC	Two Horizons New Testament Commentary—S, N, C/L
WBC	Word Biblical Commentary—T, E, C/L
TNTC	Tyndale New Testament Commentary—S, N, C

What kinds of commentaries will you find in a bookstore or in a theological library? Which ones should you use or consider purchasing?

At one end of the spectrum, you'll find commentaries written for popular or lay audiences. These often concentrate on the practical (putting biblical insights to concrete use in daily life) or devotional (showing how the texts inspire or contribute to our love for God and others) significance of biblical texts. These are also imprecise labels. Such commentaries tend to be shorter, based solely on an English translation, and rarely go into much detail about the original languages or technical details. They focus on putting the message of the Bible into practice.

Somewhere in the middle, you'll find commentaries that target pastors and teachers to help them communicate the significance of a biblical text. Pastors might author these for the benefit of their colleagues. Other commentaries focus on the significant details of the English (or original-language) text for readers who seek more depth, yet they remain in this middle area of the spectrum by relegating technical matters to footnotes (if these are included at all). Laypeople, pastors, and advanced Bible students can profit from their discussions.

At the far other end from the popular ones, you'll find academic, analytical, and technical commentaries written by scholars for other scholars and teachers. These resources rigorously explore the significance of the original languages, refer to specialized studies in English or other modern languages, and go into the fine points about all aspects of interpretation. Many of the details might be inaccessible to non-scholars or to those without theological education. Some commentaries give more weight to the ancient world of the text and historical matters; others focus on the theological significance of the texts for modern readers.

Beyond these factors, because publishers and editors of series have control over who writes the entries in the volumes, the volumes might all share a viewpoint or theological orientation (for example, conservative or liberal; Protestant, Catholic, or Orthodox; evangelical or mainline). At other times, publishers and editors might seek a cross-section of perspectives to achieve an ecumenical series. While these labels aren't always very useful, they do point to a certain reality in the publishing world. (See page 334 if you need a refresher on how I'm using these labels. Many are also listed in the glossary, which begins on page 411.)

Obviously, you have several factors to consider when you think about using a commentary to help you with your Bible study. Perhaps the key question is: What's your purpose in using a commentary? Some other considerations:

- How much depth of details and technical analysis of the biblical texts do you want or need for your study (or how much depth can you understand)?
- Are your theological moorings secure so you can weigh technical issues with proper discernment?
- Are you just starting out on your theological journey and needing issues presented on a more basic level?
- Are you a veteran Bible student?
- Are you studying the text in order to teach it to others?
- Is your study for your own devotional enrichment—and, if so, what kind of commentary will best contribute to what you need at this point on your spiritual journey?

Recognizing that these and other factors create various tensions, I can't recommend commentaries for every situation. And space doesn't allow me to list commentaries for individual biblical books. However, several sources do provide details and helpful recommendations about individual commentaries on specific books of the Bible. You might find the first three in the library of a theological seminary, or you might need to order one of them from a bookstore or online.

Glynn, J. *Commentary and Reference Survey*. Grand Rapids, MI: Kregel, 2007. Now in its tenth edition, this guide lists and ranks approximately 900 commentaries and 1,600 other biblical resources for the benefit of professors, Bible students, and pastors.

Longman III, T. *Old Testament Commentary Survey*. 4th ed. Grand Rapids, MI: Baker, 2007. The author provides a brief assessment of the viewpoints of numerous commentaries. He also indicates who would most benefit from each one (scholar, pastor, layperson).

Carson, D. A., *New Testament Commentary Survey*. 6th ed. Grand Rapids, MI: Baker, 2007. In this work, you'll find extensive entries for commentaries for each NT book. The author notes the intended audience, level of difficulty, and theological perspective of each commentary listed.

www.denverseminary.edu/resources/the-denver-journal. In this online listing, titled "Denver Journal" (on the Denver Seminary website), you'll find lists of recommended commentaries in the OT bibliography and NT bibliography. These are listed book by book and updated at least semiannually.

In what follows, I'll place some recommended commentaries into three categories to help you determine the commentaries that will best meet your needs. Under each category, I'll list the major series; some of these are still not completed. If you're close to a seminary or theological college library[2], you might be able to sample these resources before you buy them. This might be especially helpful if you aren't sure which commentary will best meet your needs.

Practical Orientation

Anders, M., ed. *Holman New Testament Commentary*. Nashville: Broadman, Holman, 1998. Based on the NIV and mostly written by theologically conservative (usually Southern Baptist) pastors and others who aren't NT specialists, these short commentaries are useful for pastors, teachers, and Sunday school teachers. Also contains helpful illustrations and points for group discussions.

Krodel, G. A., ed. *Proclamation Commentaries*. Minneapolis: Augsburg Fortress, 1978. These brief paperback commentaries on the NT, written by prominent critical scholars, are designed especially for those who preach.

Miller, P. D., P. J. Achtemeier, and J. L. Mays. *Interpretation Commentary*. 43 vols. Louisville, KY: Westminster John Knox, 2005. Written by mainline scholars for preachers and teachers, this series focuses on the meaning and application of the texts of the entire Bible.

Motyer, J. A., and J. R. W. Stott, eds. *The Bible Speaks Today* [*BST*]. Downers Grove, IL; Leicester, UK: InterVarsity, 1986. This popular-level series provides commentary on books in both testaments. Most of the authors are British evangelicals.

Muck, T., gen. ed. *The NIV Application Commentary* [*NIVAC*]. Grand Rapids, MI: Zondervan, 2001. The series aims to cover both the OT and NT. It divides comments on each biblical section into three areas: "original meaning," "bridging contexts" into today's world, and "contemporary significance." The comments on the original meaning are relatively brief. Teachers, preachers, and laypersons will profit from this accessible series that is evangelical in orientation.

Ogilvie, L. J., ed. *The Communicator's Commentary*. Nashville: Nelson, 1991-1994. As the title suggests, this series focuses on how to proclaim the meaning and application of the text. Mostly written by North American evangelical expositors or preachers, these commentaries are helpful for pastors, teachers, and Bible study groups.

Osborne, G. R., ed. *New Testament Commentary* [IVP *NTC*]. Downers Grove, IL; Leicester, UK: InterVarsity, 1991. This series of brief commentaries aims to link the pastoral heart with the scholarly mind, emphasizing the significance of the text for the church. The series is evangelical in orientation.

Teaching, Preaching, and Serious Study

The entries in the following series make significant use of the original languages. However, they usually relegate technical references to footnotes to avoid cluttering up the discussions for those not interested in or able to follow them. These commentaries tend to draw out the theological implications of the texts (some more so than others), but not all devote space to practical application, often leaving that to readers.

Carson, D. A., ed. *Pillar New Testament Commentaries [PNTC].*
Leicester, UK: InterVarsity; Grand Rapids, MI: Eerdmans,
1988. This ongoing series represents a major mid-range series,
more technical than many in this category. The authors are
generally conservative. An electronic version is available.

Clendenen, E. R., ed. *New American Commentary [NAC].*
Nashville: Broadman, Holt, 1991. This series—written largely
by Southern Baptist scholars, but including a few contributors beyond that denomination—targets pastors; in addition,
Bible students and laypersons will find these detailed but not
overly technical works very useful. An electronic version is also
available.

Furnish, V. P., gen. ed. *Abingdon New Testament Commentaries.*
Nashville: Abingdon, 1996. Ecumenical in scope, this series
seeks to provide compact, critical comments particularly for
theological students but also for pastors and church leaders.
Several volumes of the parallel *Abingdon Old Testament
Commentaries* series have also been released.

Harrington, D. J., ed. *Sacra Pagina.* Collegeville, MN: Liturgical
Press, 1991. A multivolume series on the NT written by
Roman Catholic scholars.

Harrison, R. K., ed. succeeded by R. L. Hubbard Jr. *New
International Commentary on the Old Testament [NICOT].*

Grand Rapids, MI: Eerdmans, 1965; Bruce, F. F., ed. succeeded by G. D. Fee. *New International Commentary on the New Testament* [*NICNT*]. Grand Rapids, MI: Eerdmans, 1952. Work on new volumes or revisions in both of these NIC series is ongoing. Both represent a high level of conservative evangelical scholarship, and the commentary might be described as more technical than popular. However, the comments are accessible to most serious readers.

Longman III, T. (OT), and D. E. Garland (NT), eds. *Expositor's Bible Commentary* [*EBC*] revised ed. Grand Rapids, MI: Zondervan, 2006. [First edition edited by F. E. Gaebelein; 12 vols., 1976–1992.] A complete update of the first edition is underway; the first revised volume appeared in 2006. This series includes commentaries on the books in both the OT and NT, plus introductory articles. Authors represent several nations and denominations, but all are evangelicals. They write for a wide audience to explain the meaning of the Bible, not to engage overly technical or obscure issues. An electronic version is also available.

Martens, E. A. (OT), and W. M. Swartley (NT), eds. *The Believer's Church Bible Commentary*. Scottdale, PA: Herald, 1991. This important Mennonite/Anabaptist set (historically Mennonites have been committed to nonviolence, peaceful resistance, and pacifism) provides substantial comments on the English Bible text, along with extensive applications to contemporary church life.

Wiseman, D. J., ed. *The Tyndale Old Testament Commentaries* [*TOTC*]. Leicester, UK/Downers Grove, IL: InterVarsity, 1964-99; Morris, L. ed. *The Tyndale New Testament Commentaries* [*TNTC*]. Leicester, UK: InterVarsity; Grand Rapids, MI: Eerdmans, 1956–1991. The two Tyndale series represent mainstream evangelical scholarship from both

Britain and North America. These commentaries, written for laypeople and pastors, present the theological significance of the biblical books.

The New International Biblical Commentary [*NIBC*]. Peabody, MA: Hendrickson, 1988. This commentary features prominent scholars, including many evangelicals, who write to make the best study accessible to a wide audience. The comments tend to be briefer than other entries in this category. Authors span the theological spectrum. The NT series (ed. W. W. Gasque) is complete, and the OT series (eds. R. K. Johnston and R. L. Hubbard Jr.) is near completion.

Advanced Study

Most readers of this *Handbook* won't need or be able to interact with the deepest level of commentaries. However, I'll list several series in case you'd like to check out any of them to answer technical questions. Again, you might not want to purchase these commentaries, but you can still make use of them if you're near a seminary or college theological library. To get the full benefit of these, readers need to have knowledge of the biblical languages — the more the better. Even if you don't have that knowledge, you might still profit from these sources, recognizing that you might not always be able to follow the intricacies of all discussions.

Albright, W. F., and D. N. Freedman, eds. *Anchor Bible* [*AB*]. Garden City, NY: Doubleday, 1964. This ongoing series covers the OT, NT, and apocryphal books. Many volumes are highly technical in nature and only for advanced students and scholars. Their quality varies widely, although several are truly superior. Contributors include Catholics, Jews, and Protestants.

Cross, F. M., and H. Koester, et al., eds. *Hermeneia: A Critical and Historical Commentary on the Bible.* Minneapolis: Augsburg

Fortress, 1972. This series will eventually include volumes on books in the OT, NT, as well as apocryphal books and writings by early church fathers. The most liberal of all the series listed here, it often provides the most detailed treatment of books available by top scholars. The works are highly technical and focus almost exclusively on historical and critical issues. Due to their high level of scholarship and prohibitive cost, it's likely that only specialists will find much use for the commentaries in this series.

Emerton, J. A., C. E. B. Cranfield, and G. N. Stanton, eds. *International Critical Commentary, Old and New Testaments* [*ICC*]. Edinburgh: T. & T. Clark, 1895. These highly technical volumes, which stress critical and philological matters, are written by top scholars across the theological spectrum. New volumes and revisions continue to emerge, although older volumes are rather dated. An electronic version is also available.

Hagner, D. A., and I. H. Marshall, eds. *New International Greek Testament Commentary* [*NIGTC*]. Grand Rapids, MI: Eerdmans, 1978. This NT series reflects a high level of conservative scholarship, accessible to those with a background in Greek. An electronic version is also available.

Watts, D. J. (OT), and R. P. Martin (NT), eds. *Word Biblical Commentary* [*WBC*]. Nashville: Nelson, 1999. The level of detail in these commentaries requires two (or occasionally three) volumes for some of the longer biblical books. The format of these commentaries includes sections that provide textual, structural, and literary analysis, exegesis, and conclusions about the meaning and significance of the texts. These aren't for average readers, although nearly anyone could profit from the "Explanation" sections. An electronic version is also available.

Yarborough, R. W., and R. H. Stein, eds. *Baker Exegetical Commentary on the New Testament* [*BECNT*]. Grand Rapids, MI: Baker, 1992. This ongoing series, written from a conservative, evangelical viewpoint, provides in-depth exegesis (critical interpretation) of the Greek NT texts. An electronic version is also available.

Original-Language Resources

As I noted in the previous section, advanced commentaries engage the original language of biblical texts. While you might not be able to follow all the discussions without knowledge of Hebrew or Greek, you can glean a lot of useful information if you're persistent. As a reminder, the word-study tools by W. Van Gemeren [NIDOTTE] and C. Brown [NIDNTT] that I listed earlier also study the words in the original languages.

If you have access to a theological library at a seminary or Bible college and you're really curious about doing more advanced studies of Hebrew or Greek words, you'll find four additional excellent sources listed here. In addition, if you'd like to learn more about the grammar of the biblical languages, I've listed several excellent resources to help you pursue that goal.

Word Studies

Botterweck, G. J., H. Ringgren, H.-J. Fabry (eds.). *Theological Dictionary of the Old Testament* [*TDOT*]. 15 vols. Grand Rapids, MI: Eerdmans, 1974-2006. Fifteen volumes have appeared in English translation. *TDOT* volumes present in-depth discussions of the key Hebrew and Aramaic words in the OT, written by the first rank of scholars from around the world. This is the standard, most complete, and authoritative treatment of OT words.

Jenni, E., and C. Westermann (eds.). *Theological Lexicon of the Old Testament.* 3 vols. Peabody, MA: Hendrickson, 1997. Briefer than *TDOT,* yet these volumes provide in-depth and wide-ranging investigations of the historical, semantic, and theological meanings of Old Testament concepts. This reference work can serve a wide audience, from professors and researchers to pastors and students of the Bible. Even readers with little or no knowledge of Hebrew can use it profitably.

Bauer, W. (Danker/Arndt/Gingrich) [BDAG]. *A Greek-English Lexicon of the New Testament and Other Early Christian Literature.* 3rd ed. Chicago: University of Chicago Press, 2000. The standard Greek lexicon, an indispensable tool for discerning the meanings of Greek words during the Hellenistic period. This is *the* lexicon that all students of NT Greek should have.

Kittel, G., and G. Friedrich, ed. *Theological Dictionary of the New Testament* [*TDNT*]. 10 vols. Grand Rapids, MI: Eerdmans, 1964–1978. This monumental reference work mediates between a regular lexicon such as BDAG and the specific task of exposition. *TDNT* treats more than 2,300 theologically significant NT words, including the more important prepositions and numbers as well as many proper names from the OT. Presenting the words in the order of the Greek alphabet, *TDNT* typically includes the following entries for each word: its secular Greek background, its role in the OT, its use in extrabiblical Jewish literature, and its varied uses in the New Testament.

Grammars

Pratico, G. D., and M. V. Van Pelt. *Basics of Biblical Hebrew.* Grand Rapids, MI: Zondervan, 2001. This is a systematic approach to the grammar and basic syntax of biblical Hebrew.

Waltke, B. K., and M. O'Connor. *An Introduction to Biblical Hebrew Syntax.* Winona Lake, IN: Eisenbrauns, 1990. This grammar also integrates modern linguistic approaches.

Blass, F., A. Debrunner, and R. Funk. *A Greek Grammar of the New Testament and Other Early Christian Literature* [BDF]. Chicago: University of Chicago Press, 1961. Though not easy to navigate, *BDF* is recognized as the standard and authoritative source.

Wallace, D. B. *Greek Grammar Beyond the Basics.* Grand Rapids, MI: Zondervan, 1996. This book is more user-friendly and comprehensive than the other grammar resources listed here. One great advantage is the multiple examples of grammatical features that it cites.

ELECTRONIC TOOLS AND RESOURCES

While printed materials still dominate the way most people study the Bible, publishers and others who have access to "content" are increasingly making resources available in electronic formats. By electronic, I mean both computer-resident and web-based materials. Of course, convenience is the main advantage of electronic resources. Shelf-loads of Bibles, reference books, atlases, and various other materials can now reside on a laptop computer. In the past, you'd need to rely on a book's index or table of contents to locate a specific reference, but now search engines do the same task quicker and more accurately, often searching multiple sources at once.

As with printed resources, you'll still need to weigh the many choices available and the type of resources you need for your study. And, of course, money is always a consideration. What follows are brief reviews of several software products I've found most useful. I frankly admit that dozens of other worthy products probably exist that I don't know about, including some that might be equally useful or even better than the ones I've listed here. And I further admit that putting this all into a book is highly risky, given that the world of software and electronic devices evolves very quickly. Still, here's a start.

In the first category, you'll find products that have the most features and power. Of course, these often cost the most money as well. For each product, prices vary depending upon what add-in features you select and where you purchase the product.

In the second category, you'll find products with fewer features, although some are surprisingly robust. A few are even free or web-based, so you can use them from any computer connected to the Internet.

Finally, I list several products for handheld devices.

Most Robust and Feature-Rich Tools (Top Tier)

Logos/Libronix (www.logos.com) comes in a variety of configurations, depending on the number and level of resources you want to start with. You can select from an assortment of base products and add other options if desired. Logos packages include many of the "best and latest" (and under current copyright) resources. However, they also incorporate many dozens of other products that are classics or simply because those options might interest some purchasers. Obviously, more resources means higher prices. Realistically, most users will find they don't need or won't have use for many of the resources included.

Beyond that, however, Logos has a key benefit. While other software programs have some add-ons, Logos surpasses them all. Many publishers of Bible-related materials are porting their products onto the Libronix platform—in effect, using the Logos sophisticated search engine. Because of this, you can load literally hundreds of additional products that might or might not come with one of the off-the-shelf packages. This includes commentaries, encyclopedias, lexicons, and other first-rate sources. More appear almost weekly.

All resources are fully searchable, along with the Bibles and other sources that come with the original purchase. In fact, the ability to search in one, several, or even all the resources in your software library makes Libronix a powerful tool. Theoretically, you could search for all references to John 3:16 in the hundreds of resources on your computer. In the catalog of books and commentaries listed previously in this chapter, most of the electronic versions install on the Logos platform. An edition for the Macintosh platform is also available.

Accordance (www.accordancebible.com) is a Macintosh-based program that can run on a PC using an emulator. However, if you have a PC, Logos is a better choice. Accordance is fast and has powerful search capabilities. It includes many Bible versions, as well as other resources and tools for advanced research in primary texts. Unlike some of the other programs, such as Logos and BibleWorks, Accordance doesn't include an automated update service or Internet integration. Although it lags behind the far-reaching library of research and study sources that Logos features, its capacities are extensive and expandable. For many Mac-users this is probably their product of choice, though you should seriously consider Logos.

BibleWorks (www.bibleworks.com) is the premier tool for searches and analyses of biblical and ancient texts, including sources such as Philo and Josephus, as well as in dozens of modern languages. It enables serious students to search in multiple ways for forms and occurrences of words and phrases. Pop-up windows immediately identify grammatical forms (for example, for verbs: tense, mood, voice, and so on) and cite the meanings of words from numerous lexicons. BibleWorks can be customized for different levels of users (more or less sophisticated), and it comes with hours of instructional videos.

BibleWorks is the best resource for word studies, grammatical analyses, and concordance searches on forms in various versions—biblical and extrabiblical, and comparing parallel texts—but doesn't incorporate other resources as does Logos. It will appeal mostly to scholars and advanced users who do extensive work within biblical texts. This is primarily a PC-based program. While BibleWorks does not have a specific Macintosh version, many users find they can run the software on certain Macintosh computers.

Pradis (www.zondervan.com), the search engine for Zondervan products, features that publisher's products along with many versions of the Bible in various configurations. You can start by purchasing one product, such as the TNIV or the NIV Study Bible, or you can buy various collections of products. Pradis enables Bible searches of various kinds as well as access to several of the substantial dictionaries mentioned earlier in this chapter: *NIDOTTE* and *NIDNTT,* along with the *NIVAC* commentary series. Most of Zondervan's reference products exist on Pradis. This software seems ideal for both laypersons and pastors, and it works on both PC and Macintosh platforms.

PC Study Bible (www.biblesoft.com) ships in many versions— from a very basic one that includes only a few Bibles to full-fledged versions that rival Logos and Accordance for available content. Like those two products, PC Study Bible allows users to add many additional sources. While some of the sources are very old like its competitors, others are the latest and best available. And unlike Logos, the PC Study Bible includes many of the best Zondervan dictionaries otherwise only available on the Pradis platform. The product aims to appeal to the full range of users—from average laypersons who want a computer-based Bible that they can use to search or print out texts to advanced users who need to use many tools and resources.

QuickVerse (www.quickverse.com/shopfiles/default.asp) ships in multiple editions for PC, Mac, and PDAs (Palm and Pocket PC). As with all the products already mentioned, QuickVerse allows you to view multiple reference materials—including Bibles, dictionaries, commentaries, and encyclopedias—side by side on the computer screen. A built-in QuickSearch feature allows you to highlight a word or Bible verse and find all of its occurrences in a particular text. Advanced search options also enable you to search by word, phrase, or verse in any language across multiple books.

WordSearch [www.wordsearchbible.com] is another powerful and easy-to-use tool to enhance your Bible study and research. For pastors, it can provide significant help with sermon preparation. WordSearch allows users to add dozens of Bible translations and reference works of all kinds and includes excellent features to help teachers prepare Bible lessons.

Excellent Tools (Second Tier)

In addition to the premier software programs listed in the previous section, many other software products are excellent tools to help with your study of the Bible. Some of these can be downloaded at no cost. Others are based entirely on the Internet and can be used only there.

If you don't need the more robust products I just described, consider the following tools to assist you in studying Scripture. These products tend to be more basic and might not offer the sophisticated searches or additional add-on resources that increase the costs of the products in the preceding group.

By the way, you'll find an amazing number of online Bibles and related links at the "Bible Studies" link of Tyndale House in Cambridge, England: www.tyndale.co.uk/Tyndale/links_Biblical .htm.

The Sword (www.crosswire.org) is the CrossWire Bible Society's free Bible software project. This group has amassed a library of Bibles and other Scripture-related texts that can be used by all SWORD Project–based software. The resources on this site are free and are available for PC, Mac, and PDAs.

Online Bible (www.onlinebible.org/html/eng/starterspack .htm) is a basic, free, PC-based program. The Online Bible Starters Pack contains a complete Bible study package with many powerful and fast features that — for a free program — might pleasantly surprise you.

Bibloi (www.silvermnt.com/bibloi.htm) is a PC-based program for serious users, nearly rivaling the top-tier products listed in the preceding section. This full-featured Bible study package uses the original languages of biblical texts and is user friendly. It includes the texts and tools you need for serious study and research. This program appeals mostly to professors, students, and pastors.

E-Sword (www.e-sword.net) is a free program available for the PC and Pocket PC. E-Sword is fast and effective, user friendly, and includes many features that compare with some of the commercial software packages.

Bible Database (bibledatabase.org) is a free PC-based resource. You can do online searches in many different Bible versions or download versions to your computer.

Theophilos (www.theophilos.sk) sells basic, student, and scholar editions of its PC-based software, and all are surprisingly cost-effective. It targets all age groups from pre-school to adult. However, it includes many older sources (part of why it's available so inexpensively) that many people won't use.

For PDAs (Palm, Pocket PC, Mobile Phones, and MP3 Players)

In this mobile age, you can carry your Bible and other resources in your pocket or purse on a variety of handheld devices. In addition to sources identified for PDAs in the preceding category, the following sources are very usable and surprisingly feature rich. Some are free, and some have significant search capacities, including multiple screens.

BiblePlus (palmbibleplus.sourceforge.net) is free for Palm devices. You can download many different versions of the Bible in many languages, including Greek and Hebrew. Other sources, though mostly old and out of date, are also available at no cost.

Olive Tree (www.olivetree.com) includes many Bibles and other resources, some free and others for sale. It supports original-language texts with some scholarly capabilities. Platforms include Palm, Pocket PC, BlackBerry, various mobile phones, and other devices.

Laridian (www.laridian.com) software gives you access to Bibles and Bible-related reference material (featuring Zondervan products) in a format customized for the unique features of Palm, Pocket PC, Windows Mobile-based smartphone, iPod, and BlackBerry devices.

CHAPTER 8

USES OF THE BIBLE

S uppose you found a map to a buried treasure. Too far-fetched? Let's say that you bought an old house, and as you knocked down a wall to do some remodeling work, you found original-issue IBM stock worth millions of dollars. Or what if you learned that a distant relative who you were close to as a child left you an unexpected inheritance?

We can think of the Bible as all of those things: a treasure, a valuable stock, or a rich inheritance from God. In fact, the apostle Paul told the leaders of the church at Ephesus, "I commit you to God and to the word of his grace, which will build you up and give you an inheritance among all those who are sanctified" (Acts 20:32).

Certainly, God's Word plays an essential role in the Christian's life. As we've explored various approaches and methods for studying Scripture, we've realized how important and useful believers find the Bible to be. However, rather than allowing these uses to float around in our minds, I want to emphasize the important functions Scripture plays in our lives.

I'm sure you already know about many or all of these areas. Yet you might not fully appreciate all of them. Perhaps God wants to encourage you to make use of his Word in other or more significant ways as you become more adept in your Bible study and as God uses it to transform your life.

God has provided a rich resource—a treasure or inheritance of priceless value—that his people have enjoyed and embraced for many centuries. Through the years, many Christians have discovered how to allow the Bible to permeate their lives. This chapter gives you the opportunity to ask if you've allowed Scripture to have the place that God wants in your life as well as how you can maximize this asset God gave to his people.

Let's explore seven areas where God's Word plays a primary role in our lives: spiritual growth, worship, liturgy, theology, ministry, care and counseling, and spiritual formation.

GROWTH

What does it mean to grow? A sapling takes years to grow into a strong and mature tree. An infant receiving the love and care of parents grows into a healthy and productive adult. Growth might come quickly (some insects go through their entire life cycle in a day), or it might take place slowly over the course of centuries, as with the bristlecone pine tree in the American West. The essence of living things is to grow and attain maturity. Stunted growth is a deformity of nature.

Growth is also central in the spiritual realm. Failure to mature spiritually is an aberration because God designed us to grow. Think about the sad words of the author of Hebrews: "It is hard to explain because you are slow to learn. In fact, though by this time you ought to be teachers, you need someone to teach you the elementary truths of God's word all over again. You need milk, not solid food!" (5:11-12). Although the original readers of this letter had followed

Christ for some time, they hadn't made any efforts to pursue spiritual maturity.

So how can Christians grow? God involves himself in our spiritual growth. In fact, the apostle Paul makes clear that only God causes spiritual growth. To the believers in Corinth, Paul wrote, "I planted the seed, Apollos watered it, *but God made it grow*. So neither he who plants nor he who waters is anything, but *only God, who makes things grow*" (1 Cor. 3:6-7, emphasis added).

However, this doesn't mean we just sit and wait for spiritual growth to happen to us. Just as a hardworking farmer makes it possible for crops to grow through many crucial tasks— preparing the soil, sowing good seed, watering, fertilizing, cultivating, weeding, and harvesting—we must also make efforts to grow spiritually. The apostle Peter said, "The word of the Lord stands forever. And this is the word that was preached to you. Therefore, rid yourselves of all malice and all deceit, hypocrisy, envy, and slander of every kind. Like newborn babies, crave pure spiritual milk, so that by it you may grow up in your salvation" (1 Pet. 1:25–2:2).

Although Peter's use of *word* means more than the Bible, it certainly includes the Bible, particularly in the centuries after the apostles lived. Peter urged his readers to picture themselves as infants at the breast, craving the nourishment that will sustain them. When we crave this nourishment and undertake the tasks that lead to spiritual growth, just what can we expect? In what areas does our study of God's Word allow us to grow? Let's look at several.

Growth in Knowledge and Understanding

As divine revelation, the Bible reveals God's will and his ways to us. Only when you engage with Scripture can you come to know and understand God's will and ways. Just how important is it to grow in this knowledge? Solomon, who was known for his power and wisdom, said, "The wise lay up knowledge, but the babbling of a fool brings ruin near" (Prov. 10:14, NRSV). Through the OT prophet Hosea, God said, "My people are destroyed from lack of knowledge" (Hos. 4:6). Clearly, God wants us to recognize that knowledge is fundamental if we want to be wise and survive spiritually.

The Lord commended Solomon when he requested, "Give me wisdom and knowledge, that I may lead this people" (2 Chron. 1:10). We don't know all the ways God imparted knowledge to Solomon. Perhaps some came directly; probably knowledge was imparted through godly counselors and prophets. For us, the authors of Scripture function as our godly counselors and prophets. With their writings inspired by the Holy Spirit, they convey to us knowledge that God deems critical for us to comprehend.

What do we need to know, and how can our study of the Bible facilitate that? The psalmist wrote, "Do good to your servant according to your word, O LORD. Teach me knowledge and good judgment, for I believe in your commands" (119:65-66). God's Word leads us to live well, but for it to do any good in our lives, we must embrace what it says. Knowledge leads to good judgment, which we find by following God's commands. When we immerse ourselves in the reservoir of God's revelation and act on what it says, we learn how to live.

Of course, it's possible to misuse Scripture or even to miss the point of what it teaches. That's why I've devoted so much space and effort in this *Handbook* to stress how important it is to become proficient in interpreting God's Word. Knowledge doesn't come just from spending a lot of time studying the Bible. Even diligent efforts can be futile. Jesus castigated some of the biblical scholars of his day when he said, "Woe to you experts in the law, because you have taken away the key to knowledge. You yourselves have not entered, and you have hindered those who were entering" (Lk. 11:52).

The key to knowledge comes by understanding what God's Word says and putting its message into practice in our lives. As the apostle James wrote, "Humbly accept the word planted in you, which can save you. Do not merely listen to the word, and so deceive yourselves. Do what it says" (1:21-22).

The Bible contains other kinds of knowledge beyond how to live. We discover how God has worked in history, from Creation to the founding and spread of the Christian church through Jesus' followers. In between, we learn about the Fall at Eden; Noah and the Flood; the call of Abraham, Isaac, Jacob, Joseph; and the founding and history of Israel culminating in the promised Messiah Jesus. These are facts of history, but, more important, they're the inspired interpretation of the meaning of that history. And because God stands behind his Word, we know that these accounts are reliable, so we can rely on the knowledge that the Scriptures convey.

At the center of the Bible's message, we find the grand and glorious point of it all: knowledge of God's redeeming love for his fallen creatures, and through that knowledge comes salvation and eternal life with God through faith in Christ. Paul put it eloquently: "Faith comes from hearing the message, and the message is heard through the word of Christ" (Ro. 10:17).

By responding to the message found in God's Word, we receive salvation. And through the same Word, we gain knowledge of how to live and serve. The effects of the Bible and its message on history can't be calculated. The British statesman William Wilberforce and his efforts to abolish the slave trade serve as a prime example of how biblical truth changed first one man and then an entire culture.

As we study the Bible, we grow in knowledge to help us to mature, becoming all that God intends for us to be as citizens of his kingdom.

Growth in Appreciation and Enjoyment

How sad that when you mention studying the Bible, some people recoil or cringe. In effect, they say, "Oh no, not another boring, pointless study session." For some, the Bible seems to be a hard book to understand; for others, it's bizarre, ancient, or frustrating.

I hope that some—even many—of the methods for studying the Bible I've suggested will help you overcome any obstacles you struggle with. With a modern translation or paraphrase and some fresh approaches, virtually all of us can learn from the Bible and grow in our appreciation of its wisdom.

The more we know about the Bible, the better our study and appreciation for it becomes. If you make a commitment to regular study of the Bible, your enjoyment will increase as you become more adept at mining its riches. Savor its delights. Don't treat Bible study as a duty; see it as an adventure.

Who can resist the colorful stories of the Bible—those filled with all kinds of realism, treachery, intrigue, betrayal, loyalty, tragedy, and humor? And that list just scratches the surface! In one of your extended studies of Scripture, challenge yourself to come up with your own exhaustive list of the traits the Bible's stories exhibit.

In these ways, digging into the Bible can move beyond just learning from it—you can enjoy reading it. Even unbelievers marvel at and acknowledge the Bible's profound teachings and literary artistry. How much more should this be true of God's people!

The Bible's diversity is also striking. Where else in one collection of writing could we find such ancient stories alongside poignant poems, arresting prophecies, and penetrating parables, not to mention bizarre apocalypses? Within the same volume, we find the wisdom of ancient Semites along with tightly reasoned Greek logic. If you haven't thought of the Bible this way, you might want to consult a book such as *How to Read the Bible as Literature*, by L. Ryken (see the "For Further Study" section on page 388 for details) or other books that take a similar approach. The Bible is simply a great read!

WORSHIP

Our study of the Bible also guides the way we worship God. As Christians, God is the sole being worthy of our worship. Worshipping anything or anyone else is idolatry, yet how do we know who the true God is and what he has done? We have two sources: the world and the Word.

The created world speaks of a Creator. Actually, it shouts a message something like, "An awesome and powerful Person has made what we see—from the subatomic to the galactic to the interpersonal. We acknowledge this creator God, and rightfully we bow before him." Yet not all people "hear" these words. Some replace God with alternative gods, including some of their own making, such as possessions, fame, or riches. Others replace God with objects he has made, such as the sun or even other people.

Although the natural world reveals the power and splendor of its creator, God has spoken more directly and with more clarity through what theologians call "special revelation." Special revelation consists of words that God speaks to his people. The revelation of God's Son, Jesus, also carries the title "the Word" (Jn. 1:1,14; 1 Jn. 1:1). The Bible captures some of the special revelation God has spoken to his people. For that reason, Paul calls Scripture "God-breathed" (2 Tim. 3:16).

Let's look briefly at two ways the Bible affects how we worship God.

Scripture Teaches Us How to Worship

As a corporate body gathered for worship or in our individual times before the Lord, the Bible calls us to worship. God's Word informs us what worship is as it provides examples of worship from our spiritual ancestors. Scripture's records of God's nature, words, and deeds prompt our worship. We study the Bible so we can learn how better to worship the One who deserves all praise, honor, and faith-ful service.

From Scripture, for example, we learn to worship God rather than his creation: "The heavens declare the glory of God; the skies proclaim the work of his hands. Day after day they pour forth speech; night after night they display knowledge" (Ps. 19:1-2). The apostle Paul confirmed that the natural world reveals God, the true object of our worship: "Ever since the creation of the world [God's] eternal power and divine nature, invisible though they are, have been understood and seen through the things he has made. So they are without excuse" (Ro. 1:20, NRSV).

Scripture points us to God and inspires us to give him the glory, honor, obedience, and service that he deserves. We worship in response to God. And worship is richest of all for God's redeemed creatures, those of us who have a saving relationship with him. We worship God when we respond to what he has accomplished in the world and in us, especially how he acted to save us through the death of his Son, Jesus Christ.

The Bible also provides insight that informs our worship. We learn why we worship, what worship involves, and how to worship well. Christians live "in Christ" with all the blessings and privileges that brings. This status prompts our worship, and God receives glory (see Eph. 1:6,12,14).

Scripture also tells us that worship isn't limited to the "music segment" in a church service. For that matter, worship isn't limited to the church service at all. Paul defined true worship differently:

> I appeal to you therefore, brothers and sisters, by the mercies
> of God, to present your bodies as a living sacrifice, holy
> and acceptable to God, which is your spiritual worship. Do
> not be conformed to this world, but be transformed by the
> renewing of your minds, so that you may discern what is

the will of God—what is good and acceptable and perfect. (Ro. 12:1-2, nrsv)

Paul defines appropriate worship as using our bodies to honor God—allowing God to renew our minds so that we accomplish his will rather than what the world dictates. Later Paul writes, "The rendering of this ministry not only supplies the needs of the saints but also overflows with many thanksgivings to God" (2 Cor. 9:12, nrsv). The same Greek word translated as *worship* (*latreuō*) in Romans 12:1 is translated *ministry* here. In other NT verses, it is translated *serve* (see Mt. 4:10; Lk. 1:74; 2:37; 4:8; Acts 24:14; 27:23; Ro. 1:9; 2 Tim. 1:3) or *service* (*latreia*; see Jn. 16:2; Ro. 9:4; 12:1; Heb. 9:1,6). When Christians give of their resources to meet the needs of others, they engage in worship.

This kind of ministry is worship. God receives praise for putting this generosity into the hearts of his people. We need the Bible to inform us about the nature of true worship; otherwise, we might fall into our culture's trap of evaluating a worship service on the basis of whether we liked the music. When we instead worship by the Spirit, the Spirit accomplishes nothing less than a total renovation of our beings and produces the kinds of actions that please God. We worship through our obedient service in the world.

When we diligently study the Bible, we learn all that this kind of worship involves. Through Bible study, we learn to live lives that worship. Studying the Bible enables us to become people who worship our Creator well in the ways that he deserves, by our words and in our actions.

We Use Scripture in Our Worship

While our worship of God goes well beyond gathering for church services, the Bible indeed both calls for "corporate worship" and provides elements we can use in those times of worshipping together in our churches. The apostle Paul described some of the outcomes of the worshipping congregation. He wrote, "Be filled with the Spirit, as you sing psalms and hymns and spiritual songs among yourselves, singing and making melody to the Lord in your hearts, giving thanks to God the Father at all times and for everything in the name of our Lord Jesus Christ" (Eph. 5:18-20, NRSV). When the Spirit fills the church and its members, singing fills the hearts and then the mouths of worshippers. Portions of the Bible work especially well to help us direct our worship to God.

The Psalms quickly come to mind when we think about using the Bible when we meet as a community of believers. Many Christian congregations recite some of the psalms of ancient Israel or other sections of Scripture as avenues of worship. This allows us to direct our adoration and praise to the Lord of all. Observe how these psalms invite congregations, individuals, and nations to worship God.

Not to us, O LORD, not to us but to your name be the glory, because of your love and faithfulness. Why do the nations say, "Where is their God?" Our God is in heaven; he does whatever pleases him. But their idols are silver and gold, made by the hands of men. They have mouths, but cannot speak, eyes, but they cannot see; they have ears, but cannot hear, noses, but they cannot smell; they have hands, but cannot feel, feet, but they cannot walk; nor can they utter a sound with their throats. . . . The LORD remembers us and will bless us: He will bless the house of Israel, he will bless the house of Aaron, he will bless those who fear the LORD—small and great alike. (115:1-7,12-13)

I love the LORD, for he heard my voice; he heard my cry for mercy. Because he turned his ear to me, I will call on him as long as I live. The cords of death entangled me, the anguish of the grave came upon me; I was overcome by trouble and sorrow. Then I called on the name of the LORD: "O LORD, save me!" The LORD is gracious and righteous; our God is full of compassion. The LORD protects the simplehearted; when I was in great need, he saved me. Be at rest once more, O my soul, for the LORD has been good to you. (116:1-7)

Praise the LORD, all you nations; extol him, all you peoples. For great is his love toward us, and the faithfulness of the LORD endures forever. Praise the LORD. (117:1-2)

Give thanks to the LORD, for he is good; his love endures forever. Let Israel say: "His love endures forever." Let the house of Aaron say: "His love endures forever." Let those who fear the LORD say: "His love endures forever." In my anguish I cried to the LORD, and he answered by setting me free. The LORD is with me; I will not be afraid. What can man do to me? The LORD is with me; he is my helper. I will look in triumph on my enemies. (118:1-7)

The NT also includes writings that grew out of the early believers' experiences of worship. Mary's Song (the Magnificat) in Luke 1:46-55 and Zechariah's prophecy (the Benedictus) in Luke 1:68-79 were probably expressions of individual worship. Many NT scholars believe that Colossians 1:15-20 and Philippians 2:6-11 also provide examples of early Christian hymns of worship to the exalted Christ. Paul probably had in mind the psalms of the OT as well as Christian compositions when he spoke of psalms, hymns, and spiritual songs in early Christian worship (see Eph. 5:18-20; Col. 3:16). The apostles who wrote the words of the NT had personal experiences with the risen Lord that led to words of worship. Our experiences with the risen Lord and his Word should do the same for us.

The Bible doesn't elicit worship only when we read portions written for that purpose. The Scriptures also provide vast evidence of God's mighty deeds, Christ's work for his people, and the Spirit's help and empowerment. Wherever we read of God's love and care, his gifts and call, his provisions and promises, we should be prompted to worship. For example, how can we read the following words without raising our hearts and voices in worship?

> Listen, I tell you a mystery: We will not all sleep, but we will all be changed — in a flash, in the twinkling of an eye, at the last trumpet. For the trumpet will sound, the dead will be raised imperishable, and we will be changed. For the perishable must clothe itself with the imperishable, and the mortal with immortality. When the perishable has been clothed with the imperishable, and the mortal with immortality, then the saying that is written will come true: "Death has been swallowed up in victory." "Where, O death, is your victory? Where, O death, is your sting?" The sting of death is sin, and the power of sin is the law. But thanks be to God! He gives us the victory through our LORD Jesus Christ. (1 Cor. 15:51-57)

LITURGY

We also use God's Word to form our liturgies. The English word *liturgy* comes from a Greek word related to the words for service and worship we just discussed. In contemporary usage, liturgy speaks of a rite or a group of rites that people use in formal worship. Nearly all churches, from those that hold very formal and strictly organized worship services to those that seem very informal and free-flowing, use a kind of liturgy to organize their services, even if they don't use that term to describe what they do. In any case, churches use the Bible in their services of worship—their liturgies. They also use parts of the Bible itself in those liturgies.

Individual

Although liturgy mainly describes public or corporate worship, individuals can also employ a kind of liturgy for their personal worship, often called devotional or quiet times. As with public worship services, individuals might structure their personal devotions formally or informally.

Followers of Christ have always engaged in their own private devotional times, whether or not they had access to a personal copy of the Bible or any portion of it. Early Christians might have memorized parts of Scripture they heard read in their own language. Perhaps later Christians meditated on figures in stained glass windows or icons on church walls. Certainly, Christians throughout the ages could pray: the Lord's Prayer, prayers drawn from biblical texts, and conversational prayers of their own making.

Such informal and individual quiet times continue to this day. You might pray, read, or study a portion of Scripture; read a study guide or devotional book of some kind; intercede and petition God for yourself and others; and go on your daily way. I fondly hope that some of the study tactics outlined in this *Handbook* will prove useful in your own devotional life—your personal, if informal, liturgy.

From early days, Christians also developed more formal kinds of personal liturgies, ones used both individually and in communities. An early example survives in the "Rule of St. Benedict" (about AD 480–547), which referred to the "Divine Office." That label, or the "Daily Office," came to describe the art of praying and chanting the Scriptures, eventually adding other appropriate readings from church fathers and other Christians. Benedict and others followed a fixed regimen of times throughout the day (and night) designed to produce a life of contemplation. This kind of fixed daily routine was intended to produce both individual Christians and a community of believers who focused on spiritual values.

Several denominations or groups produce variations of the Divine Office, such as the *Book of Common Prayer* of the Protestant Episcopal Church; Celtic Daily Prayers of the Northumbria Community in England; the prayer book for Orthodox Christians of the Antiochian Orthodox Community; and books produced by the Order of St. Benedictine, the Order of St. Luke, the United Methodists, and different Lutheran groups. This is just a small listing of examples.

Few laypeople can engage the seven or eight times for prayer and reading a day as some monastic communities practice. More commonly, Christians who follow the Divine Office attempt four: morning office (Lauds), midday, evening (vespers), and a short office just prior to retiring (compline). Others manage one or two times a day. What are some of the values of practicing this kind of fixed regimen?

Using one of these guides gives users a sense of community with others who follow the same regimen. In other words, they provide a sense of the body of Christ at prayer and worship, particularly if people do them at the set times. In addition, the system is designed so that in the course of several cycles (one, two, or three years), participants cover the entire Bible with readings appropriate to the church calendar.

Obviously, you can set up your own routine to accomplish the same things. Many of the study suggestions we've explored allow you to do just that. The specific regimen you follow is not nearly as important as making sure you follow some kind of plan for quiet time and Scripture study each day. Regulate your life by the constant infusion of Scripture and prayer. Engage in your personal liturgy to accomplish what St. Benedict valued: a life infused by spiritual values. How better to attain that goal than by immersing yourself in Scripture—if possible, several times—each day?

Corporate

As we've already noted, Scripture should also infuse the corporate services of Christian worship. The terms *formal* and *informal* again apply here. Some churches employ fixed and formal liturgies, even though they might adapt them as needed on particular occasions. The Episcopal Church's *Book of Common Prayer* (BCP) once more provides a good example, although many other denominations or church groups employ their own variations. In the BCP, in addition to the sections on The Daily Office, you'll find a lectionary that arranges readings from the Scriptures to read through the entire Bible over a three-year cycle. It also includes "Proper Liturgies for Special Days" as well as liturgies for other services.

The liturgies for weekly church services give the precise order of prayers, readings from the OT, Psalms, epistles, and gospels, along with other components appropriate to the occasions. Even a quick glance at any of the services will show you how the words of Scripture inform the actions, prayers, and readings of the liturgy. You might also find optional readings to select from. Services will often include the Apostles' or Nicene Creed. The BCP includes the entire book of Psalms because the liturgies make so much use of them.

Other churches and groups prefer to worship more informally, meaning that instead of using prescribed services and prayers, these churches prefer to devise their own. They select how and which portions, if any, of the Bible they'll use for a given church service. They devise the liturgy and Scripture's place in it to fit the occasion.

Of course, even churches and denominations that avoid prescribed liturgies follow their own informal liturgies very regularly. In many churches, the order of service remains fixed from week to week, the only difference being the selections of hymns, Scripture readings, and prayers. They might even recite the Lord's Prayer every week or regularly close with some benediction from the Bible.

Ideally, informal liturgies are also infused with the Scriptures, but the pastor, worship leader, or some committee decides what role Scripture will have. The liturgy might include responsive readings or the reading of the text for the upcoming sermon. Often the Bible surfaces in a song or hymn (as in Eph. 5:18-20). It might find its most prominent place in the sermon, especially if this message is expositional.

THEOLOGY

As Christians, we use the Bible as the starting point to determine our theology. The word *theology* comes from the Greek word for god: *theos.* Theology is the study of God. Various groups who believe in some concept of god have different theologies that attempt to describe what they believe, including their beliefs about God or god.

While in some abstract sense we claim that certain statements or facts correspond to the true nature of God, theology is really more of a human attempt to express our current understanding of those facts. So what do we base those expressions on? What sources do we arrive at our theology from? For Christians, the Bible initiates theology.

The Bible is also the lens we look through at other evidence — such as natural revelation — to put together our theology. In other words, while we might speculate that God is vindictive because so many people were killed in a recent tsunami, we must filter that evidence from the natural world through the lens of the Bible that allows Christians to put tragic events into perspective. The Bible declares that God loves all people—that he's a God of love. So through that lens, we sift through the evidence in the natural world and try to come to conclusions that help us formulate our theology.

While all Christians believe their theology comes from the Bible, we need to recognize two distinct approaches to arriving at theology: biblical and systematic theology. Let's briefly look at the starting point and objectives of each approach.

Biblical Theology

While the first basis or focus of formulating theology is called "biblical theology," this doesn't imply that systematic theology is not based on the Bible. Instead, this first focus is called "biblical" because it seeks to understand the theologies presented by the biblical authors themselves in the contexts of their historical situations and in their own terms or categories.

For example, in one of the study methods in chapter 6, I suggested that you do an in-depth study of an individual book in the Bible. At the conclusion, you produced your summary of the main theme and the main conclusions. In essence, although I didn't use that label, you were doing a biblical theology. Your goal was to see what the biblical author conveyed in that individual book in light of his own circumstances and those of the readers. You captured his theme and his conclusions. You ended up at the author's theology.

For example, if you did that study for the letter of James, you would have realized that one of the author's main themes is "faith." You might have concluded that for James, the faith that saves a person must be accompanied by works. That would be James' biblical theology of faith. You could then compare that view of faith with Paul's, perhaps as expressed in his letters to the Romans and the Galatians.

After your in-depth study of those two letters, you might conclude that faith is a key theme for Paul, too, and that he was also concerned about the nature of a faith that saved. But when arriving at your conclusion about what Paul means by faith, you might say something like this: Faith and faith alone (with no works) saves a person. That's Paul's biblical theology of faith. You might continue your survey of the biblical theologies of faith by next studying Hebrews, where again faith looms large.

So you can see that biblical theology seeks to express the Bible's theological themes from the perspective of the authors or groups of authors of the biblical texts. Biblical theology might compare the theology of the Synoptic Gospels (Matthew, Mark, and Luke) with the theology of the gospel of John. It might ask how Luke's portrait of Jesus compares with Mark's. It might explore how the theme of God's kingdom progresses from the OT to the NT. Or it might compare the theology of the preexilic with the postexilic prophets.

Systematic Theology

Biblical theology might cause you to ask if an overarching biblical view of faith exists. In other words, can we extract what the entire Bible has to say about the concept of faith (or any other concepts or tenets of the Bible)? The answer is yes, and that's the role of "systematic theology."

In contrast to biblical theology, systematic theology takes its categories, labels, and agenda from the modern world. It's our attempt to systematize what the Bible teaches based on what we want to know about it. We look to the Bible for answers to our questions. For example, the category or label of "the person of Christ" is probably important to most of us. So to answer the question of "Who was Christ?" we mine the Scriptures for answers and we systematize or categorize those answers in ways we find useful.

For this reason, you can also go to a library of a theological seminary or college (or even a theological library online) and locate various "flavors" of systematic theologies. You can find Lutheran, Baptist, Reformed, Pentecostal, Methodist (Wesleyan), or Catholic theologies, to name a few, as well as varieties within all those labels! Not surprisingly, for example, you find the views of the meaning and practice of baptism to differ among many of these groups. They take the biblical data about baptism and systematize it differently, arriving at different conclusions about the significance of that information.

Where scholars stand on the theologically liberal-conservative spectrum also affects the kinds of questions they raise as well as the different ways they filter the answers. Systematic theologies differ because different people ask different questions of what the Bible says, according to the needs and issues they're confronting.

Similarly, systematic theologians come from different cultures or geographical regions, and this can result in different "takes" on the Bible's theology. For example, "liberation theologians" write from the perspective of Latin America. They raise questions growing out of their experiences with the poor and marginalized. No wonder they see things in the biblical texts that wealthy North Americans might see differently or not at all. Africans, Asians, and Europeans bring their own questions and filter the answers through their own experiences.

So how do you do theology systematically well? First, you must use sound principles to analyze biblical texts that relate to the issue you want to address. For example, if you want to explore the issue of "the work of Christ," then you search for the passages that address that issue and do your best study of those texts.

Second, you need to include all the texts that explore the question at hand, not just those that allow you to slant the conclusions any way you want.

Third, you bring together all your results in a way that honors the spirit of all the evidence, and that honors all that the Bible itself emphasizes.

Finally, you show how your conclusion works in the life of the church and in the lives of Christians. An irrelevant theology isn't worthy of the God who authored the Scriptures.

Remember that when you do your own biblical studies and come up with your understandings of biblical issues, they are your understandings. If another Christian doesn't see things precisely as you do, it doesn't mean the other person is wrong, misguided, or unwilling to work as hard as you did to arrive at the right answer. You might want to reread the section in chapter 3 about presuppositions and preunderstandings (see pages 110-115). We all bring our own assumptions, beliefs, and attitudes to studying the Bible, and all of these color our outcomes.

The Place of Theology

I firmly believe that we must engage in both biblical and systematic theology. It's vital to understand biblical authors and their writings from the inside — to get their perspectives on what they decided to write about under the inspiration of the Holy Spirit. Biblical theology pursues this important agenda. And we also need to draw the Bible's teachings together into coherent patterns that we can catalog, review, apply, and teach to others. Systematic theology performs this function.

Both approaches require us to study the Bible. Because systematic theology seeks to answer questions we bring to the texts, it will more obviously reflect our worldviews and issues — and that's a good thing. As Christians, we should seek to bring God's wisdom to our specific cultures. This also implies that systematic theology is an ongoing discipline, as new questions arise and new answers need to emerge from the Bible. At the same time, we need biblical theology to study texts deeply to know how our spiritual ancestors understood God and his purposes in their worlds. And we need their understandings to assure that we don't distort the meaning of Scripture in our desires to find answers to our questions.

We need both biblical and systematic theologies. As we examine how the biblical writers learned from the struggles of their faith and how they perceived God and his ways, we can come up with our own patterns of understanding the truth to help us to live faithfully as Christians in our world.

THE MINISTRY OF THE WORD

Yet another way we use the Bible is by committing to studying Scripture and receiving God's Word into our lives, allowing it to minister to us. By engaging with God's truth in the Bible, we experience spiritual growth and transformation. God calls some people to transmit the transformational truth of Scripture to others through various ministries of the Word.

Throughout biblical history, God has chosen individuals to speak for him and communicate his message. In the OT, for example, the prophets stand out as people who spoke God's message to his people. The early church also included prophets, but the list of communicators speaking for God expanded. Apostles appointed by Christ played a crucial role in communicating the Word, as did evangelists, teachers, and pastors.

The NT includes evidence that early Christian preachers and teachers explained God's Word. Communicating the truth occupied a central place in the church's priorities. Paul urged his protégé

Timothy, "Preach the Word; be prepared in season and out of season; correct, rebuke and encourage—with great patience and careful instruction" (2 Tim. 4:2).

Because faith comes by hearing the Word of God (see Ro. 10:17), those who communicate God's Word are essential. While the distinction between teachers and preachers might seem arbitrary at times, we'll look at them as separate roles to distinguish them. We'll also look at one less formal way that God uses people to speak for him.

Teaching

God calls some people to be teachers of his truth. The prophet Ezra might claim status as the "patron saint" of teachers. Listen to these words: "Ezra had devoted himself to the study and observance of the Law of the Lord, and to teaching its decrees and laws in Israel" (Ezra 7:10). What a privilege: to be a devoted student of God's Word and teach others what you have learned!

Teaching is a central spiritual gift and function for the church. Teachers help people answer the questions, "What are God's people to believe, and how should they live?" Urging the Roman Christians to respond to God's grace in their lives, Paul exhorted them to use their gifts in the service of the church. He wrote, "If your gift is serving others, serve them well. If you are a teacher, teach well" (Ro. 12:7, NLT; also see Eph. 4:11).

During the history of Israel, the prophets typically answered these kinds of questions. Leaders of the early church taught from the OT, adding the teachings of Jesus and the words of the apostles and others. Eventually, of course, they acknowledged the entire Bible as God's revealed Word. During and after this process, teachers explained and applied the Word of God.

Teachers instruct in three arenas: the content of "the faith," what the Christian doctrines mean, and how those committed to the way of Christ must live. They also help Christians avoid the ever-present dangers of heresy and false teachings. The Bible serves as the textbook for these tasks. Paul observed, "Everything that was written in the past was written to teach us, so that through endurance and the encouragement of the Scriptures we might have hope" (Ro. 15:4). Teachers teach so God's people may be encouraged to press ahead faithfully.

Teachers also explain and show how the truth of God functions in life. Paul sent Timothy to the Corinthians to explain how Paul lived out the gospel so the Christians there could grow in their obedience. He said that Timothy "will remind you of my way of life in Christ Jesus, which agrees with what I teach everywhere in every church" (1 Cor. 4:17). Paul taught every group of Christians how to live out their faith.

When Jesus explained to his followers what it took to build disciples, he said that central to the task was "teaching them to obey everything I have commanded you" (Mt. 28:20). A disciple of Jesus must learn to follow all of the Lord's commands. For us, that encompasses the entire Bible.

God calls parents to be teachers. Moses told the Israelites as they were about to enter the Promised Land: "Love the LORD your God with all your heart and with all your soul and with all your strength. These commandments that I give you today are to be upon your hearts. Impress them on your children. Talk about them when you sit at home and when you walk along the road, when you lie down and when you get up" (Dt. 6:5-7). In order to take this role seriously, you must study. John Wesley once wrote,

I SIT DOWN ALONE,

ONLY GOD IS HERE;

IN HIS PRESENCE I OPEN,

I READ HIS BOOKS;

AND WHAT I THUS LEARN,

I TEACH.[1]

God calls and gifts some members of his body to teach his Word (see 1 Cor. 12:28). Don't seek the role of teacher for the wrong reasons; the apostle James warned that those "who teach will be judged more strictly" (Jas. 3:1). However, don't shrink from this privilege if God calls you to it, because sharing what you learn from your study of Scripture is a high calling.

Preaching

If teaching centers on instruction, preaching focuses on exhortation — urging and encouraging change and growth in the lives of those who hear. Of course, good teachers show the implications of their teaching for life, but they focus on instruction. Preaching and teaching often deal with the same content, but preaching stresses the need for people to change because of the message proclaimed.

Paul believed that God had called him to preach the message of Christ crucified and to urge unbelievers to place their trust in Christ (see Ro. 15:20; 1 Cor. 1:17,23; 9:16; 2 Cor 10:16; Eph. 3:8). The apostle insisted, "God was pleased through the foolishness of what was preached to save those who believe" (1 Cor. 1:21). For Paul, it was crucial that the saving message about Jesus be proclaimed everywhere. Consequently, he urged Timothy to preach the Word (see 2 Tim. 4:2). The Word encompasses all of God's will for his creatures. Preachers have the opportunity to proclaim God's message so their hearers can experience transformation.

If preaching has the capacity to transform those who hear the message, then the content of that message is critical. All kinds of "preachers" proclaim all kinds of messages in our world. Christian preachers have the obligation to be biblical. Serious Bible study enables the preacher to proclaim "a word from God" from the pulpit or in the marketplace.

Preachers can use their platforms to preach other messages besides biblical ones. Their words might just be their current thoughts about any variety of topics — including religious ones! Yet God's people deserve to hear God's perspective on life. They need to know how to endure or how to resist the temptations and lures of the cultures around them. How tragic if instead they hear human wisdom in place of God's. While God does use human instruments, called by Paul "jars of clay" (see 2 Cor. 4:7), the special calling of the preacher is to communicate the power of God through life-giving and life-transforming words. The Scriptures contain God's truth. If you are called to preach, "Preach the Word."

Leading Bible Studies

Preaching and teaching seem rather formal. Yet God also calls and uses many Christians in informal ways to transform the lives of people. While they don't get the same press as preachers or teachers who stand in front of larger congregations or classes, Bible study leaders might exert equal or greater impact on the lives of individual people. Review 1 Corinthians 12:14-26 for a reminder of the importance of *all* functioning members of the body of Christ, not just the prominent ones.

Unlike most preaching or teaching venues, Bible study leaders face smaller groups. However, smaller doesn't mean lesser, because study groups allow for personal interactions among the leader and group members. Teachers and preachers have to use applications they think will fit many of their hearers. But the intimacy of a small group allows leader and fellow learners to move more readily from interpretation to a personal and relevant application. Bible study leaders sit in a circle with others, allowing life-to-life contact that can be powerful.

Like preachers and teachers, Bible study leaders have the crucial role of helping others understand the truth and implications of biblical instruction. They deal with the same content from the Scriptures, face the same implications, and raise the same issues, yet they are able to tailor their lessons to their group members. To truly be Bible study leaders, they must be diligent students of the Word of God. While other kinds of small groups are useful and have their place, Bible study groups give people the opportunity to sink their teeth into the Scriptures in a nonthreatening context with great potential to change their lives.

If you get an invitation to lead a Bible study, pray and seriously consider taking up the challenge. Walking with others on the path to godly maturity will revolutionize your own personal Bible study. You'll find that many of the methods in this *Handbook* can help you succeed.

PASTORAL CARE AND COUNSELING

Many uses for the Bible we've explored in this chapter overlap with the last three we'll explore. As the source for knowledge and wisdom, and as the repository of what to believe and how to live, the Bible supports people who need guidance, comfort, and help. The writer of Psalm 119 speaks of the comfort he derives from God's Word: "My comfort in my suffering is this: Your promise renews my life. . . . I remember your ancient laws, O LORD, and I find comfort in them" (vv. 50,52).

God's promises and instructions found in Scripture comfort and support us in times of trials and difficulties. When we need to hear the truth about our circumstances, identity, or destiny, no source of encouragement is more reliable than Scripture. God's Word speaks words of life and truth to us.

When we face the many trials and challenges of life — whether physical, mental, or spiritual — we have various kinds of assistance available. In fact, I believe we need to embrace all the helps that God provides, such as the resources of physicians, counselors, and spiritual companions.

I acknowledge the danger of separating people into compartments as if our spiritual and psychological issues remain distinct from each other. But speaking at this point of the spiritual realm, I believe that Christians must guard against entrusting the well-being of our souls to false teachers. Pastors, spiritual directors, and any other advisors will guide others best when their hearts have drawn close to God through years in God's presence and when Scripture directs their outlook.

We find guidance for our souls from God because he made us in his image. The prophet Habakkuk wrote, "Woe to him who says to wood, 'Come to life!' Or to lifeless stone, 'Wake up!' Can it give guidance? It is covered with gold and silver; there is no breath in it" (2:19). If we put this warning into our contemporary culture, we might ask, "Should we give more credence to a popular self-help book or a media expert than we give to God's Word? Or will we instead follow a way that the Bible counsels because the Holy Spirit has breathed God's wisdom into it?" It's better to follow God's wisdom than the world's.

At the same time, some Bible teachers and preachers misuse the Bible and mislead God's people who seek and need help. They promise more than the Bible promises under the guise of their great faith or God's power to perform miracles if we have enough faith. They twist the Scriptures and misapply their teachings. In some cases, no one exposes their errors, with the result that people discount the Bible's effectiveness. In other cases, people become disillusioned and reject not only the Bible teacher and the Bible but also the Christian faith.

I'm not trying to minimize God's great power to heal or perform great acts for his people. And I certainly don't want to undermine the place of prayer and faith in our relationships with God. I'm simply warning against abuses of the Bible. People can receive genuine help from the Bible, yet they might be harmed by false hope. We should always keep in mind that faithful living according to Scripture might involve enduring a lifetime of pain, such as Paul's thorn in the flesh (see 2 Cor. 12:7-10), rather than experiencing a miraculous healing.

That's why the principles of studying the Bible are so crucial. Paul lauded the diligent and careful use of God's Word. He reminded Timothy, "Do your best to present yourself to God as one approved, a worker who does not need to be ashamed and who correctly handles the word of truth. Avoid godless chatter, because those who indulge in it will become more and more ungodly. Their teaching will spread like gangrene" (2 Tim. 3:15-18, TNIV). Study diligently to find out what God's Spirit intended to teach through Scripture and use those teachings to help yourself and those around you.

Scripture often supplies specific help or at least the perspective we need in our circumstances, questions, and decisions. Several of the Bible study methods in this *Handbook* urge you to enter Scripture through a specific issue in your life. The genre of Wisdom Literature in the Bible (Job, Proverbs, Ecclesiastes, and Song of Songs) excels in this function. Likewise, the Psalms often give us voices to express our joys, sorrows, and tragedies.

We can also find encouragement by reading and praying the words of Scripture. This helps us see that others encountered these issues before us. Paul's words provide comfort: "No testing has overtaken you that is not common to everyone. God is faithful, and he will not let you be tested beyond your strength, but with the testing he will also provide the way" (1 Cor. 10:13, NRSV). God's Word provides the hope and promise that we will survive. For example, Job's story reminds us that more might be going on in our circumstances than we know, and it's always better to bless God than to curse him and die. We might never arrive at the answer to our "Why?" questions, but we can still trust in God.

Of course, when you find yourself in the midst of testings or decisions, you can also engage in topical studies that zero in on your specific needs. For example, if you lose someone close to you, you can do a study on "grief" and better understand God's perspective on and provision of comfort for your sorrow.

In any event, as you read and study what the Bible teaches, keep track of the issues and answers your study reveals. You can "file" these for eventual use for yourself, or you'll find them useful when trying to help and encourage your friends.

PERSONAL GUIDANCE

One aspect of applying God's Word centers on finding what some Christians call "God's will for our lives." Faithful Christians want to obey God, so we naturally seek God's guidance in the Scriptures. This underscores how important careful study of the Bible is, because guidance in life is a serious matter. Saying, "God wants me to . . ." places a weighty obligation on a follower of Christ. We don't want to be guilty of dismissing what God wills for our lives. As we seek to apply the Bible in the area of personal guidance, we should consider several points.

We should seek God's will as laid out specifically in passages of Scripture that we have faithfully studied on the basis of valid methods of Bible study, such as the methods we've considered in this *Handbook*. Some texts use the specific language of God's will to instruct readers. For example, Paul tells the Christians at Thessalonica, "It is God's will that you should be sanctified: that you should avoid sexual immorality" (1 Thess. 4:3). In other places, Paul expected his readers to grasp God's will from what he communicated to them more generally, as in Romans 12:2: "Do not conform any longer to the pattern of this world, but be transformed by the renewing of your mind. Then you will be able to test and approve what God's will is—his good, pleasing and perfect will." The apostle insisted that the Roman Christians allow God to transform their minds so they'd know how God wanted them to live. Of course, Paul then followed these words with more specific instructions that his readers would understand as God's will (the rest of Romans 12–15). So if we're eager to do God's will, we need to allow God's Spirit to transform us, and we need to implement God's instructions as we discover them in his Word.

But what about specific guidance? Can we use the Bible to help make decisions about the person we should marry, which car to buy, what church we should attend, the job we might take, or whether or not to have children? Certainly, the Bible gives us principles to help us make decisions. We find these principles when we discover how the Bible provides instructions for the original readers. We should ask such questions as: *Why did the writer instruct the readers to take that specific action? And what was at stake in this instruction?*

While the specific application might not fit our circumstances, we need to discover what cross-cultural principle informed the original application that might also apply to our circumstances.

I believe that Christians should use their sanctified common sense to apply the meaning of the biblical text in appropriate ways. How does our common sense become sanctified? This is what Paul meant when he instructed his readers in Rome to allow God's Spirit to transform their minds. The Spirit accomplishes that as we immerse ourselves in God's Word. We should follow Jesus' example of when he faced Satan's temptations and infuse our minds with the principles of the Scriptures.

At the same time, I think it's wrong to use a Ouija-board approach to discern God's guidance from the Bible. This tactic flips open the Bible at random, points a finger with eyes closed, and reads the resulting "guidance." While that might be an extreme case, some

Christians expect God to speak to them in almost magical ways, without them doing the work of understanding what God painstakingly reveals in Scripture.

The guidance we derive from a passage never contradicts what that passage means in its context. That's why our discussion about the various principles on how to study the Bible is so vital. We need to understand what texts mean so we can arrive at proper principles to guide our lives. Because the entire Bible is God's Word, guidance from one text will never contradict what another text explicitly teaches. God doesn't speak out of both sides of his mouth. If it seems that way—if guidance we glean from a passage opposes what other Scriptures clearly teach—we're likely misunderstanding the passage.

Finally, specific guidance might be as different as God's unique call and gifts to his people. In other words, guidance isn't "one size fits all." Simply because God used the principle from a passage to guide someone else in a specific direction doesn't mean you should head the same direction. God will sanctify our common sense in light of how he wants to use his Word to direct our paths. For example, while God's will is that all his followers love their neighbors, the form or action that love takes will differ depending on many factors. However, we don't have the option to reject God's will.

SPIRITUAL FORMATION

The last use of the Bible we'll explore is "spiritual formation." While the term itself was coined within the last few decades or so, spiritual formation has always been the goal of serious followers of Christ. To *form* means to bring something into existence and shape it around certain goals. If it's clay, you might "form" it into a vase or bowl.

Using that metaphor, spiritual formation describes the process of becoming shaped in the spiritual realm of life. As Christians, how can we become spiritually formed? How do we know if we're being formed in the right way?

God's Spirit seeks to conform God's people to be like Christ. Paul put it precisely: "God knew his people in advance, and he chose them to become like his Son, so that his Son would be the firstborn among many brothers and sisters" (Ro. 8:29, NLT). Apparently, God desires an entire family of sons and daughters who resemble his Son, Jesus. In the process of spiritual formation, we cooperate with and promote that process of becoming like Christ.

We become like Jesus when we think and act like him. Conformity to Christ starts in the spiritual domain and leads to a transformed life. We love God and our neighbors as Christ loved his father and people in this world. Jesus instructed his followers to live this way: "'Love the Lord your God with all your heart and with all your soul and with all your mind.' This is the first and greatest commandment. And the second is like it: 'Love your neighbor as yourself.' All the Law and the Prophets hang on these two commandments" (Mt. 22:37-40).

Spiritual formation clearly requires transformation. In addition to Jesus' love commands, another obvious illustration is Paul's picture of the fruit of the Spirit. Spiritually transformed people will exhibit these qualities. He writes, "The fruit of the Spirit is love, joy, peace, patience, kindness, generosity, faithfulness, gentleness, and self-control. There is no law against such things. And those who belong to Christ Jesus have crucified the flesh with its passions and desires. If we live by the Spirit, let us also be guided by the Spirit" (Gal. 5:22-25).

Note what Paul adds in verses 24-25 after listing the fruit. Living according to the Spirit implies allowing the Spirit to guide us and not being ruled by our sinful natures, desires, and passions.

How do we achieve this? While guidance might come in many ways, the Spirit uses God's Word as a prime means to produce in us the kind of life that God desires: a life that is like Christ. Many Christians are adept at learning and growing in knowledge (not bad in itself), but knowledge alone can be a trap. As Paul said, "Knowledge puffs up while love builds up" (1 Cor. 8:1, TNIV). We need to learn how to love (as Jesus commanded), and that takes spiritual transformation.

In many of the Bible study methods in this *Handbook*, I've emphasized the essential steps of first asking and then allowing the Spirit to use what you discover to transform your life. Both steps are crucial. What's the point of asking God to show you what you need to do and then ignoring what he shows you in his Word? That's a dangerous approach! God isn't pleased with people who honor him with their lips while keeping their hearts to themselves (see Is. 29:13).

Prayer and Bible study together are crucial. Pray that God will show you what he wants to change in you, especially at the heart level. As you begin each time of studying the Bible, pray David's prayer: "Create in me a clean heart, O God, and put a new and right spirit within me" (Ps. 51:10, NRSV). Ask God to make sure that the information you uncover in your study of his Word results in transformation. Be a "doer of the Word."

In our culture, we deal with all kinds of pressure to steer our lives and values into selfish quests. When you decide to pursue a life that pleases God and become more like Christ, you'll constantly face the foes of the world, the flesh, and the Devil. Peter urges, "Be self-controlled and alert. Your enemy the devil prowls around like a roaring lion looking for someone to devour. Resist him, standing firm in the faith" (1 Pet. 5:8-9).

God gives us his Word to fortify our faith. By immersing our minds in what God has revealed, his Spirit can do the inner work of transformation we desperately need for becoming like Christ.

FOR FURTHER STUDY

Growth in Appreciation of the Bible as Literature

Gabel, J. B., et al. *The Bible as Literature: An Introduction.* 4th ed. Oxford, UK: Oxford University Press, 1999.

Ryken, L. *How to Read the Bible as Literature.* Grand Rapids, MI: Zondervan, 1985.

Worship

Carson, D. A., ed. *Worship by the Book.* Grand Rapids, MI: Zondervan, 2002.

Peterson, D. *Engaging with God: A Biblical Theology of Worship.* Downers Grove, IL: InterVarsity, 2002.

Webber, R. E. *The Biblical Foundations of Christian Worship.* Peabody, MA: Hendrickson, 1995.

Liturgy

Benedict, D. T. *Patterned by Grace: How Liturgy Shapes Us.* Nashville: Upper Room Books, 2007.

The Book of Common Prayer. New York: HarperCollins, 1991. (Many editions exist.)

Eslinger, E. S., ed. *Upper Room Worship Book: Music and Liturgies for Spiritual Formation.* Nashville: Upper Room Books, 2006.

Pfatteicher, P. H. *Liturgical Spirituality.* Harrisburg, PA: Trinity, 1997.

Senn, F. C. *Christian Liturgy: Catholic and Evangelical.* Minneapolis: Augsburg Fortress, 1997.

Webber, R. E., ed. *Twenty Centuries of Christian Worship.* Peabody, MA: Hendrickson, 1995.

Theology
Biblical
Brueggemann, W. *Theology of the Old Testament: Testimony, Dispute, Advocacy*. Minneapolis: Fortress, 1997.

Hasel, G. *Old Testament Theology. Basic Issues in the Debate*. 4th ed. Grand Rapids, MI: Eerdmans, 1995.

Ladd, G. E. *A Theology of the New Testament*. 2nd ed., ed. D.A. Hagner. Grand Rapids, MI: Eerdmans, 1993.

Marshall, I. H. *New Testament Theology*. Downers Grove, IL: InterVarsity, 2004.

Smith, R. L. *Old Testament Theology: Its History, Method, and Message*. Nashville: Broadman, Holman, 1993.

Thielman, F. *Theology of the New Testament*. Grand Rapids, MI: Zondervan, 2005.

Systematic
Erickson, M. J. *Christian Theology*. 2nd ed. Grand Rapids, MI: Baker, 1998.

Grenz, S. J. *Theology for the Community of God*. Grand Rapids, MI: Eerdmans, 2002.

Lewis, G., and B. Demarest. *Integrative Theology*. Grand Rapids, MI: Zondervan, 1996.

McGrath, A. E. *Christian Theology: An Introduction*. 3rd ed. Oxford, UK: Blackwell, 2001.

Ministry of the Word
Preaching
Goldsworthy, G. *Preaching the Whole Bible as Christian Scripture: The Application of Biblical Theology to Expository Preaching*. Grand Rapids, MI: Eerdmans, 2000.

Greidanus, S. *The Modern Preacher and The Ancient Text: Interpreting and Preaching Biblical Literature*. Grand Rapids, MI: Eerdmans, 1994.

Robinson, H. W. *Biblical Preaching: The Development and Delivery of Expository Messages*. 2nd ed. Grand Rapids, MI: Baker, 2001.

TEACHING

Bredfeldt, G., and L. Richards. *Creative Bible Teaching*, rev. ed. Chicago: Moody, 1998.

Blair, C. E. *The Art of Teaching the Bible: A Practical Guide for Adults*. Louisville, KY: Geneva Press, 2001.

Coleman, L. E. *How to Teach the Bible*. Nashville: Broadman, Holman, 2000.

Mabry, S., and B. McNabb. *Teaching the Bible Creatively*. Grand Rapids, MI: Zondervan/Youth Specialties, 1990.

LEADING BIBLE STUDIES

Davis, D., and S. Nikaido. *Discipleship Journal's Best Small-Group Ideas*. 2 vol. Colorado Springs, CO: NavPress, 2005.

Kuhatschek, J., and C. Bunch. *How to Lead a LifeGuide Bible Study*. Downers Grove, IL: InterVarsity, 2002.

Munro, M., and J. Couchman, eds. *Discipleship Journal's Best Bible Study Methods*. Colorado Springs, CO: NavPress, 2002.

Pastoral Care and Counseling

Buchanan, D. *The Counselling of Jesus*. Downers Grove, IL: InterVarsity, 1985.

Collins, G. R., ed. *Christian Counseling*. 3rd ed. Nashville: Nelson, 2007.

Watson, J. *Biblical Counseling for Today*. Nashville: Nelson, 2000.

Spiritual Formation

Cunningham, S., and K. J. Egan. *Christian Spirituality: Themes from the Tradition.* New York: Paulist, 1996.

Demarest, B. *Satisfy Your Soul: Restoring the Heart of Christian Spirituality.* Colorado Springs, CO: NavPress, 1999.

Demarest, B. *SoulGuide.* Colorado Springs, CO: NavPress, 2003.

Dixon, N. *Companion to the Revised Common Lectionary: Praying with the Scriptures.* London: Epworth, 2004.

Jeremiah, D. *Life-Changing Moments with God: Praying Scripture Every Day.* Nashville: Nelson, 2007.

Klein, W. W. *Become What You Are: Spiritual Formation According to the Sermon on the Mount.* Waynesboro, GA; Bletchley, Milton Keynes, UK: Authentic/Paternoster, 2006.

Mulholland Jr., M. R. *Shaped by the Word: The Power of Scripture in Spiritual Formation,* rev. ed. Nashville: The Upper Room, 2001.

Thompson, M. J. *Soul Feast: An Invitation to the Christian Spiritual Life.* Louisville, KY: Westminster John Knox, 1995.

Webber, R. E. *The Divine Embrace: Recovering the Passionate Spiritual Life.* Grand Rapids, MI: Baker, 2006.

CHAPTER 9

A LIFETIME OF BIBLE STUDY

We live in a fast-paced world. We expect quick fixes, abbreviated therapy, high-speed travel, instant results, three-step easy solutions, and microwavable macaroni and cheese.

Unfortunately, many of us place studying the Bible on this same level. We decide, "Since I can't do it fast, I can't fit it in at all." Who can find time in a busy day to study the Bible? It's a great idea, but other activities and events inevitably crowd it out. If pressed, many of us might confess that the "results" of studying Scripture just don't seem to justify the time and effort. Or we might admit to fits and starts—periods of success and spells of inactivity—that leave us feeling frustrated and even guilty.

Maybe you were born with a disposition that makes doing things regularly and repeatedly a natural process. You change the oil every three thousand miles, just as the manual says! If you have this natural bent, regular times with Scripture come more easily.

On the other hand, maybe you have a temperament that resists fixed structures. You pay the bills eventually, and you tend to navigate through life as it comes at you. For you, a fixed routine seems stifling, and naturally you approach regular Bible study the same way.

Or maybe you don't study the Bible because you don't have a definite plan that works well for you. You struggle to sustain the task of reading a certain number of verses or for a set period each day.

Finally, maybe you fall into the category of Christians who just don't realize the value of studying the Bible. You don't consciously avoid it; you simply don't realize how useful it could be for you.

Glance in the mirror to see if any of these descriptions reflect you. Perhaps you'd raise other issues. However, you'd also need to ask yourself, *How can I grow to maturity as a Christian with little or no input from God's Word?*

Wherever you land, please know that I'm not trying to make you feel guilty; instead, I want to inspire you to grasp just how wonderful and beneficial studying God's Word can be for you. Remember how the apostle Paul commended his young friend Timothy:

> Continue in what you have learned and have become convinced of, because you know those from whom you learned it, and how from infancy you have known the Holy Scriptures, which are able to make you wise for salvation through faith in Christ Jesus. All Scripture is God-breathed and is useful for teaching, rebuking, correcting and training in righteousness, so that all God's people may be thoroughly equipped for every good work. (2 Tim. 3:14-17)

THE NEED FOR BIBLE STUDY

The benefits of Scripture go far beyond opening up God's salvation to us. In Scripture, we discover teaching, rebuking, correction, training to become righteous, and equipping to do good. If we're following Christ, we should want and need all these functions performed in our lives. We can trust God's words to guide our journey. What else could accomplish these tasks to help our growth into mature and productive people?

We have so much to gain by embracing God's Word, and we have so much that we forfeit if we neglect it. It's a lot like trying to eat a well-balanced diet to nourish our bodies and making efforts to exercise to foster a healthy life. Many people spend hours in a gym every week, even hiring personal trainers to make sure they get the right kinds of exercise. When we practice a healthy lifestyle, we have a greater chance of living a vigorous and long life than if we sit on a couch all day eating Twinkies and drinking beer.

Let me put it some other ways. If you're a marathon runner, then you eat and train well because that's what successful runners do to maintain their ability to perform. If you're a successful salesperson, you study your product well, master its capabilities, and learn how to communicate its virtues effectively. In these cases, you do what you *do* because of who you *are*.

The same is true when you're a follower of Jesus—one of his disciples. Engaging God through his Word should be what you *do* because of who you *are*. Jesus said, "If you continue in my word, you are truly my disciples; and you will know the truth, and the truth will make you free" (Jn. 8:31-32, NRSV).

What we discussed early on in this *Handbook* bears repeating: Bible study isn't the *end*; it's our *means* of connecting with the God who loves us so much. To continue in Jesus' Word requires regular and consistent encounters with him. Jesus' friends meet God primarily in the Bible. While God speaks in other ways, in the Word is where God speaks most clearly and most definitively, so his Word should be the place we want to inhabit. Our goal is to encounter God; the Bible is a primary means to reach that goal.

So how will you meet with God consistently? What decisions do you need to make? The first might be to decide if you're truly a disciple of Jesus. If so, you'll continue in his Word. How do you do that?

Find Time

First, you need to find the time to meet with God consistently. If you struggle with finding time, perhaps you need to eliminate or shorten other activities to allow you to spend time with Jesus. Can you spend less time surfing the Internet, text-messaging, or chatting with friends? Do you need to read all those blogs or watch all those TV shows? Or maybe you need to get up earlier in the morning to recover time to spend studying God's Word. What's crowding out time with God?

Of course, you need to make these decisions for yourself. However, if you claim to be a friend of Jesus but find yourself too busy to fit him into your schedule, something is drastically wrong.

Set Aside Ample Time

Once you've carved out some regular time to spend with God, you need to decide on an amount of time. Again, this is a personal decision. My only advice is to be reasonable with yourself if you're just starting out. You'll find that the time can expand or contract depending on how you use it. However, what you require to encounter God — not the busyness of your schedule — should determine the length of time. Busy people manage to do many good things, partly because they set priorities to make sure they accomplish the important things. Don't squeeze out God.

One component of determining how much time you spend studying the Bible is deciding the best time in your day to meet with God. You'll probably find that the same time or times each day will help you be consistent. You'll know where this appointment with God is on your schedule, and you'll begin to look forward to it.

Decide How to Spend Your Time

Now that you've found time to study the Bible and you've decided how long to spend in your pursuit, what will you do with your time?

Much of this book seeks to answer that question. Try the various methods (or variations of them) that fit your needs.

You might decide to stick with one method for a season because it fosters communion with your Father in heaven. But at some point, if you realize that one approach no longer nourishes your relationship with God, head down a different path to knowing God better.

In their book *The Critical Journey: Stages in the Life of Faith*, Janet Hagberg and Robert Guelich trace the journey of faith as a series of stages. As you approach studying the Bible, you might want to think about how Christians grow and mature and what the life of faith looks like in the process. Your current stage in the Christian life might dictate what you need in your spiritual diet. If you're a fairly new Christian, you need a certain diet to get you on firm footing in your life with God. If you've been a Christian for some time, you shouldn't assume the diet that worked for you at an earlier point in life will still provide the nourishment you need at your current stage.

Don't be discouraged if some methods fail to meet your needs. Drop them and look elsewhere. Don't assume that an alleged "one size fits all" method of Bible study will meet your needs, even if it's the latest and greatest approach endorsed by some celebrity Christian. At one stage, you might benefit most from using guided studies where you answer questions. Later in your journey, you might write those kinds of books.

Remember your target: It's not to *do* Bible study and prayer; it's to meet with your Lord. Use methods that help you achieve that goal. When you meet with God and grow in your relationship with him, you won't want to give up your practice of Bible study and prayer. They'll become as vital as breathing oxygen and eating daily food.

REGIMENS TO CONSIDER

While the word *regimen* might make you think of such words as *rigidity, inflexibility,* and *life-draining drudgery,* don't think of regimen as a negative term. In medicine, for example, it refers to a systematic application of remedies to bring about a cure. You'd be happy to follow a regimen if you were sick and you knew it would make you well. But more broadly, a regimen refers to any system meant to promote health or achieve some positive effect. Certainly, you'll want to consider a regimen for studying the Bible in order to get well and stay well spiritually.

Let me suggest several regimens, moving from the shortest to ever-increasing lengths of time.

Daily Quiet Time

You can set aside time to meet with God, whether it's first thing in the morning, during a midday interval, or at some quiet period in the evening. Various labels for this time include "The Daily Office," "Morning (or Evening) Watch," "Devotions," "Appointment with God," and "Quiet Time." Whatever you call it, you need to find time each day to pray and to reflect on Scripture with a view toward building your life of faith.

In her book *Feeding Your Soul,* Jan Fleming explores "the nuts and bolts of quiet time." Her discussion includes some practical questions you should consider. In essence, they are:

- *Where* will you meet with God?
- How *long* can you spend with God?
- *How* will you engage God at this stage in your life?

From your answers to these questions, you can develop a plan for studying Scripture and praying. In this *Handbook,* I've tried to provide many approaches and resources you can use to carry out your plan.

For example, you might want to try using the Divine Office, also called Daily Office, that I mentioned while discussing liturgy in chapter 8. This approach breaks up the day into a series of times for reading Scripture, praying, and meditating. Prayer books, also called lectionaries, contain a list of readings of Scripture for individual or corporate use. Lectionaries list the readings for each of the office's daily times, or they might simply list all readings for the day. Some lectionaries include Scripture, prayers, and other readings.

An alliance of North American Catholics and many traditional "mainline" North American Protestant denominations produced *The Revised Common Lectionary*, publicly released in 1994. Based on the Anglican and Episcopal *Book of Common Prayer*, *The Revised Common Lectionary* covers the entire Bible in a two-year cycle of readings. You might consider using this or a similar guide if you find this structured approach useful.

Weekly Schedule

Lectionaries are also set up on a weekly cycle, outlining readings for an entire week, sometimes specifying ones for individual days of the week. *The Revised Common Lectionary* lists readings for each Sunday that you can read and meditate on for the entire week at various times. The readings include a passage from the Old Testament; a passage from one of the psalms, another from either the book of Revelation or the Epistles, and a passage from one of the four gospels. It follows a three-year cycle. Other books in this genre take similar approaches.

Longer Programs

You might decide to embark on extended studies to further foster your spiritual growth. If so, you might want to adopt a regimen other believers have found helpful and tested over time. One example is the spiritual exercises of St. Ignatius, which have been adapted for laypeople. Another is the two-year Academy for Spiritual Formation, sponsored by The Upper Room. In this program, you travel to a retreat center every three months for a five-day retreat. See the "For Further Study" section at the end of this chapter for more information on these.

Even if you don't use St. Ignatius's spiritual exercises or the Academy for Spiritual Formation's retreats, you can still add the concepts behind these approaches to your Bible study regimen. Here are a few ways to do that.

ANNUAL CYCLE

Since the earliest years of the Christian church, Christians have celebrated an annual cycle that begins with advent in November and December. Waiting for Jesus' birth puts us in the posture of expectation. Like the Israelites of old, we find ourselves longing for the fulfillment of God's promise to send the Son of David, the Messiah. Although the dates fluctuate each year, the annual cycle follows this rhythm:

- Advent Season (the four weeks prior to Christmas)
- Christmas (December 25)
- The Twelve Days of Christmas (December 25–January 5)
- Epiphany (and Ordinary Time until Lent) (January 6–Ash Wednesday)
- Shrove Tuesday, or Mardi Gras (the day prior to Ash Wednesday)
- Ash Wednesday (the seventh Wednesday prior to Easter)
- Lent (the period between Ash Wednesday and Easter)
- Holy Week (from Palm Sunday to Easter)
- Maundy Thursday (prior to Good Friday)

- Good Friday
- Easter
- Pentecost (the seventh Sunday after Easter)
- Ordinary Time (from Pentecost to the beginning of advent season)

This annual cycle reminds believers to celebrate the central events of the Christian faith. In our modern era, we easily forget our spiritual heritage, including how our ancestors in the faith marked the passage of significant biblical events. We can do more than read about these events; we can experience and celebrate them by acknowledging the seasons when they occurred.

We also have the tendency to look for the flashy events—to want to be impressed and dazzled. Special effects impress us, not the long and drawn out "same old, same old." Yet in the annual cycle, the longest periods are "ordinary time," a good description for most of life. As Christians, we must plod along faithfully, knowing that God works despite our inability to see or understand what he's doing. Even when God seems silent or absent, we must still trust him.

Then God breaks through and performs one of his mighty acts! We celebrate God's fulfillment of his promise to redeem sinful people, and we acknowledge his goodness and faithfulness. Jesus did come. Jesus died for our sins and rose again. The Holy Spirit descended just as Jesus promised he would. Then we wait and work faithfully, fully expecting that Jesus will come again—the Second Advent. You can experience this rhythm by using the church calendar, not merely the holidays of Christmas and Easter.

Personal Retreats

You probably know about retreats. We use them in both secular and sacred arenas of life as opportunities for people to step back from the normal routines and focus on special issues, training, and team building, among other things. Churches regularly schedule retreats for various groups, such as youth, the staff, and lay leaders.

Have you ever retreated from normal life simply to spend time with God? If your spiritual life feels stagnant and you need a new direction or renewed motivation, you might need to carve out some extended time for a personal retreat. During a retreat, you can engage more deeply with some methods of Bible study that don't fit easily into your normal routines. Or a retreat might help you transition from one stage of faith to the next, providing you with time to reflect on what God is calling you to be.

Some organizations and institutions facilitate spiritual retreats that you can attend. This approach has several obvious virtues. Experienced spiritual guides plan and structure the time. They select the topics and gather the necessary resources. If the topic fits your needs and the dates fit your schedule, a facilitated retreat is a great option.

Allow me to express just one word of caution. If you choose a preplanned retreat, carefully choose a Christian spiritual retreat that enables you to commune with God. Keep in mind that the word spirituality has a broad meaning these days. In addition, many "how-to" retreats simply push techniques or the latest steps for accomplishing something. Some of these retreats have their place; however, a spiritual retreat provides time and space to pray, study, and reflect. You want a retreat that helps you deepen your relationship with God, not just a time and place that fills every moment with activities, lectures, and discussions. Choose wisely.

Many retreats provide times for input as well as solitude. Some retreat locations have a qualified person to talk to you and help you plan your retreat. Often called spiritual directors, these individuals can suggest ways you can listen to what God is saying to you.

Keep in mind that you can also arrange your own retreat. This might be a half day, full day, or longer. I suggest starting with a half-day retreat so that you don't find yourself overwhelmed with silence and inactivity. You can increase the length of your retreats as you find the times useful and life-giving. Regular retreats could easily become a habit you can't break!

Don't attempt to cover too much ground in a retreat. In our fast-paced culture, most of us naturally want to maximize our time—and that means multitasking and lots of activities. Instead, during your retreat, adopt the adage that "less is more." You need time to read, reflect, and pray about your relationship with God during this time, not to cover a lot of ground. Turn off your cell phone; leave your laptop at home. You get the point.

Once you decide how long you want to retreat, you need to answer several questions. The first is where you'll go. You might try a spot in your own house, a friend's house, or a local coffee shop, but most likely you'll find those surroundings too distracting. Search for a quiet place where you'll be free of interruptions the entire time. Perhaps you can locate a nearby retreat center, church, or monastery that will allow you to use some space. Insert "personal retreat" into your favorite Internet search engine, and you'll discover many options.

You'll also need to determine what will occupy your time. You might want to plan the time carefully, perhaps use one of the Bible study methods in this *Handbook*. Or you might want to keep your time flexible and proceed as you sense the Holy Spirit leading you. I suggest preparing at least a basic agenda even if you decide to alter it as you proceed.

Of course, spending time with God through the Scriptures and prayer is essential. Give yourself space for listening and reflection, perhaps with your journal. If your location allows some reflective time outside, break up your study time with walking and praying in God's creation. Consider some devotional readings if their input might inspire or encourage your relationship with your Lord.

My Parting Shot

We all face the same question: "Is my relationship with God worth cultivating?"

If you answer yes, then you need to decide how you'll connect with the God who made you, loves you, created the world for you to live in, and sent his Son, Jesus, to rescue you from sin and death. In prayer, we respond to God and speak to him with our words. In the Bible, we listen to God's words spoken to us through people like us.

If we really want to hear God's voice, we need to learn to slow down and listen very carefully. The Bible doesn't shout to us. The Spirit speaks with a quiet voice that requires serious and sustained attention.

I love Jesus' words to one of his churches: "Look! I stand at the door and knock. If you hear my voice and open the door, I will come in, and we will share a meal together as friends" (Rev. 3:20, NLT). Can you hear his knock at your door?

Jesus loves us and desires to meet with us just as you might share a meal or a latte with a best friend. Won't you open the door to him? Don't worry about the past. Now is the time for new beginnings in your relationship with the Lord.

For Further Study

Many organizations sponsor online sites that list readings and prayers for each day or week. For example, *Discipleship Journal* (published by NavPress, also the publisher of this *Handbook*) offers two free daily Bible-reading plans: "The New 5X5X5 Bible Reading Plan" and the "Book-at-a-Time Bible Reading Plan." They also offer the *"Discipleship Journal* Bible Reading Plan." All three

are available at www.navpress.com/Magazines/DiscipleshipJournal/
BibleReadingPlans/. If this approach appeals to you, you can also do
some searching to see if others available online fit your needs. They
are too numerous to list here and are, of course, subject to change
occasionally.

Pursuing the Spiritual Life

Demarest, B. *Satisfy Your Soul.* Colorado Springs, CO: NavPress,
1999.
Foster, R. *Celebration of Discipline: The Path to Spiritual Growth.*
San Francisco: HarperSanFrancisco, 1984, 1998.
Hagberg, J. O., and R. A. Guelich. *The Critical Journey: Stages in
the Life of Faith.* 2nd ed. Salem, WI: Sheffield, 2004.
MacDonald, G. *Ordering Your Private World.* Nashville: Nelson,
2003.
Thompson, M. J. *Soul Feast: An Invitation to the Christian Spiritual
Life.* Louisville, KY: Westminster John Knox, 1995.
Watkins, K. *The Great Thanksgiving.* St. Louis, MO: Chalice Press,
1995.

Quiet Time

Eyre, S. D. *Drawing Close to God: The Essentials of a Dynamic Quiet
Time.* Downers Grove, IL: InterVarsity, 1995.
Fleming, J. *Feeding Your Soul: A Quiet Time Handbook.* Colorado
Springs, CO: NavPress, 1999.

Daily and Weekly Office

Benedict Jr., D. T. *Patterned by Grace: How Liturgy Shapes Us.*
Nashville: Upper Room Books, 2007.
Collins, W., ed. *The Daily Book of Common Prayer: Readings and
Prayers Through the Years.* Grand Rapids, MI: Eerdmans, 2000.

Consultation on Common Texts. *Revised Common Lectionary.* Nashville: Abingdon Press, 1992.

Job, R. P., and N. Shawchuck. *A Guide to Prayer for All God's People.* Nashville: Upper Room Books, 1990.

Johnson, M. E., ed. *Benedictine Daily Prayer: A Short Breviary.* Collegeville, MN: The Liturgical Press, 2005.

McKnight, S. *Praying with the Church: Developing a Daily Rhythm for Spiritual Formation.* Brewster, MA: Paraclete Press, 2005.

Northumbria Community. *Celtic Daily Prayer.* San Francisco: HarperSanFrancisco, 2002.

Shorter Morning and Evening Prayer: Divine Office. Collegeville, MN: The Liturgical Press, 2006.

Tickle, P. *The Divine Hours: A Manual for Prayer.* 3 vol. New York: Doubleday, 2000-01.

Tickle, P. *The Night Offices: Prayers for the Hours from Sunset to Sunrise.* Oxford, UK: Oxford University Press, 2006.

Wakefield, J. I. *Sacred Listening: Discovering the Spiritual Exercises of Ignatius Loyola.* Grand Rapids, MI: Baker, 2006.

Retreats

"The Academy for Spiritual Formation" of The Upper Room. A Ministry of the General Board of Discipleship, The United Methodist Church.

Cooper, D. A. *Silence, Simplicity, and Solitude: A Guide for Spiritual Retreat.* New York: Bell Tower, 1992.

Del Bene, R. *Alone with God: A Guide for Personal Retreats.* Nashville: Upper Room Books, 1992.

Jones, T. *A Place for God: A Guide to Spiritual Retreats and Retreat Centers.* New York: Image Books, 2000.

Silf, M. *Going on Retreat: A Beginner's Guide to the Christian Retreat Experience.* Chicago: Loyola Press, 2002.

NOTES

Introduction

1. Of the numerous editions of Luther's *Table Talk*, one useful example is T. S. Kepler, ed., *The Table Talk of Martin Luther* (Mineola, NY: Dover, 2005). It may be found online as well.

Chapter 1: How the Bible Came to Us

1. Judas was the third son of Mattathias Hasmoneus, a Jewish priest who with his five sons began a guerilla movement to throw off the yoke of the Syrians who were oppressing the Jews. Nicknamed "Maccabeus" (the Hammerer), he defeated the Syrians in major battles, setting the stage for Israel's eventual independence a few years after his death.

2. For the reference to this action, see the apocryphal book 2 Maccabees 2:14. Second Maccabees contains records of the exploits of the Jews and their revolts against the Syrians from about 180-161 BC. In general, any Catholic version of the Bible will include the apocryphal books, between the OT and NT. You can also find them in various Bible software versions and online at http://wesley.nnu.edu/biblical_studies/noncanon/apocrypha.htm.

3. See 1 Macc. 9:27. This book covers the period from about 336–104 BC.

4. See *De Vita Contemplativa* 25. Philo was an important Jewish philosopher who lived and wrote in Alexandria, Egypt, from about 20 BC to AD 50.

Chapter 2: Preparing to Study the Bible

1. The Tetrapharmacon, an Epicurean formula that likely dates to Epicurus. See Gilbert Murray, *Five Stages of Greek Religion* (Garden City, NY: Doubleday, 1955), 205.

Chapter 4: The Spiritual Discipline of Bible Intake

1. Peter Lewis, *The Genius of Puritanism* (Haywards Heath, UK: Carey Publications, 1979), 54.
2. Nielson Media Research, Inc. reports that Americans overall average 4.5 hours of TV watching per week.
3. Dallas Willard, *The Spirit of the Disciplines* (San Francisco: Harper & Row, 1988), 150.

Chapter 6: Bible Study Methods

1. By William Mounce (Grand Rapids, MI: Zondervan, 2006).
2. Paul D. Gardner, *New International Encyclopedia of Bible Characters* (Grand Rapids, MI: Zondervan, 2001).

Chapter 7: Resources and Helps for Studying the Bible

1. The National Association of Evangelicals' statement of faith reads as follows:
   - We believe the Bible to be the inspired, the only infallible, authoritative Word of God.
   - We believe that there is one God, eternally existent in three persons: Father, Son, and Holy Spirit.
   - We believe in the deity of our Lord Jesus Christ, in His virgin birth, in His sinless life, in His miracles, in His vicarious and atoning death through His shed blood, in His bodily resurrection, in His ascension to the right hand of the Father, and in His personal return in power and glory.
   - We believe that for the salvation of lost and sinful people, regeneration by the Holy Spirit is absolutely essential.

- We believe in the present ministry of the Holy Spirit by whose indwelling the Christian is enabled to live a godly life.
- We believe in the resurrection of both the saved and the lost; they that are saved unto the resurrection of life and they that are lost unto the resurrection of damnation.
- We believe in the spiritual unity of believers in our Lord Jesus Christ.

The mission of the NAE is to extend the kingdom of God through a fellowship of member denominations, churches, organizations, and individuals, demonstrating the unity of the body of Christ by standing for biblical truth, speaking with a representative voice, and serving the evangelical community through united action, cooperative ministry, and strategic planning. For more information on the NAE, see www.nae.net.

2. To locate graduate theological institutions, go online to the website of the Association of Theological Schools in the United States and Canada (www.ats.edu). Similarly, one can search online using the keywords "theological schools and colleges" to locate the location of undergraduate institutions.

Chapter 8: Uses of the Bible

1. As quoted by John Telford, *The Life of John Wesley*, Wesley Methodist Book Room, 1899, chapter XX [cited on http://wesley.nnu.edu/wesleyan_theology/telford/telford_ch20.htm].

GLOSSARY

abridged concordance: Lists the occurrences of the main words that occur in a translation of the Bible or Testament, contrasted with an "exhaustive" concordance that lists all the occurrences of all words.

acknowledged (Greek: *homologoumenon*): Early church leaders used this term to describe texts they believed certainly belonged in the NT Canon.

Acts: NT narrative about the origin and spread of the message of Jesus from Jerusalem throughout the Roman world.

allegory; allegorical: (1) Literary genre, often a story, where details and characters often symbolically represent a deeper level of meaning. (2) Tactic of interpreters who find deeper meanings and often multiple senses in biblical texts.

annual cycle: Method for reading through the entire Bible in the course of one to three years. Various plans might include reading through the Psalms more frequently.

Apocalypse: NT genre that gets its name from the transliteration into English of the Greek word that means "revelation" or "unveiling." The sole example is the book of Revelation.

apocalyptic: From the Greek word *apokalypsis* (meaning "revelation"), it refers to a genre of literature (the NT book of Revelation is a prime example). The works in this genre purport to be revelation from God that comes through an angelic mediator to a human seer or prophet who discloses what God plans to do in the future.

Apocrypha: Thirteen books written by the Jews prior to the first century AD. They are often placed between the OT and NT in Bibles used by Roman Catholics or Eastern Orthodox Christians and are not included in Jewish Scriptures and not accepted as canonical by Protestants. These books do supply many valuable historical and theological insights into the Jewish world in the time between the OT and NT.

apostasy: Religious rebellion against *Yahweh* (God).

apostolicity: A criterion for including books in the NT Canon; refers to writings originating with or closely connected to one of Jesus' apostles.

application: Responding to God's Word by putting it into practice in our lives. The significance of a text in view of its meaning.

Aramaic: A northwest Semitic language of the ancient Aramaeans that spread through Mesopotamia and eventually west. It became the dominant language in the Middle East and was the language Jesus spoke.

Ark of the Covenant: The piece of furniture in the Jewish tabernacle (or Tent of Meeting) that held the stone tablets containing the Ten Commandments and other sacred objects; symbolic of God's presence.

assumptions: Fundamental beliefs and commitments that we bring to a task and that determine how we conduct it; also called presuppositions.

authority: The weight or power we attach to the Bible. As God's Word, it has the last word on matters of faith and practice.

autograph: Original copy from a biblical author (no matter who actually put pen to manuscript).

basic Bible study method: Limited to the essential steps in observing, interpreting, and applying the message of the Bible as found in its various genres.

basic verse: Single reference that stands out as a passage or chapter is read.

Bible atlas: Provides maps of the lands where biblical events occurred. Because events occurred over a long span of time, duplicate maps show how place names changed over the years.

Bible dictionary: Contains articles on most biblical names, places, images, themes, and important words in alphabetical order.

Bible encyclopedia: Includes in-depth discussions of significant biblical topics. It is larger than a Bible dictionary and is often a multivolume work.

Bible introductions: Provides readers with essential background to study each book of the Bible, including issues of authorship, recipients, date, genre, purpose for writing, and essential message.

Bible surveys: Includes some material contained in Bible introductions. Surveys give additional attention to the content or message of biblical books.

biblical theology: Seeks to discover the theologies of the biblical authors themselves, given the contexts of their historical situations, and in their own terms or categories.

Canon: From the Greek word that means "rule" or "standard." Refers to the "measuring stick" that defines what's "in" and what's "out" of Scripture.

catholicity: A criterion for including books in the NT Canon. Refers to writings embraced widely (catholic in the sense of universal) over the entire realm of Christendom.

codex: The "book" that results when individual sheets of papyrus or parchment are sewn and bound together at the edges, one on top of the other; the ancestor to modern books.

cognates: Words that have common origins.

comedy: Story where the plot moves from tragedy to triumph and has a happy ending.

commentary: Provides expert analysis of biblical texts with more detail about the background of biblical books than found in study Bibles, Bible introductions, or dictionaries and encyclopedias. Explains the meaning and significance of individual verses or sections.

concordance: Lists all the places where a word occurs either in the original Hebrew or Greek languages or in a specific translation of the Bible. Some concordances bridge the biblical languages by identifying both the original language words and their English translations.

conservative: As applied to theological positions, describes those who hold traditional views that liberals might view as old-fashioned or restrictive.

contemplation: Act of listening to God, freeing ourselves from our own thoughts, and being open to hearing God speak.

context: Framework within which an element is located. A literary context is the larger section (paragraph, discourse, or book) in which a passage occurs. A historical or cultural context is the world from which the passage emerged.

corporate worship: Responding together as a body of believers to who God is and what God has done, as the result of diligent study and application of the message of the Bible.

counseling: Support and help in the crises and events of life.

cultural expressions: Features that display particular values or practices of a group of people. Might include preferences in food, dress, and ways of farming.

Daily Office: See **Divine Office**.

descriptive: Account that reports what happened or what an observer described.

deuterocanonical: Books considered secondary to the

universally accepted books of the Canon of the Bible. Includes the Apocrypha.

devotions: See **quiet times**.

Diaspora: Scattering of Jews from their homeland. Also called the Dispersion.

disaster prophecy: A subtype of prophecy announcing God's catastrophic judgment.

disputed (Greek: *antilegomenon*): Early church leaders used this term to describe biblical texts they were uncertain about including in the NT Canon.

Divine Office: Daily practice that includes prayer, Bible reading, and other devotional practices designed to promote spiritual growth. Might include several occasions during the day (such as morning office, midday office, vespers, and compline).

divine revelation: View that the Bible contains the message that God has spoken to his people.

dynamically equivalent: Bible translations that strive for as close a correspondence as possible to the thought or impact of the original biblical text.

ecumenical: (1) Seven councils of the fourth through eighth centuries that brought together leaders from all wings of Christendom to affirm emerging Christian theology and settle on the NT Canon. (2) A wide collection of religious positions or leaders, as in the recent "ecumenical movement."

embedded genre: Smaller features within a larger work — such as popular proverbs, riddles, fables, parables, songs, and lists — that make a story more interesting and lifelike.

Epistles: Genre of literature in the NT through which several of the apostles communicated to early Christian churches in the Roman world. Also called letters.

eschatological: Meaning of a biblical text for understanding the "end times."

etymology: Study of a word's history or its root or component parts and how words have come to their current form and meaning.

evangelical: The conservative Christian movement that stresses a personal commitment to Christ through spiritual rebirth (being born again), the authority of the Bible, and orthodox views on essential doctrines and personal ethics.

Exile: Period when the Jews were forcibly removed from their lands (721 BC, northern kingdom of Israel fell to the Assyrians, and 587 BC, Judah fell to the Babylonians) until the returns allowed under the Persian rulers beginning in about 538 BC.

Exodus: Liberation of the Jews from slavery in Egypt when Moses led the Hebrew people to the Promised Land.

external evidence: Employed by textual critics concerning the manuscripts themselves—the number, dates, and types of biblical manuscripts that scholars can access and evaluate.

fictive kinship: Practice of applying family titles, privileges, and responsibilities to others as if they shared the actual relationships implied by the titles. For example, followers of Jesus called themselves brothers and sisters, embracing both the duties and privileges of family members.

formal liturgies: Corporate worship governed by strict rules and prescribed practices.

formally equivalent: Bible translations that strive for as close a correspondence as possible to the structure and wording of the original biblical text.

genre: Category of literature distinguished by a particular style, structure, or content. Fiction, biography, poetry, and prophecy are examples.

gnosticism: Early rivals of Christianity, the gnostics divided the material realm from the spiritual realm.

gospel: From the Old English word *godspel*, which means "a good story." It translates the Greek word *euangelion*, which means "good news."

gospel harmony: Book that presents the text of the four gospels in parallel columns in alleged chronological order.

gospel synopsis: Book that presents the text of the four gospels in parallel columns to allow comparative study.

Greco-Roman: The ancient world dominated by Greek and Roman cultures. The world into which Jesus was born.

Greek: The language of the Greek peninsula. Classical dialects merged into a common language (*koine*) during the Hellenistic period that prevailed from about 300 BC to AD 300.

Hebrew: Semitic language of ancient Israel that continued in common use until superseded by Aramaic in about 400 BC (although it continued in religious use). Most of the OT was written in Hebrew, with a few sections in Aramaic.

historical and cultural background sources: Resources that allow modern readers to understand issues in the ancient world and help them grasp the message of biblical passages.

imprecatory psalms: The twenty-five or so psalms that vigorously denounce the writer's enemies, seeking their sudden ruin (see 35:8), their death (see 55:15), their misery (see 109:10), the massacre of their children (see 137:9), and their relegation to the pit of destruction (see 140:10).

in-depth Bible study method: A rigorous and time-intensive study of a biblical text. Also see **basic Bible study method**.

informal liturgies: Corporate worship governed by informal rules and often spontaneous practices.

interdenominational: Located within or moving among many religious bodies and sects.

interlinear: A Bible "translation" that seeks as closely as possible to substitute a word in the target language for each word in the source, with as minimal rearrangement as needed to produce an acceptable reading.

internal evidence: Employed by textual critics. It concerns: (1) what we know about how scribes operated and what they were likely to do when making copies of texts; and (2) what we know about the original authors of the texts (thought, theology, language, writing style, and background) and what they were more likely to write.

interpretation: Process of determining the meaning of a passage—what the author intended to say and what the original readers most likely understood.

intertestamental period: Broadly, the period between the close of the writing of the OT (c. 424 BC) and the birth of Christ (c. 5/4 BC). The starting point for the events recorded in the NT.

Israel: (1) Name God gave to Jacob (see Gen. 32:28) that came to identify the Hebrew people. (2) When distinguished from Judah, Israel refers to the Northern Kingdom of ten Jewish tribes that split from Judah under Jeroboam in c. 928 BC and then fell in battle to the Assyrians in 721 BC.

Judah: (1) Fourth son of Jacob and Leah (see Gen. 29:35) and the Hebrew tribe that descended from him. (2) When distinguished from Israel, Judah refers to the Southern Kingdom of the tribes Judah and Benjamin that fell to Babylon in 587 BC.

Law: Refers to the Torah (especially the first five books of the Bible), the Ten Commandments, or the several codes of conduct prescribed for God's people in the OT.

lectionary: A schedule of readings from the Bible for Christian church services or for individuals for a prescribed period of time.

letters: Also called the Epistles, the letters in the NT are messages of instruction and encouragement sent by apostles to individuals or churches.

lexicon: Another word for dictionary, it contains the inventory of words in a given language and supplies the range of meanings of those words. Often used to refer to the biblical languages.

liberal: As applied to theological positions, describes those who hold tolerant or progressive views that conservatives might view as departures from the orthodox faith.

liberal-conservative spectrum: Range of theological positions from more progressive to more moderate to more traditional. *Example*: One who is theologically liberal might deny that Jesus literally rose from the dead; a theological conservative would affirm that Jesus did.

literal: Often used to refer to Bible translations that adhere more closely to the original wording and structure of the biblical text. A more accurate term is *formally equivalent*.

literary context: The larger section in which a specific passage or text is located.

liturgy: From a Greek word related to the words for service and worship. In contemporary usage, it refers to a rite or a group of rites people use in formal worship.

Maccabean revolts: Under the leadership of Judas Maccabeus and his brothers in the 140s BC, Israel recovered its independence as a nation from the Syrians.

Maccabees: Jewish warriors during the Intertestamental period who took their name from Judas Maccabeus (c. 168 BC), one of the Jewish leaders who led the revolt against the Syrians.

Magisterium: Roman Catholic Church's teaching authority to interpret correctly. That church's guarantor of orthodoxy.

mainline: Churches that tend to be more ecumenical and liberal (they prefer the term moderate) in outlook than evangelical groups. Frequently, they belong to interdenominational organizations, such as the National Council of Churches and World Council of Churches. They formerly held a numerical majority or dominant presence in mainstream society—hence, the name.

Masoretic Text: Abbreviated as MT, the main Hebrew text available today produced from about the seventh to eleventh centuries AD by Jewish scribes known as the Masoretes.

meaning: The goal of studying the Bible should be to discover the *meaning* the author intended and that the original readers most likely understood.

meditation: Memorizing a verse of Scripture to reflect on it at any time. Christian meditation involves filling your mind with God and truth.

metaphor: Compares two items directly by equating the two: *The Lord* is *my shepherd.*

metonymy: Substitutes one idea with something closely related to it.

Midrash: (1) Hebrew word meaning "interpretation." (2) Body of rabbinic commentaries on OT texts.

ministry of the Word: Various ways of transmitting the transformational truth of Scripture to others, whether by preaching, teaching, leading Bible studies, or other means.

Mishnah: The compilation of the Jewish oral traditions and commentaries on OT Law, eventually incorporated into the Talmuds.

monotheism: The worship of a single deity. The position of religions such as Judaism, Christianity, and Islam.

moral: Principles or standards for acceptable conduct that grow out of the Bible's teachings.

narrative: Literary genre, usually involving characters and a plot, that tells a story or explains how something happened.

observations: What we discover after seeking to see and clarify things as they are. To observe carefully is a crucial first step in

Bible study.

orthodoxy: A criterion for including books in the NT Canon. Refers to writings that affirmed the church's understanding of truth and theological soundness.

parable: A favorite literary device of Jesus that uses a concrete image, story, or saying to teach a corresponding spiritual truth. Places a story and a spiritual lesson side by side.

paraphrase: Bible translations that take more liberties in departing from the wording and structure of the original language texts, often using more distinctive language targeted to a specific culture.

pastoral care: Supporting people by helping them know what to believe and how to live. The message of the Bible provides guidance, comfort, and help.

Pentateuch: The five books attributed to the prophet Moses. The first five books of the OT. Also called "the Law."

personal retreat: A withdrawal (for a portion of a day to multiple days) from the routines of normal life to spend time with God, discover a new direction or renewed motivation in the spiritual realm, or help in the transition from one stage of faith to the next.

personification: Speaking of an inanimate object as human or as having human abilities or traits.

Pesher: Hebrew word meaning "interpretation" in the sense of bringing out the full significance of texts previously only partly known.

poetry: A genre of OT literature that includes rhythm (or meter), parallelism, and concentration of meaning, though all might not occur together and might not be apparent in translations from Hebrew.

polytheism: Worship of multiple gods or deities.

postmodernism: Meaning "after modernism," a twentieth-century movement that tends to reject modernist claims about the existence of absolutes, truth, and universal principles of reason that are supposedly merely products of the European Enlightenment of the eighteenth century.

prescript: The section at the beginning of a NT letter identifying the writer, recipients, and perhaps other elements, such as a prayer or wish.

prescriptive: An account that reports what an author or observer asserts should occur or ought to be the case.

presuppositions: Fundamental beliefs and commitments that we bring to a task and that determine how we conduct it; also called *assumptions*.

preunderstandings: The combination of all the information, beliefs, attitudes, and methods we bring to studying the Bible.

Promised Land: Land that God promised to his people first through Abraham (see Gen. 12:7) and then granted under Moses and his successor, Joshua.

prophecy: (1) A message from God to his people through his spokesperson (a prophet). Prophecies might comment on present circumstances or predict what God plans to do. (2) Genre of the OT that records the message conveyed by one of God's spokespersons. Declares divine statements of admonition or comfort to God's people and might include the foretelling of future plans that God has determined.

Protestant: Name given to branches of Western Christianity that in the mid-1500s protested against perceived abuses in the Roman Catholic Church, rejected the authority of the Catholic Church and the pope, and split from Rome to form their own religious bodies. Leaders prominent in the initial movement included Martin Luther, John Calvin, and John Knox.

Protestant Reformation: Sixteenth-century Western religious movement that led to the formation of church bodies separate from the Roman Catholic Church.

Pseudepigrapha: "Falsely written." Refers to books falsely attributed to famous biblical characters or writers.

qualifications: The traits of readers that put us in the best possible position to understand the meaning of the Bible.

quiet times: Private, individual occasions that typically include such elements as Bible reading and study, meditation, and prayer.

Qumran: Settlement near the northwestern shore of the Dead Sea. Beginning in 1947, the Dead Sea Scrolls were discovered in caves in nearby cliffs.

rationalism: System of thought that believes that reason and logic are the primary sources of truth and knowledge.

redeemed: Those formerly enslaved to sin and death but who have a saving relationship with God.

regimen: System for studying the Bible in order to get well and stay well spiritually.

Renaissance: Cultural movement in Europe that signaled the end of the Middle Ages. Spanning roughly the fourteenth through the sixteenth centuries, it revived learning based on classical culture and resulted in the rise of science and geographic exploration.

Revelation: NT genre. See **Apocalypse**.

Roman Catholic: The word *Catholic* (universal) points to this church's claim to be the church from its earliest time. Acknowledges the supreme authority of the bishop of Rome, the pope. Believes itself to be the only true expression of the church, whose bishops are traced in unbroken succession back to Peter (to whom, Catholics believe, Christ gave authority over the church).

salvation prophecy: A subtype of prophecy announcing God's impending rescue and deliverance.

Samaritans: Descendants of Jews in the northern region of Israel who intermarried with Gentiles and devised their own religious traditions and version of the Pentateuch.

secular: Of the world, in general. Often used in contrast to *spiritual* or *sacred.*

semantic fields: Meaning that a word or group of words covers.

Semitic: The group of languages in the Afro-Asiatic family spoken in North Africa and Southwest Asia. Includes Hebrew, Arabic, Aramaic, Maltese, and Amharic. The people who speak these languages.

Septuagint: Translation of the Hebrew Scriptures into Greek (abbreviated as LXX) in the third and second centuries BC.

Shema: Hebrew word that means "hear." The first word of Deuteronomy 6:4. "The Shema" has come to refer to the entire central affirmation of Judaism (see Dt. 6:4-9).

significance: Although what a text *meant* and *means* doesn't change (a text can't mean today what it did not mean to its author), its *significance* will change as time and cultures dictate. Another term is *application.*

simile: Compares two items using *like* or *as.* For example, "His whole body was like a hairy garment" (Gen. 25:25).

sola Scriptura: Latin for "Scripture alone," a central principle of the Protestant Reformation that insisted that the church's faith and practice be based only on the Bible.

special revelation: Words that God speaks to his people through the Scriptures.

spiritual director: A spiritual companion who facilitates a person's recognition of God's work in the normal experiences of life.

spiritual discipline: Practice or activity that cultivates spiritual growth; the discipline devoted to studying the Bible is often called *Bible intake*.

spiritual formation: The process of becoming shaped in the spiritual realm of life through sustained study of the Bible as well as other means.

spiritual growth: Process of maturing in the Christian faith as the result of diligent study and application of the message of the Bible.

spurious: Writings considered heretical and rejected from the NT Canon.

syncretism: Combining elements of a variety of religious beliefs and practices.

Synoptic Gospels: Synoptic means "viewed together." The first three gospels in the NT, whose accounts often parallel each other.

systematic theology: Our attempts to systematize what the Bible teaches based on what we want to know, according to our categories, labels, and agenda.

Talmud: Ancient Jewish writings compiled in the third through seventh centuries AD that constitute the basis of Jewish religious law. Based on earlier scriptural interpretations (the Mishnah) and later commentaries (the Gemara).

Tanach, Tanakh: The Jewish Bible. What Christians call the OT.

Targums: Aramaic paraphrases of select biblical texts.

Testament: Covenant or promise.

text cluster: Small group of verses that highlights the central message of a passage.

textual criticism: The process of establishing the original version of a biblical text (the "autograph"). Textual critics sift through variant readings (where two or more manuscripts differ at a given point) to "recover" as much of the original text of a biblical book as possible.

theological biography: The NT gospels, which convey the significance of Jesus for salvation history.

theological dictionary: When used of the biblical languages, a discussion of the words that have theological significance. Typically they trace the history of a word's uses and meanings.

theology: What we come to understand from our study of the Bible about God and related topics.

traditional viewpoints: Perspectives and values that people have followed and revered over the course of many generations.

transformation: The goal of spiritual growth. Becoming more like Christ (see Ro. 8:29). Another term is *spiritual formation*.

tribute: Payments of submission or allegiance.

typology: In biblical texts, identifying patterns of God's working in history.

unchurched: People who don't attend a church. Sometimes a synonym for those who haven't trusted Jesus Christ as Savior.

variants: Differences found when two or more biblical manuscripts are compared. Instances where the manuscripts contain different readings.

vassal state: Group of people or nation dependent on and owing allegiance to a more powerful one.

wisdom: Genre of OT literature that provides practical teaching about how to live appropriately given the challenges of life. Often wisdom is extracted from the daily experiences of life.

worldview: Individal's outlook or view of life and the world. Might be based on many factors, including ethnicity, gender, religion, and vocation.

worship: Responding to who God is and what he has done.

INDEX

AUTHOR

William Klein has written several books and is published in many magazines and journals, and has served as a pastor. He is currently Professor of New Testament and Chairman of the Division of Biblical Studies at Denver Seminary.

Other great resources to include in your reference library!

The Complete Book of Discipleship
Bill Hull
ISBN-13: 978-1-57683-897-6

As the first book in The Navigator Reference Library, *The Complete Book of Discipleship* is a definitive A-to-Z resource on discipleship and disciplemaking for every Christian. It pulls together into one convenient, comprehensive volume relevant topics such as spiritual growth, transformation, spiritual disciplines, and discipleship in the local church and beyond.

The Message
ISBN-13: 978-1-57683-916-4

The best Message on earth just got better. An improved design and enhanced readability make the all-new version of *The Message* numbered edition the contemporary translation of choice. And when paired up with your favorite study Bible, The everyday language *The Message* is known for delivesr a reading experience that is relatable, energetic, and amazingly fresh.

The Message Concordance
ISBN-13: 978-1-60006-978-9

The Message Concordance Including Phrase and Synonym Finder offers three study tools in one: a word concordance featuring the contemporary words unique to *The Message*, a phrase concordance referencing its distinctive phrases, and a synonym finder enabling readers to bridge words from the *KJV* and *NIV* with their equivalents in *The Message*.

To order copies, call NavPress at 1-800-366-7788
or log on to www.navpress.com.

Discipleship Inside Out™